Friday's Footprint

Wesley Morris

Friday's Footprint

Structuralism and the Articulated Text

Ohio State University Press: Columbus Ohio

Library of Congress Cataloging in Publication Data

Morris, Wesley.
Friday's footprint.

Includes bibliographical references and index.
1. Structuralism (Literary analysis). 2. Languages—Philosophy. 3. Language and languages—Style. I. Title.
PN98.S7M67 808 79-14147
ISBN 0-8142-0302-7

for Barbara Alverson Morris

Let the earth speak, therefore, since the men are beyond our grasp. Over and above the delights which it had given me by the river's edge, let it at last answer up and yield the secret of its unspoiledness. What lay behind those confused appearances which are everything and nothing at one and the same time? If I take any particular scene and try to isolate it, that tree, that flower could be any other tree, any other flower. Could it also be a lie, that whole which gave me such delight, that whole whose parts vanished as soon as I tried to examine them individually? If I had to admit that it was real, I wanted at least to master it, all of it, down to the smallest detail. I turned a prosecutor's eye upon the enormous landscape, narrowing it down to a strip of clayey river-marge and a handful of grasses: nothing there to prove that when I next raised my eyes to the world about me I should not find the Bois de Boulogne stretched out all round that insignificant patch of ground which was trodden daily by the most authentic of savages but from which Man Friday's footprint was absent.

Lévi-Strauss, *Tristes tropiques*

Contents

Preface: A Model for the Reader

The writing of this book has been accomplished over a four-year period and not in strictly chronological order. The subjects of language and style first presented themselves to me and emerged as independent texts, but I found I could not long remain in the rarified air of pure theory. Parts 2 and 3, then, lay dormant while I rushed to test my original impulses against the recalcitrance of literature itself, and slowly Parts 1 and 4 arose, more or less simultaneously, to round off my essay. It was not until this latter stage of development that I discovered precisely (or at least vividly) what I was writing about, and this discovery convinced me, more terribly than could any abstract conjectures, of the impossibility of formulating a complete statement on the interpretation of literary works. I have awakened at times to the frantic urgency with which I was writing, to a feeling of frustration juxtaposed with exhilaration. Yet this intensity of feeling did not arise because I was on the brink of formulating truly new and original ideas; rather I found myself confronting a crisis of consciousness, a disruptive moment of revolutionary transition both professional and cultural.

The insignificance of this present work in the face of such grand feelings should be obvious to any reader; but if I have not been adequate to it, the following pages must reveal that I have been faithful. This short preface reflects both my unwillingness to stop writing, my fear that I have not finished, and my doubt about what I have done that must be explained at least another time. The occasion for my writing comes from what seems to me an instructive division in the world of literary criticism. This division is not the same as the often-noted fragmentation of modern theory in our post-romantic world, not the same as our comfortable play with multiple perspectivisms. Our century in

Western society has been dominated by a multitude of romanticisms, but romanticisms nonetheless. We have engaged in endless debates over the adequacy of various interpretive methodologies, battles between New Critical formalism and historicism, between symbolism and realism, between phenomenology and explication de texte, between existentialism and aestheticism. We have supported countless volumes of quibbles between subgroups of larger groups; we have spawned schools within schools, and countermovements to countermovements. Each fragmented system proclaims its newness, its achievement of greater insight, and its inviolable integrity. But all of this conflict has been no more than internecine war; the context has always been romanticism, and even the self-proclaimed classicists of the early twentieth-century Anglo-American literary world were, on some reflection, merely extensions of post-Kantian aesthetics.

I do not mean to say that this extended romantic period renders all of these schools identical; I do claim, however, that they have all been trapped within the fundamental problematics of romantic philosophy. It is perhaps not much more than the tyranny of a specific terminology, the ubiquity of a vocabulary sustained by words like "becoming," "organicism," "symbol," "metaphor," "experience," "humanism," "time," "pastness," "subject," and a host of others too numerous to list. Now in the nineteen sixties and seventies one must be blind indeed not to sense the presence of a truly "other" movement, what I here will call (for lack of a better term) a new classicism, which *seems* bent on the total destruction of romantic meanings and values. It is no wonder that we, who are so steeped in the agony of our post-Kantian universe that it has become familiar and safe, tend to lash out against this encroachment on our sacred territory. We reject, condemn, engage in ad hominem attacks, even try to ignore the penetrating questions leveled at our cherished beliefs, although we do so to little avail.

It is particularly the specter of a many-headed giant called "structuralism" that disturbs us; its several mouths shout antihumanism, antisubjectivism, antihistoricism with belligerent forcefulness, and we respond somewhat quixotically with cries of our own well-worn phrases. I have been throughout this book consistently reluctant to give up much of my romantic heritage, but I discovered that some territory had to be yielded in order to reach firmer ground. Once having done this, I found that my world survived this strategic move, and at that point the encounter with the enemy became more familier than I could have possibly imagined on our first meeting. What suddenly disclosed itself was that the enemy was a projection of myself, that classicism was no opposition at all but a companion to romanticism in a world greatly enriched and more expansive than that I had previously inhabited. My temptation was to give this new world a romantic twist, to describe structuralism (like all other twentieth-century movements) as an aberrant form of romantic aestheticism, to put a neat Hegelian schema on it so that the new classicism seemed to be an antithetical system generated in the belly of romanticism itself. Yet none of these solutions worked; structuralism, in terms of the practical effects of its explanatory models, was not simply a version of romanticism. Any historical schema of contrasting theoretical movements was distorting, for romantic and classical methods of interpretation both belong to a more encompassing, a more universal, problem of "knowing." Interpretation is both an act of consciousness (a condition of consciousness and thereby subject to time) and a context for consciousness (a prior condition for thought itself, which provides the necessary basis for knowing and thereby transcends time).

Classicism and romanticism are different visions of human experience and knowledge that define the limits of man's capacities to know. If this sounds like a surrender to structuralism, I hasten to add (still defensively) that this nontemporal, expanded point of view is neither included by nor excludes historicity, subjectivity, and humanism. A theory of man *in* in the cosmos (structuralism) does not cancel out a theory of man *as* the cosmos (romanticism). Thus if Kant succeeded in recentering man in his world through a counterrevolution of Copernicus's earlier decentering, Lévi-Strauss has decentered man once more with a third revolution that brackets the transcendental subject of Kant's philosophy. The extraordinary fact in these seemingly cataclysmic whirlings and turnings is that man remains firmly on his earth throughout. Although shifts of universal perspective betoken alterations of social structure and culture, no shift is possible without the two terms of difference.

Lévi-Strauss, of course, has not given us a mere reproduction of the pre-Copernican, Ptolemaic cosmology. The world is not merely repeating itself; but man finds from time to time that his world has grown inward or expanded outward too far, and he wants (both in the sense of needs and desires), at these extreme times, to reorder his perspective. All in all, man's finitude remains unchallenged; whether we see him as uniquely individual with the romantics or as a minute and anonymous fragment of the infinite cosmos with the new classicists, man's role in life's game remains pretty much the same: his identity and security are never assured, and his responsibility and moral accountability are ever present but never static.

So too must we view man's actions and creations as always a projection of his finitude, as struggles to join his dreadful sense of self and his sublime sense of grander systems in an identity-guaranteeing work. I will be accused here of having returned to romanticism, but I plead for tolerance since my struggle against romantic terminology remains deadlocked despite my best efforts. To make my point clear I am forced to resort to a device that I see as both classical and romantic: the telling of a story. As a classical device it is intended to function as a model for all I want to say in the pages that follow, as a text about a text that does not explain the latter text but at least recognizes it as text. As a romantic device it takes the form of a parable, or, perhaps better, a fragment of narrative that is partly true, partly imagined, and recounts a moment of insight.

In the south-central highlands of Mexico, in the state of Oaxaca, above the low coastal shelf on either side that separates this region of mixed heritages and topographical contrasts from the Gulf of Mexico on the north and the Pacific Ocean on the south, beyond the dry deserts and humid rain forests that must be torn through to open the valley, is the tiny village of San Bartolo de Coyotepec. Touched by the paved highway that man's insistent progress has poured in a thin, sterile ribbon over the fertile, living earth, the village holds its silent space, forgotten by travelers who rarely pause as they pass by. It rests anonymously on the floor of the valley, in full view of the dark green mountains that surround it—if its space were not so insignificant from a distance, and if its earth-formed brick buildings were not so continuous in color with the ground out of which they arise. There is dignity in the stillness of the village, in the tinkling sounds of bells on red-brown goats moving slowly along the dusty streets, of a radio blaring somewhere, unlocatable but distinct, of an occasional human voice; there is a dignity unmindful of the fact that a neighboring village, less than a kilometer away, has stolen its name, Coyotepec, and of the more crushing nonexistence conferred on it by Mexican roadmaps. There is a highway marker, a wide gravel shoulder where some have turned because they missed their destination, and there is a sign that points laconically to the hacienda of Doña Rosa.

Oaxaca is famous for a most unusual black clay pottery made in the region. My wife and I had come there, at least in part, to buy some typical examples. We found it in the shops that came with the opening of the valley by the roads, in stalls at the Saturday Indian market, in every shape from simple mescal bottles to tiny toy whistles formed as birds or other animals for tourists. Barbara and I had traveled two thousand miles to find these treasures, but we were bewildered by their plentifulness. Can fame be valued by the commonplace? At the market pots lay in neat rows on the dusty streets like curious pebbles arranged by a playful child. In shops they were stacked row upon row in precarious mounds that seemed in constant danger of toppling over, shattering, and mingling once more with the indistinguishable earth from which they came. Indeed they did drop, from time to time, slipping from the seemingly careless fingers of the Indian women who sold them; they cracked, chipped, and caught dust from the heavy stale air that hung over the market. I turned hundreds of them over in my strange hands, examining them for indications of shoe polish that would mark them as inauthentic, as having been mass-produced instead of slowly molded, stroked swiftly with a rough stone in a process that turned the finished product to a glossy rather than a dull black, and lingeringly fired in an oxygen-poor kiln. We found some that interested us, bargained for pennies of value, and stuffed our purchases gingerly into our shopping baskets.

I wondered always if we had detected the polish; was the telltale soot of our possessions really soot or was it a lingering deposit of bootwax? Yet I was not sure why it mattered. Who, after all, would know? Was not the result of each process equally glossy, equally unusual in its bright blackness? Among the plenitude of such pots, so casually regarded by the artisans who made them, why did we show this ostentatious concern for authenticity?

Monte Alban is located on a small outcropping of mountains just south of Oaxaca City, towering above the valley and holding view for miles in all directions. The top of the highest peak is leveled, and there, in extraordinary symmetry, are the magnificent ruins of civilizations that hide under curtains of vegetation and erosion. Oaxaca is a vast storehouse of such ruins, a preserving area where the ground one stands on breathes with the monumental traces of worlds removed from our view but that now and again thrust upward into the air. The main plaza on Monte Alban is composed of expansive, open terraces, marked at regular intervals by swiftly rising pyramids, layers upon layers, hand-hewn and arranged so that they give clear evidence of the two cultures once centered there and now scattered throughout the region. The ruins are partly excavated, but on this day they were utterly deserted to the winds that rush with soft, lonely sighs across the plaza. Monte Alban is marked with hundreds of burial tombs, now numbered in random sequence, but most still unexplored and veiled with rumors of riches a thousand times greater than the stunning gold and silver necklaces dotted with semiprecious stones already unearthed. Following a crude tour-guide map, we struggled down the steep mountainside, clutching roots and loose stones, in search of the famous burial chamber where archaeologists had worked for eight days without sleep to sift the dust for more and more of the delicate filigree that now glares from glass cases in the tiny Oaxaca museum. We did not find it, but every swelling of the earth seemed a mark inscribed outside of time, the absent footprints made by men from mysterious civilizations, rich cultures filled with immensities of lived experience, of religious rituals and bewildering, alluring myths. Excited far more from half-seen riches than from harsh, opened storehouses where jewels once lay, we returned to the plaza and stood holding hands for long moments listening to voices speaking in the ageless freedom of the wind.

The technique of making black pottery had been lost, had

faded back into the dust of crumbling ruins to be unearthed by curious scholars in shards that seemed insignificant when placed beside the exquisite jewelry. Thus entering the realm of time and history, it awaited the moment when, by "accident" the legend goes, it was rediscovered by Doña Rosa. She unknowingly scraped a pot before firing; it came out glossy instead of powdery black. The day after our visit to Monte Alban, Barbara and I decided to drive to Doña Rosa's hacienda in San Bartolo de Coyotepec. She was famous now; her hacienda was the largest and the finest in the village; she displayed proudly the pictures of her visit from the president, and she gave regular demonstrations of her technique to tour groups. She also signed her work—or rather her son signed for her. She could not write.

I was troubled still by the dilemma of authenticity, but I was sure that on this day we would find the real thing. As we drove, the mountains around us hid behind a haze spawned from the marriage of warm summer sun and the humid air of the rainy season. Yet I could see the outlines of Monte Alban, and the vividness of the open terraces floated across my mind. Yesterday we had stood on the central pyramid, alone as rainclouds gathered over the mountains, looking down as the mountain looked down on tiny farms, narrow roads, on the city of Oaxaca with its cathedral of pale green stone—but unaware of San Bartolo de Coyotepec. Now, as we turned off the paved highway onto the rutted dirt street that led to Doña Rosa's hacienda, I was aware of the imposing presence of Monte Alban as never before, towering over the anonymous village.

It was Sunday; no one was at Doña Rosa's for a demonstration. We hesitated outside the plain brown walls that enclosed her gardens, walls precisely like those of other smaller houses where other village potters lived, continuous with their walls and with the dusty road. There was something of reverence in our motion, and in my voice as the tiny Indian woman with her brownish, furrowed skin came toward us. I asked if the shop was open, but it was no shop, only a corner of her home dedicated to the ageless pottery that had made her famous. She nodded to us and sat at a wide, crude table under the portico facing the garden, lush, green, filled with flowers blooming; she sat staring not at us, perhaps not at anything, while we browsed self-consciously through several simple shelves of glossy black pots. We held hands and whispered, not because we were afraid she would hear, for she spoke no English, but because it was Sunday, and because this tiny woman with miniature hands of dark skin made richer by the earth she molded for eighty years, whose hands could not sign her name but whose name was famous because of her hands, guided by what deathless spirit no one knows, discovered a technique as old as Monte Alban itself, and older yet, because this was Doña Rosa, and this was Sunday, and this ground was sacred to strange gods that filled us with awe and peace.

I turned the pots in my hands as I had done a hundred times before in the Oaxaca market, with the same awkward carefulness of one who is afraid to break the silence with some clumsy accident, yet in the presence of their creator whose unconcern ridiculed my care. We selected a few, but almost in silence and completely free of that ostentatious show of testing their authenticity we had affected in the market shops. It was not the guarantee of the name crudely scratched in the clay, not the prideful claim of ownership that Doña Rosa would not and could not express, not the simple, graceful, yet wholly functional and only faintly decorated shapes of the pottery, but the slender, clay-colored hands of the silent woman, those hands that touched the same earth of other civilizations with the same magic as the other craftsmen who also made fragile, useful, glossy black shapes, those hands that accidentally worked the clay in the same way as the other craftsmen, yet whose discovery made her famous, named her Doña Rosa for a world of people she will never see.

My exaggerated care for our purchases was less important than before as we thanked Doña Rosa and turned to go, although our treasures were far greater than any others we were to find. The feeling that swirled around us with the wind on the mountainside at Monte Alban descended to the valley and raised the dust from the barren ground, and touched us lightly and settled on our clothes and our Doña Rosa pots. We talked excitedly, full of that energy released when one emerges from a cathedral, with a happiness of discovery like that of the archaeologists who did not sleep for eight days while they sifted the treasures of an ancient tomb. We, too, would take our finds from their native soil to rest awkwardly on our display shelves two thousand miles away. No one would know, of course, if they were authentic or shoe polish imitations, yet the dust of Doña Rosa's porch would appear on our treasures no matter how often we wiped them—as if the clay, fired hard and glossy black, emitted some of its own substance to turn the little, encased world around them once more into the dry brown dirt of Oaxaca. As we bumped slowly back onto the paved highway and forced the car out of the dusty ruts that gathering rainclouds would turn into mud, and summer sun behind the rain would bake hard, and soft sobbing winds would brush once more into dust, a glimmer of sunlight pierced my eyes, a flash of green trees and bare stones that rose out of the valley floor toward the obscuring clouds. Looking down on San Bartolo de Coyotepec, and on the strangers bearing their treasures, was Monte Alban.

ACKNOWLEDGMENTS

The conversations that eventuated in this book began several years ago with my friend and colleague Mark Scheid. Since that time my course has taken many turns, but I remain conscious of these origins. I am grateful to Alan Grob for his encouragement at a moment when my commitment to this project wavered; it is quite possible that without his efforts on my behalf I would not have the opportunity here to express my thanks. Hayden White read the manuscript with unusual care and thoroughness; his critique was invaluable, and his gift of time to evaluate and correct my project is the highest compliment that I could wish for my work. I am equally indebted to Frank Lentricchia, whose knowledge and judgment I respect most highly; he has read my work and responded not only with encouragement but also with the critical concern of true friendship. I owe, far beyond the scope of this work, lasting appreciation to Murray Krieger; he is a teacher, colleague, and friend for whom simple thanks are insufficient. Finally, I renew here again my prayers for Blake and Michael Morris that theirs will be a future of happiness and fulfillment.

Friday's Footprint

Part One

The Pilgrimage of Being

THE USES OF MYTH

Standing in the present, we have been taught to look with somewhat haughty indulgence upon all the past, "primitive" cultures that flourished within their comforting and accommodating myths. Those myths appear to us as the ruins of ancient fortresses erected against the ever-threatening invasion of manifold reality or as crumbling towers of communication thrust upward toward heaven. We reluctant, proud moderns may begrudgingly admit that the societies of the past evidence a simpler, happier, more innocent world, the loss of which gives validity to man's contemporary existential anguish; yet one who would brashly seek to revive myth today, or suggest the "need" for (not so much as the existence of) a modern myth, risks being scorned as a borrower of convenient fictions or as a romantic dreamer. The relentless onrush of time, virtually hypostatized by idealistic philosophy (even against its will), has breached the fortress walls with waves of phenomenal plentitude and brought down the tower with disharmonious blasts from the trumpets of absurdity. In all, however, myth has shown remarkable resilience. It endures not merely as curious narratives labeled and filed by the scholar, but with persistent vitality in culture and culture's guardian spokesman, literature. Myth has proved impervious to man's intellect and has only recently revealed its richest resources in the deep unconscious levels of man's being. Here it gains indisputable victory over time, not by denying it but by making it meaningful.

The rediscovery of myth has occasioned something like apocalyptic enthusiasm, although this rediscovery is, in truth, an illusion covering a newly expanded understanding of human cognition, which is at once simpler and more complex than we had dreamed. Moreover, despite the various disciplines that now claim to have myth under close scrutiny, only the slenderest threads of accord foreshadow a general agreement. Thus in this first essay I will somewhat boldly anticipate what exists only in potentia, yet I do not hope to offer a definition of myth. From the anthropologists, historians, linguists, literary critics, philosophers, psychologists, sociologists, and theologians I will draw insights about myth in order to discuss its "uses" in literature. Through this process a better understanding of myth may evolve, but the focus of my essay will remain on the problems of literary interpretation. My method, then, describes a lopsided circle: on the basis of a few preliminary assumptions about the general nature of myth I will examine its specific uses in William Faulkner's *Go Down, Moses*; in turn, the specific uses will no doubt help refine the original assumptions. But at this point the trajectory of my discussion will divert toward generalizations about the essential structure and language of literature; and, as a curious by-product, it will raise for us the most problematical aspect of modern literary theory: the determination of literature's socio-historical involvement.

To focus on literature's uses of myth indicates no cavalier disregard for the latter's broader cultural dimensions. Indeed, I am anxious not to overshadow such "functions," although this is frequently the result of myth-oriented literary criticism. For example, Northrop Frye's very successful *Anatomy of Criticism* eventuates in a peculiar, aestheticized version of myth; the myth that Frye speaks of is wholly literary despite his struggles to give it a socio-historical respectability.[1] It is better, though I confess more clumsy, to keep literature and myth at least at an arm's length from one another. The illuminating studies of myth by contemporary ethnographers, myths very unlike the traditional literary versions we have come to know through the history of western art, may yield an even more significant "myth criticism," but not if we continue to see them in the same light that we view, to cite only the most familiar instance, the marvelous myth stories of our ancient Greek ancestors. Myth criticism must break free of the "allusionist" domination; the literary use of myth does not simply convey the idea of an author's esotericism. Such an approach confuses the relationship between myth and literature because allusions are almost always to other literary uses of myth rather than to myths themselves. Only slightly less objectionable is the idea that literature takes narrative fragments of myth stories to use as plot structures. The theory of "displaced" myth,[2] like allusionism, implies a recognition theory of literature; the critic's task is to expose the writer's half-clad borrowings to a near-sighted and ignorant audience.[3]

At best, allusion and displacement are only partial explanations. The assumption supporting both is that complete, preformed myth structures exist in order to be alluded to or displaced, but it is difficult to establish the "objective" reality (either cultural or psychological) of any myth. In the broadest sense, a myth is no more and no less than the *expression* of a cognitive strategy that defines man's sense of belonging to his world. "Expression" here, however, is an inclusive term ranging from elaborate and aesthetically oriented narratives of highly acculturated societies to simple pragmatic actions asserted through patterns of culturally organized behavior. A myth, therefore, is not so much a "thing" as a psychosocial process; it is not a collection of old stories but a cognitive system that fades into the vague outlines of general culture. As Claude Lévi-Strauss argues, "there is always something left unfinished. Myths, like rites are 'in-terminable.'"[4] Thus, what a literary work alludes to is at least partly an unreal construct in the critic's mind; what is displaced is no more than the "literary tradition" as defined by T. S. Eliot and transformed into "myth" by Frye.

This aspect of allusionism and displacement is in itself instructive. A myth in the broad sense need not be written down and preserved in the cultural archives of human history. There is, to be sure, no better way to establish the death of a myth than by finding it indexed in an encyclopedia and shelved in one of our vast libraries of knowledge. Myths belong to societies and not to individuals. They are unconscious systems of thought and not "beliefs" in the form of dramatic manifestations. *Myth* is not synonymous with *religion*.[5] The function of myth is to organize material phenomena and to structure human behavior. For an observer to become aware of a myth *as* myth very likely betokens the cessation of that myth's cognitive functioning for that observer, and this defines roughly a distinction between the user and the analyzer of myths. For the latter we might substitute the more traditional term *interpreter*; but in a very real way the user of myths also interprets, although his deeper and more basic activity is best labeled *understanding*. The task of analysis is to identify and describe a myth structure; yet because the myth has no "real" existence prior to the analysis, the analyzer must do more than merely describe. He must bring the myth into being; he "objectifies" it over against the messy empirical background of its general culture.[6] To do so precludes immediate interest in any particular uses of myth, for he has moved on to what we might call, following the trend of recent philosophical jargon, the level of "meta-interpretation."[7] On the other hand, borrowing terminology from Wittgenstein, the uses of myth can be "shown" but not "said": one can "experience" the force, function, and energy of myth only if it has not been objectified.[8] Once its energy has been "conserved" in a self-regulating, whole, and "visible" structure, one can only "know" the myth in its density as object. The analyst/interpreter of myths is confronted by a "principle of indeterminacy" equally as confounding as that faced by the modern physicist in quantum theory. Nevertheless, the use of myth lies in the dynamic nature of its cognitive functioning, and myths are used when, as Lévi-Strauss says, they "operate in men's minds without their being aware of the fact."[9]

The division of myth into "functional" and "objective" structures is, of course, a mere device for the purposes of my explication.[10] Nonetheless, it enables me to discuss a peculiar aspect of the underlying cognitive potential of any myth. The structuring "power" that operates unconsciously in men's minds has an explanatory force that exceeds the empirical limitations of any user. That is, the structuring capacity, which is necessarily whole and adequate, cannot be exhausted in the life span of any one man or in the duration of the collective social group.[11] It is this potential that transcends individual and race and can be abstracted into a roughly adequate structural model by the analyzer of myths. To use the familiar linguistic analogy, the finite structure or system of grammatical rules is capable of generating an infinite number of individual utterances, more than any individual or group could possibly formulate in their day-to-day speaking to specific occasions or experiences.[12] There is, therefore, a "surplus" of explanatory power built into the system, the "ghost" of perfect knowledge that leaves its lingering "trace" in every specific use of the system.[13] But this powerful structure is only "potential" in any individual culture or any single member of a culture; it is "real" only in the analyzer's objectification. On the empirical level we find that particular experience comes fragmented, momentary, and infinitely plentiful, defying the totalizing powers of this incipiently synchronic system with the diachronic nature of discrete experience. If there is a surplus of explanatory power in the system, there is also a surplus of experience to which the system may be accommodated.[14] The analyzer who abstracts the synchronic structure in order to penetrate to the source of man's potential for knowing and, hence, reach the very ground of what Dilthey long ago called "intersubjectivity" must bracket the empirical dimension of his studies, yet in so doing the myth he identifies becomes a "fundamental form of inauthenticity."[15]

The analyzer engages willfully in an act of "bad faith" in order to objectify a cognitive system; it is never a wholly satisfactory movement, for the vitality of the experiential manifold, which brings the unconscious forward into conscious activity, defies abstraction. Moreover, we know the logical possibility or "necessity" of such a system of surplus explanatory power, its existence as "Cartesian mind," only in its particular manifestations. The reality of the system is revealed in a sense of "absence," as a system always with inadequate content that pushes man toward the experiential world, forces him to speak the system to the plentiful, and truly surplus, particularity. Both system and discrete experience, form and content, are sterile and meaningless in themselves. Each shows a fundamental lack that needs completion in the other. It is true, as Lévi-Strauss says, that man is more possessed by his structuring myths than he possesses them, but so too is he possessed by experience. The key to any myth, then, is in its uses, in its confrontation with the world of surplus content, in its assertion of man's Heideggerian "being-in-the-world." It is a twofold action designed to exhaust both system and experience, to achieve a prefect equilibrium between inner and outer worlds, but because each is an infinity of surplus this is a never-ending quest.[16]

The analyzer of myths, therefore, must first "understand" them as a user before he can interpret and describe them.[17] The interpreter must penetrate to the deepest and most profound levels of the myth where he experiences its cognitive force, where he "thinks" it not as abstract or propositional but in its specificity, with direction and active purpose toward the empirical world. Ironically, here he becomes a part of the very system he is to analyze, but only in this way can he "intuit" the "rich and rewarding" nature of myth.[18] This intuitive level of interpretation involving the use of myth concerns me directly in this chapter. It is only at the level of understanding that one comes near the native user's unconscious, natural thinking, and it is this understanding that defines the literary use of myth.

For the ethnologist, understanding demands field work; he must live within the culture he studies where the day-to-day manifestations of myth in the thoughts and actions of the members of the culture are not merely observed but are to some degree open to participation. As imperfect as this living the culture may be, it is indispensable, for only at this level can one see myth thinking itself to (it does not think about) experience in the gestures and words of the natives. The ethnologist must find myth on both the sacred and profane levels of society. Yet one particular manifestation of myth has a special value; myths "told" or "sung" by an official singer of myths have a privileged position in culture. The singer is not an analyzer but his act of singing raises the myth out of the diffuseness of general society; the energy of normal, daily functioning is transformed into the gestures and words of singing. The official act of singing, however, does not sever the myth from culture; on the contrary, it reinforces the cultural basis of the myth through the dynamics of its psychosocial process. The singing of a myth asserts the individuality of the singer who, nevertheless, works only within the collective sanction. The individual voice of the singer of myths involves the hearers in the very form and activity of his performance, yet the willingness of the audience to be involved is tantamount to the granting of permission for the singer to sing, the making of a contract.[19] If the analyzer's myth, as objectified structure, represents a meta-interpretive dimension, a general code that is, according to Lévi-Strauss, "anonymous," nonfunctional, even contentless,[20] the myth articulated by an official singer is open to subjectivity, privileged functionality, and the full range of the culture's experiential content. It is somehow more than the private, daily, unconscious operations of myth in each individual member of the society, but it is less than the abstract, anonymous myth of the analyzer. Its privileged function is to reinforce the hearers' sense of "belonging" to the group,[21] and it is filled with the familiar, immediate, experiential content of the singer's and hearers' world.

The articulated myth, existing between the purely functional reality of ordered material phenomena and the anonymous structure of the analyzer's abstractions, creates an ideal mental space in which the singer and hearers dwell. It is here that the surplus of explanatory power in the structure and the surplus of empirical content play a crucial role. Neither sacred nor profane, this ideal mental space reveals a trace of the whole, self-regulating system, the ghost of perfect knowledge and order, while it grounds its expression in the concrete, immediate, familiar experiential plenitude. This myth, which exists only in the act of articulation, is, nonetheless, more than mere momentary experience, for it implies membership in an enduring community. The singer creates, then, what Heidegger calls "world," a dynamic space wherein he and his audience dwell by virtue of his act of articulation.

> The world is not the mere collection of the countable or uncountable, familiar and unfamiliar things that are just there. But neither is it merely an imagined framework added by our representation to the sum of such given things. The *world worlds*, and is more fully in being than the tangible and perceptible realm in which we believe ourselves to be at home. World is never an object that stands before us and can be seen.
>
> . . . By the opening up of a world, all things gain their lingering and hastening, their remoteness and nearness, their scope and limits.[22]

The articulated myth shows a more radical form of mythical thinking than that represented by the structuralist studies of Lévi-Strauss. Beneath the collective system, "belonging" implies the existence of an individual "ego" who belongs; the act of singing a myth, in order to function as a reinforcement of the individual's awareness "of his roots in society,"[23] must also make him aware of himself *as* member.

In this creation of world, or an ideal mental space, we glimpse what Ernst Cassirer calls the rudimentary symbolic level of mythical thought. He too describes the symbol as combining raw sense experience and abstract formal totalities in such a way as to be reducible to neither. "It is only in these activities as a whole that mankind constitutes itself in accordance with its ideal concept and concrete historical existence; it is only in these activities as a whole that is effected that progressive differentiation of 'subject' and 'object,' 'I' and 'world,' through which consciousness issues from its stupor, its captivity in mere material existence, in sensory impression, and affectivity, and becomes a spiritual consciousness."[24] This fundamental basis of mythical thought and mythical consciousness defines the subjectivity of the myth singer, yet it allows him to create a world wherein he and all individual members of the society, with their own individual identities, may truly belong. This is not, then, the agonizing self-consciousness of modern existentialist philosophy, but it is the emergence of personal identity in what might be called, with acknowledged paradox, a "collective individuality."[25]

We know too little about the sanctioning of myth singing in most societies, ancient or contemporary, to do more than speculate about its limits and purposes. Some cultures do not seem to encourage such activity, and much of the material of "sung" myths has come to us either in written, literary form or in abstract accounts of ritual ceremonies. It is clear, however, that the singer's subjective role is important and that there is a significant "provincialism" in sung myths that consists of both an emphasis on specific local detail and in the suggestion of broader limits to social belonging.[26] It seems a necessary component of articulated myths that they be localized, given a familiar ground against which is raised the somewhat unfamiliar but embracing ideal mental space.

Herein the privileged articulation provides an obvious and instructive analogy to the literary use of myth. The singer of a myth must concern himself with the aesthetic problems of language, form, and execution (performance), but he must do so within the psychosocial and historical limits placed on him by his subject matter and the "occasion" for articulation.[27] This latter factor is both helpful and a hindrance; the occasion is generally "given" to him by the homogeneous situation of his singing. His audience is already familiar with the language, tradition, locale, and cognitive system, but because this is so they function not merely as passive receivers but as active and critical participants in the performance. The product of this given occasion is the strong provincialism of mythic thought—a provincialism that is not a matter only of shared geographic and historical details, of familiar facts, themes, and actions, but is more broadly experiential in that singer and audience share a system of mental constructs, a "local system . . . of significant choices,"[28] that organizes mere familiar material phenomena and social behavior into ideal mental spaces, into what finally must be seen as an ideological context that does not so much determine individual thinking as it delimits the field of discursive possibilities.

The literary use of myth is similar in that it involves the individual "voice" of a writer who would articulate a myth or cognitive system to particular, familiar experience; yet the writer cannot assume the "givenness" of his occasion for articulation, and he must struggle against the limitations of his written language, which lacks the experiential immediacy of oral speech.[29] He must create or recreate the occasion within which the myth as a "system of significant choices" can speak to appropriate material phenomena, and he may utilize any number of verbal devices, the creation of metaphoric or poetic forms, to give the illusion of oral singing. The literary use of myth, therefore, is situationally, though not functionally, different from the "natural" or cultural use of myth.

The response of writers to the need for a created occasion varies widely; in the specific example of this chapter Faulkner brings forth, out of his own "real" experience, a fictional, homogeneous culture within which he works in almost all of his individual performances.[30] He provides his readers with the "province" of Yoknapatawpha County, Mississippi,[31] but the province is not under the same constraints as the individual performance (work). This occasion for articulation is no more than a necessary assumption of homogeneity and familiarity. The reader unfamiliar with Faulkner's total corpus is sometimes frustrated, but the province manifests itself in the "attitude" the writer takes toward details and fragments of experience that, without proof or demonstration, he simply treats as a loosely woven fabric of background. These fragments remain loose and unarticulated until the work is raised into the foreground against them. Yoknapatawpha County, like the given occasion of the myth singer, remains an endless possibility, an infinite manifold of potential discrete experiences, taking on meaning when raised into the ideal mental space of the created work.[32]

One very significant constraint placed on the native myth singer arises from the narrow sanctions of his given occasion. His intuitive understanding of both tradition and local detail will be strictly measured by his audience, and a failure of understanding would result in an improper use of myth, what we might generally term "failed interpretation." More than mere inaccuracy of detail, such failure is, in effect, improper thinking and results in either the failure to create an experientially viable and, hence, embracing ideal mental space or in a revolutionary cultural expression; it results in nonsense or new ideas. For the literary user of myths the problem is at least partly (but only partly) aesthetic, since the province or occasion is also created. The literary artist will not be judged only by fellow tribesmen on the basis of a singer/hearer homogeneity (although he will in part be so judged), but rather by his heterogeneous audience according to how convincingly he gives the necessary details of occasion. The materials of this created province, the sense of time and place, which circumscribes but is not circumscribed by the work, has traditionally been treated as irrelevant detail, local color, or texture. It is, of course, not at all irrelevant and can be seen as such only by critics who focus on abstract structure or theme as the "soul" of the work. The necessary and given provincialism of the myth singer's performance must, for the writer, be removed one step from his "real" world. The experiential detail of the writer's world enters into the fabric of his created occasion and is thereby realized for the reader. The action gives the artist aesthetic control over it, but no less an obligation to understand it as the most basic ground of his act of articulation. Unable to assume the familiarity of his audience with this detail, he must first selectively, and hence aesthetically, make it familiar, then raise out of this familiarized detail the unfamiliar but embracing ideal mental space.

In a novel like *Go Down, Moses*, however, it is not enough to say that characters misunderstand one another or themselves or their situations; rather, the complex structure of failed and successful interpretations involves the reader directly and creates the novel's powerful affective dimension.[33] The reader learns the characters' limitations in regard to their fictive worlds only by coming to terms with the process of understanding and interpreting that enables him, as reader, to achieve a sense of belonging in his own real world. Through participation in the order of language created by the author's articulation, the reader experiences the basic human struggle to stabilize his own, always tentative, being. The world of the novel is what Susanne Langer called "virtual" space and time[34]; therein we experience Faulkner's "vision" of his world as we live in his articulated version of that world. It is a continuous and profoundly historical struggle that brings the affective and expressive dimensions of art into a true communion. The author invites his readers into his world not simply to see "what" he saw but to experience "as" he experienced. The provincialism of the artist's articulation transports the reader to another place and time not in the fragments and details of material phenomena "pictured" for him but in the vision in which the reader dwells through his intuitive or sympathetic understanding. No single work, moreover, exhausts the experiential possibilities of the author's or reader's real worlds. Thus we find authors continuing to write, each work calling forth a new vision and building a "collectivity" of works. Beyond the corpus of any single writer there is an even looser composite of works that form the collectivity of a general literary tradition.

New articulations arise, transforms occur *as a result of* man's driving need to speak his myths to the endless variety of experience. The tradition composed of these efforts is neither linear nor homogeneous; it is a conglomerate of fits and starts. The goal, unconscious but fundamental, is to exhaust the surplus of experience, to fill the surplus of structuring potential with infinite content and achieve therein a oneness with the world that precludes the need for ideal mental spaces or virtual symbolic orders. It is this oneness that Frye proclaims "the total dream of man";[35] but because it remains a dream the tradition is never closed. Man's "pilgrimage of being"[36] is an endless quest for the future perfect, the "I will have been" that is stronger than "I will be" (the always unattained), weaker than "I am" (the always illusory and fleeting), and more hopeful than "I was." Human history is the record of this struggle, filled with great moments where it seemed, but only for a moment, that the dream had been realized and the "I am" fixed. Dispersed in this history, part of it but not fully symbolic of it, the greatest works of our literary tradition stand forth as privileged monuments, articulated out of their own time, enabling us to return to the ideal mental space spoken on an occasion at another hour in another land. These monuments are, perhaps, the only still vital expressions of man's agonizing pilgrimage.

BELONGING AS TYPICAL: SAM FATHERS

As much as any of Faulkner's works, his short story "The Bear" has attracted almost universal critical acclaim. It has been frequently and revealingly interpreted, yet one structural peculiarity has never been fully explained: what is the relation of the long fourth section to the other, chronologically arranged parts that narrate the hunt for old Ben? Perhaps the answer lies hidden in Faulkner's remark that the fourth section belongs to the novel, *Go Down, Moses*, as a whole;[37] thus, instead of trying to integrate this obviously different section into the traditional narrative of adventure, we might emphasize its contrast with that narrative. Considerations of "The Bear" in its larger form apart from the whole novel have resulted in partial explanations. The relationship of section four to the rest of the story has been said to be mediated by the character of Isaac McCaslin, who learns of his family heritage in the fourth section and who is the self-conscious hero of the hunt sequences. In an allegorical interpretation that follows this emphasis on character, section four is seen as depicting a fallen world tainted by original sin and in conflict with the innocent world of the forest and the hunt. Still further, the world of part four, viewed sociohistorically, describes an economy where blacks are dominated and exploited by whites while the Edenic world of the hunt denies such social hierarchies. All of these observations are true to some extent, but instead of explaining away the difference they clearly emphasize it.

We must begin with the assumption that the insertion of section four marks a break that signifies a necessary difference, a structural and thematic juxtaposition of different, though not simply opposed, elements of the complete novel. On further investigation we will also find that the elements so juxtaposed are not merely stories or moral lessons; they are disjunctive cognitive systems, one clearly mythic and the other (initially historical) aspiring to the condition of myth, perhaps in a form we can legitimately call "anti-myth."[38] There is a tension between these two systems; but there is also a structural congruence in their manifestations, and on the basis of this complex relationship Faulkner is able to comment on the limits of human understanding and action. He posits on the one hand the extreme of fragmented and discontinuous experience and on the other hand the extreme of order, wholeness, and continuity. This is not to suggest that in *Go Down, Moses* he creates a modern myth.[39] Rather in his use of myth he tests its integrity and durability, while at the same time he asserts the viability of history as a mode of thought, not unlike myth, born of the interplay of collective and individual consciousness.

The most obvious mythical dimensions of "The Bear" concern the hunt for old Ben. Traditionally this is characterized as a primitive nature myth (a sloppy and inaccurate designation) or as a totemic myth involving a ritual of initiation. The latter is accurate but frequently given a misdirected focus that illuminates the role of old Ben but excludes other crucial factors. The totemic aspects of the myth are expressed not through Ben but through Sam Fathers, through the cognitive strategies that define his world, his being and belonging. To fully understand this myth we must separate Sam from the romanticized version of him fostered by Ike McCaslin. It is only in Ike's eyes that Sam recalls a watered-down version of Rousseau's "noble savage" or embodies the rather simplistic Christian virtues of humility and prelapsarian purity. Perhaps the most obvious example of this misconception is found in the different treatments of the name "Fathers."[40] For Ike the word raises questions of genealogy and patrimony. Hence, Sam belies his name and betokens a terrible sense of an ending for the noble Indian race (already tainted in Sam's mixed blood) "now drawing toward the end of its alien and irrevocable course, barren, since Sam Fathers had no children" (p. 165).[41] The factual accuracy of Ike's observation joins two ideas that Sam himself might not associate; that Sam has no children and that the Indian race is disappearing have almost a causal connection in Ike's mind, but the name "Fathers" does not function to make the same connections for Sam. We should see his treatment of his name in the same context as the title he applies to the great buck of "The Old People," the breathtaking animal he addresses: "'Oleh, Chief . . . Grandfather'" (p. 184).[42]

Sam is a chief[43] although the privileged, hierarchical nature of this role is played down; he is a chief without a tribe; he rules not by election or rights of descent but by a "natural" right. In part, Ike recognizes this: "there was something running in Sam Fathers' veins which ran in the veins of the buck too" (p. 350), yet Sam's reverence before the stag means neither that he confuses his actual parentage with that of the animal nor that he recognizes his human grandfather reincarnated as a deer. Either belief would prevent him from hunting these sacred animals. Rather than taboo, the buck is a totem animal for Sam. It identifies his tribal belonging, membership in what we might call the "deer tribe" whose primary social and "economic" activities are hunting.[44] We should remember that Sam is never at home in civilization, and he leaves his "shop" to return to the forest as a hunter (pp. 173-74). The great buck "mediates" conflicts inherent in the hunt between forces on which the tribe's very existence depends. Deer are both the product for sustaining life (food) and the focus of an activity that ends life (death as the goal of the hunt). Sam's identity, therefore, is bound up with the totemic myth of hunter and prey and is not dependent on "humility" and sinless "purity." His hunting prowess is natural, not supernatural or mystical, and his myth gives him certain charter rights to the forest, detailing for him autochthonus origins that take no notice of the white man's legal "ownership."[45] Sam is not confronted with the problem of patrilineal inheritance that disturbs Ike; he does not feel, as Ike does, that it is a "sin" to sell the wilderness (in fact his father did sell it), and he does not (nor, ironically, could his father) even conceive of that manner of ownership.

He belongs to the forest, to his tribe, and to the practical function of hunting; his membership in this collective group confers on him an individual identity that is at the same time a kind of "typicality." Here, as Cassirer says, "the feeling of *self*" is "immediately fused with a definite mythical-religious feeling of *community*."[46] But it is not therein a loss of self, for "Myth is one of those spiritual syntheses through which a bond between 'I' and 'thou' is made possible, through which a definite unity and a definite contrast, a relation of kinship and a relation of tension, are created between the individual and the community."[47] Sam, without confusing the self and the other, identifies with his grandfather through the mediating totem of the deer, which is not a symbol of generation but a unity of opposites—life and death, food and the kill. Sam's sense of belonging is an assertion of his collective individuality. "The whole [community or myth] and its parts are interwoven, their destinies are linked, as it were—and so they remain even after they have been detached from one another in pure fact."[48]

Accordingly, Sam's attitude toward the hunt for old Ben is very different from Ike's. As a hunt it demands the testing of strength between opposing forces; it necessitates, in this particular instance, the proper dog. This is both a practical need and a reflection of the eternal conditions of hunting, a paradoxical balancing of life and death. Sam accepts the conditions without apparent emotion just as he matter-of-factly states that "'somebody is going to [kill Ben] someday'" (p. 212). When the proper dog arrives, Sam greets him with "neither exultation nor joy nor hope," and Ike thinks that "Sam had known all the time . . . it had been foreknowledge in Sam's face that morning" (pp. 214-15). It is, of course, "foreknowledge" based on recognition and simple faith. The arrival of Lion, the proper opposing force for Ben, is guaranteed by Sam's natural world of the hunt, a continuous, orderly tension between hunter and prey that defines the extremes of life and death for him. This is the heart of the lesson that Sam tries to teach Ike: that, to use Ike's own cryptic and not quite comprehending terms, "by possessing one thing other, he would possess them both." (p. 296).

Ike's response to Lion is wholly different, a repeated refrain: "So he should have hated and feared Lion" (pp. 209, 212, 226); the dog's sudden and seemingly magical appearance foreshadows for him an apocalyptic ending and a permanent loss. "It seemed to him that there was a fatality in it. It seemed to him that something, he didn't know what, was beginning; had already begun. It was like the last act on a set stage. It was the beginning of the end of something, he didn't know what except that he would not grieve. He would be humble and proud that he had been found worthy to be a part of it too or even just to see it too"

(p. 226). His nostalgia, fitted out with stoic acceptance, reawakens a questioning sense of moral worthiness and freedom from sin. The end here is an end of innocence, and he argues but gets no response from Sam, that "'it must be one of us [to kill Ben]. So it won't be until the last day'" (p. 212). None of these considerations occurs to Sam; there is for him no temporality eventuating in fatalism; there is only the recurrence of the eternal act of the hunt here raised to the level of the typical. Typicality, therefore, is more than the mere familiar plenitude of experience, but less than the apocalyptic. "Out of the mass of impressions which pour in on consciousness in any given moment of time certain traits must be retained as recurrent and 'typical' as opposed to others which are merely accidental or transient; certain factors must be stressed and others excluded as non-essential."[49] Typicality results from man's most basic efforts to order his experience, efforts that can be shared in a sense of community but that resist, then, intrusion from alien cultures. Ike attempts to impose his attitudes on Sam, "It was almost over now and he [Sam] was glad" (p. 215); for Sam, however, the hunt is no end but a culmination of the vital forces of life, no last day but a most typical day. The inevitable conflict between Lion and Ben betokens for Sam an embracing, participatory, continuation of life, not an apocalyptic moment that, as Ike sees it, excludes all those who are unworthy.

Significantly, Ike's most unselfconscious moment of participation comes not in the hunt but in listening to Sam's stories. Here Faulkner promotes Sam Fathers to the role of myth singer, and through his voice Ike is drawn into Sam's world.

> As he talked about those old times and those dead and vanished men of another race from either the boy knew, gradually to the boy those old times would cease to be old times and would become part of the boy's present, not only as if they had happened yesterday but as if they were still happening, the men who walked through them actually walking in breath and air and casting an actual shadow on the earth they had not quitted. And more: as if some of them had not happened yet but would occur tomorrow, until at last it would seem to the boy that he himself had not come into existence yet. . . . [P. 171].

This passage is an instructive one for several reasons, some of which I will merely set forth here as anticipations of later discussion. The focus is on both the affective and expressive (creative) dimensions of story telling, and in the self-conscious repetition of "as if" our attention is called to the narrow gap that exists between fiction and factual history.[50] It is an act of articulation to experience wherein "the one who speaks is able to effect a rebirth, through his discourse, of an event and his experience of that event."[51] The discourse itself, of course, is an event, an "as if" event that presents a past event as present experience. It is the storyteller's lie; words uttered in the here and now can evoke, refer to, events, persons, things that have no present existence. The affective import of this special event, however, is primarily a characterization of young Ike's growing romantic consciousness. The storyteller's lie is an act of illusionary presencing (literally a rebirth), a filling up of space and time in what we might call a narrative "digression" from temporal flow. Ike's driving passion is (will be) to dwell in the virtual space of a timeless world as a digression from life. The immediacy of Sam's oral narrative, the nowness and hereness of the event of telling the story, is transferred to the world of historical eventuality in order to stop time in a dream of timelessness. The romantic association of oral language with presence will serve as a refuge from the "written" world that threatens to dismantle Ike's dream wish.

No greater tribute could be given to the singer of tales than recognition of his powers of resurrection, his ability to grant corporeal existence through the "breath and air" of his voice. The experiential world of Kantian spatiotemporal unity is therein contracted into an immediate and present consciousness. As he listens, Ike feels nearer to belonging to Sam's world than he does at the moment of ritual initiation over his first kill (pp. 164, 177-78),[52] or when he shares in the vision of the great buck Sam calls "grandfather," or even in his confrontations with old Ben (pp. 208, 211). The timelessness of Sam's stories requires of Ike the total surrender of his own, separate-world identity if he is to participate in them, and only this once can he manage to resign the time-dominated apocalypticism that haunts him throughout his life.

The experience is not the same for Sam as it is for Ike. The radical disjuncture of temporality that twists the past into the future reflects a kind of "mythical memory" through which Sam knows what was and what will be in terms of what is. Like his foreknowledge of Lion, his memory of the past is confirmed by the eternal presentness of his world, and both serve as a guarantee of the future. Sam belongs to the forest world, as Ike never can, because his world expresses for him a pattern of belonging. It is not, one may assume, a pattern that he could describe as an abstract structure, but it is one that he naturally articulates in his stories. It is orderly, though not peaceful, and organized by a code of relationships that have a fundamental and infinite explanatory power for him. His lack of surprise at the arrival of Lion robs the event of any suggestion of the merely accidental; in Sam's world, predicated on the eternal balancing of the hunter and the hunted, Lion's appearance is not mere chance but meaningfully necessary in terms of Sam's myth. It is *merely* a matter of time. Such a code, of course, explains Sam's attitude about his own death, for we cannot say with the country doctor that Sam (nor Joe Baker) just "quit" as old people do (p. 248). What appears to Ike and the others as stoical acceptance is, in fact, a carrying out of the code of his existence. Here too it signifies less an ending than a continuation, and Sam "helps" Joe Baker in a ritualistic death as Boon Hogganbeck helps Sam (p. 254).

Boon, himself one-quarter Indian, is logically the only one of the hunting party to perform this crucial function. But his Indian blood is insufficient to confer on him membership in Sam's cognitive world even though his mixed heritage excludes him from the world of the white hunters. Moreover, Boon is a perpetual child of ten (p. 232) and, hence, never a "man" in Ike's terms (Ike crosses into "manhood" at twelve). He is condemned to time-innocence "as though time were merely something he walked through as he did through air" (p. 228). Because of Boon's simple-mindedness Ike misjudges him, believing that it will not be Boon who kills old Ben (p. 235), that Boon, clearly, is not worthy. Yet it is Boon, along with Lion, who accomplishes, unknowingly, the mythical repetition of the eternal hunt. Boon gains temporary entrance into Sam's world by "marriage," through the half-comic, sexless wedding of the mongrel dog, Lion, and the mongrel manchild, Boon, described by Faulkner with self-conscious confusion of sexual identities (p. 220). The final mythical struggle, therefore, is a conflict between the hunter, Boon-Lion, and the prey, Ben. They meet, with a further extension of the sexual imagery, in an embrace that is "almost loverlike" (p. 240). For a moment they seem to arrest time in an enduring stillness that "almost resembled a piece of statuary" (p. 241), but the hesitating terminology of this passage (the repetition of "almost") defies the apocalyptic freezing of the moment. The conflict of hunter and prey in a violent act of courage and self-destruction is not an end but, Laokoön-like, is an act of love, a preservation and continuation of life in its most typical actions.

At the same time Boon's fragile belonging is shattered, first by the death of Lion and finally by the ritualistic death of Sam in which Boon finds his own last and self-expelling act of participation. Unlike Ike and the other hunters, he cannot return to the world of business and city dwelling. He is left alone, reduced in his last scene to a terrifying madness. This last appearance of Boon in the novel, carefully placed after Ike's long internal struggle with his own identity and heritage in section four, stands as a warning that belonging is more than mere choice, mere acceptance or repudiation, more than an act of will. Boon's only home, humorously yet tragically, is as sheriff of Hoke's lumber camp, halfway between civilization and the wilderness, between two different yet potentially embracing worlds. His fate, not properly attributable to either his simple-mindedness or his confused parentage, is to be excluded from both of the cognitive worlds of significant choices that define being and identity for the other characters. An even more frightening, though similar, fate awaits Isaac McCaslin.

BELONGING AS ARCHETYPAL: LUCAS BEAUCHAMP

The fate of Boon Hogganbeck would lose much of its affective force were it not for the startling disjuncture of section four, which infuses another cognitive structure into the narrative. This structure, composed of the piecemeal fragments of the McCaslin genealogy, describes a world apart from and clearly in conflict with the wilderness of the hunt. Though it is not a myth in the familiar sense of the term, it nevertheless defines "being" and "belonging" and even at this level of generalization reveals some qualities similar to the totemic myth of Sam Fathers. Like all myths it functions to mediate contradictions on the level of "mythical logic" (as Sam's deer totem mediates the forces of life and death) that cannot be resolved on the empirical level. But these similarities serve also to point up significant differences between the myth of the hunt and the anti-myth of the McCaslin family. The latter resembles what Edmund Leach, braving the contradiction, calls "the precipitate of the development of an historical tradition"; its importance in the total structure of *Go Down, Moses* grows from its emphasis on the same kinds of structuring myths Leach finds in his analysis of the Old Testament.[53] No doubt this results from the influence of a southern Biblical tradition on Faulkner himself, making the concern with "kinship," with culturally operative systems of "exchange," marriage rules and property ownership, of central thematic and structural importance to his novel.

The fragmentary manner in which the McCaslin family myth is presented to us makes it a more problematical structure than the seemingly comforting totemic myth of Sam Fathers. Yet neither myth is inherently more orderly, complex, or adequate to experience than the other. Both meet the challenge of the empirical manifold with an exhaustive system of classifications, although the McCaslin myth, involving as it does questions of patrimony and descent, is more continually and self-consciously open to the threat of time and mere chance. To combat the dehumanization of a world ruled by accidentals, the myth of genealogy establishes a permanent, explanatory sense of origins, a genetic nexus that allows any member of the kinship chain to defy chance with the bravado of the reversible claim: "in my beginning was my end." Rather than a chaotic, linear temporality, therefore, such a strategy proves the legitimacy of belonging by transforming temporal succession into the circular structure of a spatially deployed myth; its genetic characteristics do not emphasize origins and final ends in the traditional linear sense but utilize genealogical charts of descent in order to define a perpetually present sense of belonging. That is to say, genealogy become myth, in its spatiality, draws its historicalness into a circular structure around a defining center or mediating figure. This center need not be the "first of the line" but becomes the most legitimate measure of belonging to the line; the center is an archetype that functions as a prototype for those who claim to belong to the family.

There is, then, a crucial distinction to be made between this historical myth and the nongenealogical, nonhistorical myth of Sam Fathers; the mediating element of Sam's totemic myth embraces the contradictory extensiveness of his experiential reality through the cognitive ordering of "typicals." Sam's world has no center because its identity-conferring power comes not from a kinship chain but from an integral interpenetration of discrete parts in an eternal natural order. On the other hand, the legitimizing function of the archetype is a powerful organizing principle that grants not only identity through kinship but titular rights to family property. The totemic myth of Sam Fathers with its playing down of blood kinship and assertion of autochthonous origins and natural "charter" rights regularizes time into patterns of repetition that are, in their typicality, of little threat to the myth structure's stability. But genealogical myth, with its emphasis on succession and kinship rules made stable only through the enduring power of its archetypal center, seems always open to self-destruction. Legitimacy is often measured in terms of length of tenure; the oldest family has a privileged position. Yet the center is prey to both inner and outer forces of corruption; the purity of descent is threatened by exogamous marriage and by decay through the weakness of memory. Indeed, the genealogical myth, once it has achieved stability, seems to deliberately open itself again to the challenge of linearity and the threat of chance.

Faulkner begins his use of genealogical myth by emphasizing the vague sense of beginnings in the McCaslin family. The title of the first story of *Go Down, Moses* is simply "Was," and it opens for the reader, almost without his being aware of it, a series of questions about origins. The copula "was" suggests that "something" was at "some" undefined time in the past. Faulkner has forced the verb form to serve as a noun, and we ask not only "what was?" and "when?" but also "what is the particular significance of this pastness?" The title, however, gives only a direction, and the story itself gives only partial answers. The McCaslin family is without a clear genetic nexus (a reflection of

Faulkner's sense of the fractured history of southern aristocracy); and before it can be transformed into genealogical myth it must find an organizing center—a center that, as it turns out, never defines the "original origin" very clearly.

The function of the copula, then, becomes a crucial structural key. Because it grammatically joins both anterior and posterior elements, it suggests not only pastness but linear and homogeneous temporality; in a word, it suggests history. The function is essentially metonymic: the emphasis on a linear arrangement of elements in a structurally coherent chain; but it is also open at both ends, and this sets up a sense of structural (and spatial) play. "Was" evokes both a feeling of system (the potentially closed or limited) and a feeling of boundless movement, transformation, and change within the very concept of infinite systematicity. Its metonymic nature is historicity in small, the shuffling and organizing of endlessly plentiful particularity (moments or events) under the ever-present suggestiveness of order; one could say that history so conceived is "fallen" mythology or, conversely, a special form of discourse that aspires to the condition of myth (although it must never be confused with myth). Faulkner takes this complex suggestion of history, however, and adds another dimension to it. By using the verb "was" in the traditional position of a noun, he opens up another structural order that allows the infinite possibilities of meaningfulness in the individual moment or particular event to defy either historical or mythical reductiveness; the particular stands on its own significance yet without denying its dependency on more comprehensive structural orders.

The subject of the first story, the subject element of the copula "was," is the first story itself, but there is a typical Faulknerian disjuncture in this self-reflexiveness. The story is a separable element with its own adequate structure or Aristotelian wholeness. The theme of marriage, which drives the plot to completion, is neatly wrapped up in the case of the slaves Tennie and Terrel, and the parallel marriage plot, involving the whites Sophonsiba Beauchamp and Buck McCaslin, has at least a false resolution in Buck's temporary escape from the persistent Sophonsiba. In its seeming internal wholeness the story presents itself, therefore, as a privileged moment, an objectified fragment of the past, but the suggestion of infinite regression in the title denies this moment, and any moment, privileged status. This conflict implanted in the reader's mind forces him to acknowledge the discrete "presence" of the individual story, its humorous and lively characterization, rich descriptive detail, and satisfying plot while it also raises the question of "absence," the "when" and "where" of a covering structure to which this isolated moment belongs as one moment among many. The reader's response to such a conflict is reinforced by the unexplained and surely abrupt "naming" of the novel's hero, Isaac McCaslin, on the first pages of "Was." Ike is not a part of the story itself, nor even present to remember the action (p. 4); the moment took place before he was born. "Why," the reader wonders, "is he introduced here; who are the people told about and what is Ike's relation to them?" We are trapped between the moment and the pattern.

The plot of "Was," activated by Terrel's plan to marry Tennie over the objections of their respective masters, suggests a most significant set of relationships for the novel as a whole. Terrel, somewhat cryptically, reveals his strategy to Ike's cousin McCaslin Edmonds: "'Anytime you wants to git something done, from hoeing out a crop to getting married, just get the women-folks to working at it.'" (p. 13). The idea is to entangle his own fate with that of Sophonsiba and Buck, and the device Faulkner uses to convey that entanglement is a poker game. It is marvelously adequate to this end; humorous and entertaining, this supposed game of chance establishes the crucial terms of the McCaslin genealogy through a superficially confusing but finally logical system of bluffs and betting ploys. Slaves, women, money, and property function as equivalent media of exchange. Moreover, in the process of the games the two major branches of the McCaslin family interact; the black and white descendants of old Carothers McCaslin share a common fate without, however, clear thematic association.

The interaction of the two McCaslin lines continues throughout *Go Down, Moses*. This is the central action of the second story "The Fire and the Hearth" whose hero Lucas Beauchamp is the son of Terrel and Tennie. The question raised here involves the legitimacy of various claims to the McCaslin land. Lucas is one of only two patrilineal descendants of the patriarch, Carothers McCaslin, but Lucas is black. The other direct male-line heir is

Isaac McCaslin, the son of Sophonsiba and Buck, who is white but has repudiated his claim to the land. Thus, actual possession of the farms has fallen to the matrilinear line beginning with McCaslin Edmonds, and continuing through his son Zack and grandson Roth. The legitimacy of ownership is as complicated as the poker game of "Was," but lacks even the suggestion of the element of chance. The problem is to establish the proper rules, and this involves the primary consideration of laws of exchange, the proper transference of women, slaves, money, and property within the kinship system. Lucas Beauchamp expresses the confusion neatly in an excellent Faulknerian inversion: "'Old Cass [McCaslin Edmonds] a McCaslin only on his mother's side and so bearing his father's name though he possessed the land and its benefits and responsibilities; Lucas a McCaslin on his father's side though bearing his mother's name and possessing the use and benefit of the land with none of the responsibilities'" (p. 44). This conflict within the kinship structure makes the fundamental questions of belonging and being subject to the same confusion.

The system of exchange established in "Was" is reactivated in "The Fire and the Hearth"; the conflict between the black and white, patrilineal and matrilineal, lines comes to a focus on Lucas's wife Mollie. It is resolved only through a ritual confrontation that gives rise to a mediating, archetypal figure. On the empirical level, however, there is only contradiction. Lucas, even after the ritual action has mediated the conflict, still ponders its experiential impossibility: "'How to God . . . can a black man ask a white man to please not lay down with his wife? And even if he could ask it, how to God can the white man promise he wont?'" (p. 59). Yet as he muses on this dilemma he has already asked for and received the promise, not so much as a verbal agreement but in an archetypal moment of union through conflict. Lucas has already asserted his rights within the kinship rules, the patrilineal rights that make his wife taboo to other men. These rights (though empty of "legal" import) are guaranteed against the encroachment of Zack, the matrilineal descendant, but they are not guaranteed against Zack's assertion of his white supremacy. When Lucas tells Zack, "'I wants my wife,'" he speaks in the legitimacy of his blood descent; he is the grandson (and great grandson) of old Carothers McCaslin, whose incestuous relations with his own half-black slave daughter resulted in the birth of Terrel, Lucas's father. Under the laws of patrilineal descent it is unclear whether or not Carothers's taking of his own daughter is forbidden; it is clear, however, that the doubling of Lucas's patrilineal rights gives him strong claim against Zack, for Mollie cannot be freely exchanged without risking a break in the line of male descendants. Carothers, however, has also broken a social taboo that separates the black and white races, and in this sense Zack's taking of Mollie represents a continuation, a mythic repetition that will be repeated again.

The sense of repetition for a brief time stymies Lucas; there is a social and genealogical inevitability to Zack's actions. Significantly, Lucas recalls the events leading up to the the taking of Mollie in mythological terms. He is sent across swollen rivers to fetch a doctor for Zack's white wife dying in childbirth (the child is Roth). It is a journey into and return from death, a rebirth from the river "Lethe" only to find "a world . . . subtly and irrevocably altered" (p. 46). At this point Lucas wishes to reestablish his life the way "it had used to be" (p. 48), but this wish is fulfilled not simply by returning to the "good old days." The wish actively raises the inherent conflicts of his heritage (reawakened by Zack's taking of Mollie to replace his dead wife) to a mythical level—a level where mediation is possible. Lucas's rebirth is, therefore, rebirth into essential knowledge; memory is transformed from nostalgic yearning to that "mythical memory" that is of past, present, and future.

Thus Lucas realizes what he must do almost as if he had already done it; he asserts his patrilineal rights by taking Mollie back. He challenges Zack to a physical confrontation and carries the fight to him when Zack seemingly will not respond. He enters Zack's bedroom in the early dawn for what is, on the empirical level, a final confrontation between black and white, yet as he does so he begins to make manifest in his actions the conflicts of his and Zack's family heritage. Holding his open razor prepared for the sacrifice of the peaceful, sleeping victim—a sacrifice that in actuality will never be—Lucas forces the empirical to the level of myth. "In the first of light he mounted the white man's front steps and entered the unlocked front door and traversed the silent hall and entered the bedroom which it seemed to him he had already entered and that only an instant before, standing with the open razor above the breathing, the undefended and defenseless throat, facing again the act which it seemed to him he had already performed" (p. 52). Here in an instant of timelessness past and future are joined in a present composed of the conflicts between black and white, patrilineal and matrilineal lines. The two men, though significantly unlike, are, Lucas tells us, "'brothers, almost twins'" (p. 47). The potential for mediation is here in the dioscuri, but only if Lucas can force Zack into an active response. The process is gradual but finally successful, and the climactic moment comes (so much like the violent moment of the killing of Ben) over the "center of the bed" (p. 57), the sacred spot that functions as what Leach calls the "middle ground, abnormal, non-natural, focus of all taboo and ritual observance."[54] In a moment of time transformed by ritual action into the echo of a myth, the precarious balance of irreconcilable opposites is held in tension.

The significance of this moment reverberates throughout the novel. Indeed, the conflict of crossed cultural codes is a frequent narrative structure in Faulkner's novels that speaks nothing less than a cultural myth, the myth of the author's South. Complex and unresolvable in their many manifestations, the fundamental terms of this contradiction in *Go Down, Moses* are relatively simple. The codes involved express two immutable laws: (1) that lines of descent are measured through the heritage of the father and son, are patrilineal, and (2) that marriage rules are racially endogamous, thereby supporting the cultural hierarchy where whites rule blacks. The endogamous system, however, is severely restrictive upon the white group; it depends upon a plentiful supply of white females in the culture—on availability. It is further restricted by another code (only vaguely present in *Go Down, Moses* but explicit in many other Faulkner novels) outlining the taboo against incest. As a result of this complex of rules certain exceptions have arisen. To preserve the scarce supply of white women and the racial "purity" of the feudal South an extraordinarily strict code bars relations between white females and black males, but the inverse is not true. Relations between white males and black females are "permissible" with the crucial provision that no offspring of such a union be given "legal"

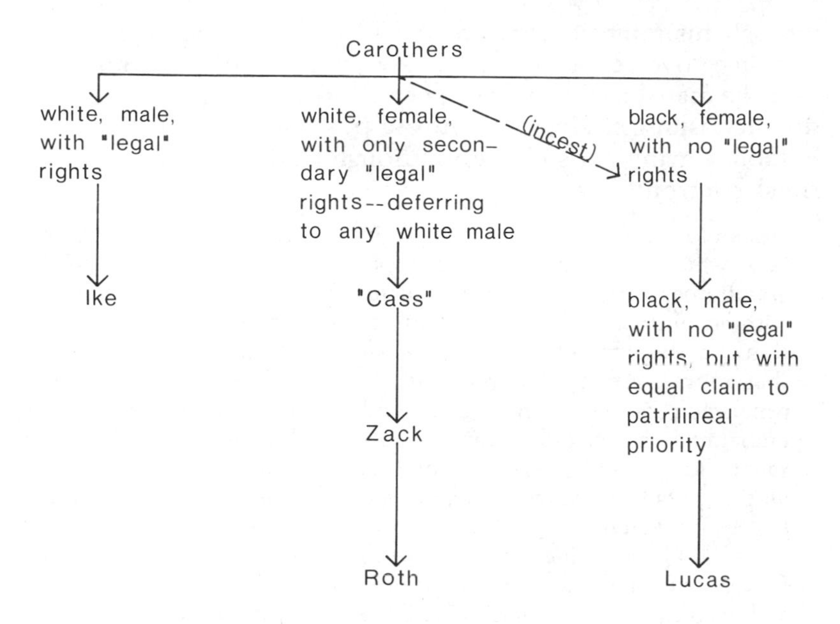

rights to the inheritance of property, that is, be allowed to join the ruling white class.[55]

The McCaslin family patriarch, old Carothers, has, with one "possible" exception, abided by these codes, but that exception has seemingly raised an unresolvable conflict. A simplified chart of these codes may help in visualizing the problem. It is the broken line of "incest" that disrupts the balance of the chart; this is, of course, what Ike sees as the McCaslin "sin," but more importantly it is the act that gives Lucas equal status with Ike in the patrilineal system. The confrontation between Lucas and Zack, therefore, brings several codes into play. Zack, as a white, has the advantage over Lucas, a black, but Lucas, as a "double" direct male descendant, has the advantage over Zack, a descendant on the female side. They are not quite equally balanced, and the symbolic "marriage" of the dioscuri only momentarily mediates the conflict.

As the tension breaks itself apart, Lucas emerges into an archetypal presence through his confrontation with the "other." It is he who possesses the icon of the struggle, the misfired bullet, still "live" as it contains "two lives" (p. 58); it is Lucas who, through his mixture of white and black blood, gains the slight advantage over Zack in order to assert his patrilineal dominance over the matrilineal line. He is, henceforth, the centering force of the McCaslin genealogical myth—a position recognized by Roth Edmonds many years later even though he does not know of the ritual confrontation (p. 114).

> He could see Lucas standing there in the room before him . . . the face which was not at all a replica even in caricature of his grandfather McCaslin's but which had heired and now reproduced with absolute and shocking fidelity the old ancestor's entire generation and thought—the face which, as old Isaac McCaslin had seen it that morning forty-five years ago, was a composite of a whole generation of fierce and undefeated young Confederate soldiers, embalmed and slightly mummified—and he thought with amazement and something very like horror: *He's more like old Carothers than all the rest of us put together, including old Carothers. He is both heir and prototype simultaneously of all geography and climate and biology which sired Old Carothers and all the rest of us and our kind, myriad, countless, faceless, even nameless now except himself who fathered himself, intact and complete, contemptuous, as old Carothers must have been, of all blood black white yellow or red, including his own.* [P. 118]

For Roth, Lucas centers the myth so completely that he contains more of life than that represented in the McCaslin line; he stands for the conflicts of the whole southern tradition, unresolved, preserved, and born again in another form.

> It was as if he were not only impervious to that [McCaslin] blood, he was indifferent to it. He didn't even need to strive with it. He didn't even have to bother to defy it. He resisted it simply by being the composite of the two races which made him, simply by possessing it. Instead of being at once the battleground and victim of the two strains, he was a vessel, durable, ancestryless, non-conductive, in which the toxin and its anti stalemated one another. . . . [P. 104]

Ultimately, Ike too affirms Roth's conclusion, in charactistically more romantic terms. He argues that Lucas takes only "three quarters" of his grandfather's, Lucius Quintus Carothers McCaslin's, first name, "'taking the name and changing, altering it, making it no longer the white man's but his own, by himself composed, himself selfprogenitive and nominate, by himself ancestored, as, for all the old ledgers recorded to the contrary, old Carothers himself was'" (p. 281).

It is crucial to note here the subtle distinctions between Roth's and Ike's descriptions of Lucas. Ike's romantic imagination is obsessed with origins and endings, with the romantic idea that time can be overcome in the archetype of self-creativity; the act of self-naming is conflated with the egocentric dream of self-progenesis. Roth, though tempted by the egoism of the archetypal center, perceives the endless reverberations and echoes through time, across space, that shatter the family myth in order to project a more encompassing cultural myth of the South. For Roth, Lucas represents a "loop" in the narrative flow of family (genealogical) and cultural (southern) history, a repetition that turns back upon itself and stands as an archetype for the history of the culture. In Lucas a mediating answer is found for the infinitely regressive temporality of "Was." The necessity of origins, missing from the McCaslin ledgers, emerges in Lucas; it is, of course, a violent emergence, momentary, metaphorical in its expression through the "click," a tenuous centering of the genealogical/cultural (mythical) conflicts that cannot hold against its own internal tensions, although Ike desperately wants the center to hold against the threat of time.

Whatever Ike desires, the novel makes us aware that this is no more and no less than a symbolic centering; Lucas reverses the master/slave roles in order to symbolically replace, act as "supplement" for, the absence of an "original" family patriarch. He takes the "Name" of the (great) (grand)father thereby displacing all other claimants, including Ike,[56] but this is not to say that Lucas transcends his own position *in* the family structure, that he becomes the present, timeless, apocalyptic, egocentric embodiment of the genealogical myth. The distinction I want to make here concerning Lucas's role in the novel can be expressed in two different ways. Linguistically, Lucas's act of self-naming is a form of catachresis, a misuse of language involving a disjunction in transmission or etymology. "Lucius" (old Carothers) is corrupted into "Lucas," the latter bearing, as Ike notices, a dissimilar similarity to the former. The catachresis reveals not only change and alteration (Ike's temporal terms) but also the timeless process of linguistic substitution (the paradigmatic function where one term is allowed to take the place of another). Free exchange in the Lucius/Lucas ratio speaks for a free inversion of the master/slave roles. It is, therefore, the idea of a centering archetype (overextended by Ike) that "Lucas" (the name) represents in the narrative; we are encouraged to read "Lucas" with every mention of "Lucius" and, conversely, "Lucius" for "Lucas." Such is the force of patronymia, which in this present issue tells us much about the McCaslin (and Southern) desire for a stabilized family (cultural) myth marked by originary presence.

This desire can be expressed in another way: in terms of the psychosocial relationships of the family. Family history, genealogical myth, in *Go Down, Moses* must not be interpreted literally, that is, in the familiar (visual) manner we all often use in saying that a child is the "image" (Roth uses the term "replica") of one or the other parent. Lucas is the "image" of old Carothers through the act a "mapping."[57] Lucas fills the function-role of imaging forth old Carothers because it is designated to him by the other members of the family. After all, Roth has never seen old Carothers, and Ike's claim that Lucas consciously corrupted Lucius's name is mere speculation. This designatory action (which Lucas only gradually comes to accept, never understands, and learns to exploit) expresses an intense sense of "need" (familial and cultural). For Roth the need arises from the "inherited" weakness of his matrilineal claim to the McCaslin land, but it also springs from a sense of guilt (familial and cultural), even if unconscious. Lucas is established in a role of circumscribed power, as authority and yet as ward, as father and yet as child. Lucas's archetypical function bears, for Roth, the ambiguity of the McCaslin and southern codes, both threatening and comforting, self-destructive and conserving. This twofold movement is even more clearly represented through Ike, whose romantic delusions of selfprogenesis designate Lucas as the image of McCaslin origins in a direct countermovement to his own great repudiation of the role of family patriarch. That repudiation is an unsettling, an opening that not only needs to be filled but also calls attention to the self-destructive potential hidden within the family and southern social structure, in the revolutionary idea that one *can* reject one's heritage.

The significance of this patterning for the narrative of *Go Down, Moses*, for Faulkner's work as a whole, and, perhaps, for the general theory of narrative, cannot be overstated. It reflects *both* a theory of language usage and of cultural functioning. The matter is hopelessly tangled, for Ike, in the issue of original sin: the fact of the sin is clear but the origin and consequences remain clouded in the infinite regression of "Was." That "initial" story opens the door partway by establishing the social economy of the family and culture based on the exchange of women, slaves, money, and property; yet it remains for Ike, in the fourth part of "The Bear," to discover the value restrictions of that social economy in the McCaslin ledgers. There money, writing, property, slaves, marriage, and sin are mingled, and because of this mingling "original" sin may not be established as "originary." The sin is not a beginning act but an enabling act, the very essence of the exchange system itself, which, therefore, reflects no beginning or ending, no before or after. This, then, is the source of Ike's neurotic fear of time.

The system of exchange as it is presented in "Was" equates women, slaves, money, and property, but such an exchange economy is too simple for an agrarian-capitalist system (which still bears traces of feudal morality) like that of the old South. The later stories make the value restrictions much clearer. Women who are not slaves (white women) are exchangeable, through marriage contracts (conventions), only on specific levels of society. The exchange has to do with a heirarchy of the ruling white class (land owners) that permits upward mobility for white women only when scarcity of class-equal white women is intense (see Faulkner's *Absalom, Absalom!*). Women who are also slaves (black women) function in a freer system of exchange because they cannot function as media for the transmission of "legal" rights. They can, ironically, transmit a "name" insofar as we are justified in seeing "Lucas" as a corrupt borrowing of "Lucius." This name is a mark of biological kinship, but it is not a sign of legal rights; it is not the family name. As a result of this set of restriction-distinctions, the exchange of white women is remarkably limited, whereas the exchange of black women is potentially unlimited.[58] Moreover, the distinction between white women and black women as media of economic exchange involves a radical distinction in function value; it is a distinction not unlike that in linquistics between "icon" and "sign."[59] The white woman as "icon" *is* society (hence, the antithesis of an antisocial act like incest). As icon she embodies a host of seemingly incompatible ideas: (1) the idea of repression and postponed gratification of sexual desires (in the sacralizing of the marriage ritual),[60] (2) the consequent displacement of "natural" desires (values) into artificial "needs" (values) as in the amassing of wealth or in the artificial inflating of values like those of the icon itself, (3) authoritarian control of the medium of exchange (money),[61] (4) conservatism, and (5) scarcity and exploitation. The black woman functions as a sign possessing only "exchange value,"[62] as in the "free" substitution one for another. The black woman as sign expresses: (1) unrepressed desire or promiscuity, (2) consequently, the ideal of "natural" or nonartificially inflated values, (3) unrestricted flow of the medium of exchange, (4) anarchy, and (5) the ideal of plenitude.

This is a cultural myth considerably more inclusive than can be expressed by any one or all of Faulkner's novels. Yet the disturbances of family/cultural stability that drive forward the narrative of *Go Down, Moses* uncover these mythic patterns; those disturbances arise for two reasons. First, the extraordinarily restrictive exchange value of the icon makes it less functional (less available and artificially more valuable) in social commerce than the sign. Second, these two functions, icon and sign, are not discrete elements in the social structure: if black and white women are distinct as to race, they are indistinct as to gender and the function of transmitting biological kinship (recall Lucas's corrupt name). This latter function must not be misunderstood (as, for example, Ike misstates it); the black woman conveys biological kinship even if the black child of a white father inherits no legal rights. We cannot, therefore, dismiss the distinctive treatment of black women and white women by drawing a line between sex (promiscuity) and marriage (purity), for biological kinship is a possible issue of both. Old Carothers's sin must be viewed ambiguously, as sin and not-sin, as both the affirmation and questioning of a social law that runs to the very heart of the social structure. One cannot say simply that incest taboos apply to white women and not to black women, for that would necessitate an absolute distinction between white women as "of society" and black women as "outside society" (as "natural").[63]

The genealogical obsession with forefathers in *Go Down, Moses* exposes a complex of cultural attitudes. There is expressed in this an Oedipal subjugation to the father/archetype, a sense of guilt that has as its basis little more than the awarding of priority to the father/archetype (hence, Roth's inability to take action against Lucas). Yet it also asserts the longing to be at one with the forefathers (the desire for atonement). This "at-oneness" is unavoidably repressive; it is the basis for a differentiation between belonging and exclusion, between master and slave. On the cultural level it is the basis of segregation, the ideology of racial purity, and authoritarian political power. Repression here appears as the foundation of social order by defining through prohibitions the distinction between culture and nature. The incest taboo, in fact, can be said to create (promisicuous) desire in order to exclude it from culture, and thus southern culture can be said to invest in the black woman all of those promiscuous desires that, through prohibition, negatively define the culture of the white (master) race.[64] Black women as slaves, however, are an essential medium of exchange *in* society. They are not absolutely distinct in function from white women who are also a medium of exchange (if highly restricted) in social commerce.

What Ike discovers as the family "scandal"[65] is the conventional emptiness of the incest taboo, its arbitrary or "sign-function" value. It is not the fact of incest as sexual act or even as psychological desire that is shocking. It is the ambiguous manner of its social encoding. The word "incest" never appears in the ledgers, and its absence tempts us to assign it magical powers, as a kind of negative icon asserted by its exclusion from the articulate, written world of family/social orderliness. The ledgers, as a commercial narrative history of the McCaslin family, assert their existence (and the family's existence) over against the non-existence of the term "incest." The iconic presence of the family/social order is based on the prohibition (repression) of incest, its absence. But the illusion of negative iconicity here proves to be just that, an illusion. The ledgers' wilfull silence on the matter does not really exclude it from society. What should be guilt for sin is expressed in terms of an exchange of money. Sin, literally, can be bought off; incest has a price in the commercial structure of exchange. More importantly, the confusion of money, slaves, property, and women (white and black) argues for a series of linguistic exchanges that explains the economic as well as moral basis of the family/society.

For example: (+ or –) *incest* correlates with (black or white) close-kin woman. The distinction is nothing more than a matter of convention, for presumably (−) incest or incest prohibition comes into play when the (white) option is selected as an attribute of close-kin woman. But the ledgers overreact to this convention by "silencing" the term "incest" altogether, and that overreaction (guilt) creates the family riddle that Ike is compelled to solve, to articulate. He must speak the unspeakable, a paradoxical activity that forces him to see that (−) incest or incest prohibition *does* correlate with (black) woman, otherwise the money payoff would not have been necessary and the primary clue to the riddle's solution would not have been *written*. Finally, if (−) incest or incest prohibition is not the mark that separates family/society from "nature," from anarchy and promiscuity, if it is not the basis for an absolute distinction between the "icon" or culture (as racial purity and authority) and the "sign" of nature (as unrepressed desire), then anarchy and desire creep into the very fabric of culture itself. The icon is little more than an overdetermined sign; the class structure contains the seeds of its own destruction; revolution is contained in the potential of inversion of terms (e.g. master/slave, white/black) through unrestricted exchange (substitution).

It is not the dog Lion, but the McCaslin ledgers that Ike fears. It is an attitude that causes him to fear writing in general, to prefer the oral society of Sam Fathers as a type of Rousseauistic retreat. Ike's Rousseauism, however, is confounded by the same contradictions that underlie the McCaslin family myth. Expressed in a series of geographical/moral clichés, the "South" is opposed to the "North" in order to define cultural value on the basis of privileged origins. Rousseau's oppositional categories easily merge with similar distinctions articulated by defenders of the American South. The South is associated with passion (often expressed in the desire for origins), with agrarian love of the soil (or the primeval forest), and the illusion of eternal presence or plenitude. The South is tribal; it is preliterate (a lingering ideal still extant in the special treatment of oral contracts in the South, the giving of one's word), and, therefore, it is not only the repository of, but is also possessed by, oral language. The North replaces passion with cold logic, replaces love of the soil with the commerce of restricted commodity exchange, and replaces the dream of plenitude with the fear of scarcity that creates artificial need (the basis of industrial productivity and overproductivity for profit/wealth). The North is national or international as opposed to tribal; it is essentially literate (emphasizing the supplementarity of exchange involving ownership of real property and contractual communality). The southern myth establishes the North as destroyer of the idyllic South, and it is a natural association that allows Ike to fix the destruction of the South in the very fact of writing (the ledgers).[66] The North is the dreaded otherness, foreign, inauthentic; the North debases southern passion (desire for origins) into northern need/scarcity (originless supplementarity).

But the fatal irony of Ike's discovery is the revelation of the dreaded northern otherness within the South itself. Insofar as the southern myth is embodied in the icon of the white woman (purity, innocence) it is, from the beginning, threatened by need/scarcity, by the too great restrictiveness that necessitates exceptions to the rules of exchange for the sake of self-preservation. Thus northern supplementarity (sign-functioning) comes to "be" at the very moment that the southern icon is "conceived." Rules of restrictive usage like the incest taboo operate as repressive forces on one level (with regard to white women) and are relaxed as an indulgence of passion on another level (with regard to black women). Ike discovers in the McCaslin ledgers the written evidence of supplementarity within the myth of presence, which is to say that he discovers writing (as corruption) already there.

There is, of course, some justification for the southern claim that a northern invasion is a prelude to a fatal dispersal. The oppositions—industrial versus agrarian, technological labor versus human labor, centralized government versus local control, liberal versus conservative (as a series of not quite congruent pairs)—express the dread of the fall from plenitude and authenticity, the dread that paternalistic authority can be replaced by an anonymous authority. The North, as representative of industrial capitalism, is attacked for its dispersal of the biological family unit in order to replace that unity with the "company family," in order to replace the biological father with the "corporate father." The dehumanizing effect on the worker (child) of the corporate family is easily seen in the free substitution that takes place throughout the national/international structure of the company; "transferrals" are the same as free "sign-supplements." Northern industrial capitalism, of course, may not be any more dehumanizing and exploitative than southern agrarian capitalism; southern bond slavery itself substitutes easily for northern wage slavery. But the issue here is not at this level moral (although it *must* ultimately be so understood). What is to be grasped is that otherness, as a necessary element in self-definition, self-preservation (or even using Ike's term, selfprogenesis), is not a simple outwardness to be excluded by an easy differential definition. Endogamy discovers within itself a necessary exogamy (as reciprocity);[67] oral language as myth of plenitude and presence reveals an inward "writing" as scarcity and supplementarity;[68] belonging (as to a family or a society) is a matter of conflicting impulses between repression and rebellion. Lucas's emergence as the McCaslin archetype articulates this conflict; he is the origin (preservation) and self-destruction of the McCaslin family.

Lucas's archetypal presence, however enduring and mythical it is, does not rob him of his individuality or particularity. He lives in the world, in its petty, daily circumstance, supported by the confidence of his position in the family myth. His status in that world gives him certain power over it, and his freedom to act within the permissive limits of his myth (the myth that he himself centers) often results in Faulkner's best humor. Lucas's comic willfulness is the subject of the other half of "The Fire and the Hearth," the action that results from the finding of a buried gold coin. The scene is filled with mythic possibilities; the money comes from the earth, from a potentially sacred place called the "Indian mound." But Lucas sees it in terms of his own myth, as money once buried by old Buck and Buddy McCaslin and, hence, his own property by rights of inheritance. Lucas is tempted by an apocalyptic view of the incident worthy of Ike, but all this is wrapped in the temporality of his own genealogical myth. "For the next five hours he crawled on hands and knees among the loose earth, hunting through the collapsed and now quiet dirt almost grain by grain, pausing from time to time to gauge by the stars how much remained of the rapid and shortening spring night, then probing again in the dry insensate dust which had yawned for an instant and vouchsafed him one blinding glimpse of the absolute and then closed" (pp. 38-39). The phrasing of the passage is extraordinarily rich, measuring Lucas's "absolute" right to the money as "heir and prototype" against the moment by moment, "grain by grain," "time by time" (and later in the same passage, "coin by coin"), temporality of his existence. The story of Lucas's search for gold takes on the form of the tall tale, the frontier humor so prevalent in Faulkner's later work. Lucas becomes here the trickster, duping almost everyone and narrowly escaping terrible calamity, but this is a confirmation of his archetypal status, not a denial of it. He is a version of Jung's trickster, the clownish figure who represents the fact that "some calamity or other has happened and been consciously understood,"[69] that, we might say, some conflict or other has been momentarily mediated.

The archetypically centered genealogical myth, however, does not confer upon all of its members the same reassuring barriers against temporality. The historicity of such a myth challenges time in a manner very unlike Sam's totemic myth, for the archetypal center draws into itself the diversity born of unmediated conflict and forces all to accept its paradoxical embracing of difference. Only Lucas manages to operate, clownishly, within his mixed and conflict-ridden heritage. Roth Edmonds, in his acknowledgment of Lucas's centrality, falls victim to the myth he belongs to. As a child he knew only Mollie Beauchamp as a mother; yet she is not his mother, and she cannot confer on him the patrilineal heritage of Carothers McCaslin nor the black blood that would allow him to rival Lucas. In the innocence of childhood Roth accepts the fire and hearth of Mollie's cabin as the center of his world. "Even before he was out of infancy, the two houses had become interchangeable: himself and his foster-brother [Lucas's son, Henry] sleeping on the same pallet in the white man's house or in the same bed in the negro's and eating of the same food at the same table in either, actually preferring the negro's house, the hearth on which even in summer a little fire always burned, centering the life in it, to his own" (p. 110). But the symbol of the hearth cannot prevent his fall into experience; the archetypal center does not deny time and reality but organizes it, gives it meaning. The "interchangeable" function of the "houses" (family divisions) is not innocent but problematical. For Roth this necessitates an entering into the conflicting terms of myth. "Then one day the old curse of his fathers, the old haughty ancestral pride based not on any value but on an accident of geography, stemmed not from courage and honor but from wrong and shame, descended to him" (p. 111).

The presence of the centering archetype contains the nemesis of myth in the accident of geography. The myth confers on the accident a special meaningfulness, but Roth is, nevertheless, caught in the relentless history of the old ledgers, the "fading sequence" returning to the "anonymous, communal, original dust" (p. 261). The same fate does not await Lucas: he seems beyond time. He will, Roth says, "'not only outlive the present Edmonds as he had outlived the two preceding him, but [will] probably outlast the very ledgers which held his account'" (p. 117). For Roth the awareness of his plight is swift and final. "Then one day he knew it was grief and was ready to admit it was shame also, wanted to admit it only it was too late then, forever and forever too late" (p. 112). In the story "Delta Autumn" he is condemned, by the force of the centered myth, to repeat the sins of his fathers without resolving them, to repeat old Carothers's sin and bring the family full circle again around Lucas as the center. But by this point in the novel such matters cannot be assigned to mere accident. "Delta Autumn" opens with what seems like an irrelevant discussion of "circumstance" and "Happen-so" (p. 346) and closes with Ike's lament that Roth's partially black child was born "'just because a box of groceries happened to fall out of a boat'" (p. 360), yet to leave it at this point is too easy. Roth, once again like old Carothers, tries to buy his way out of the incestuous guilt of his actions with the black woman, and once more the family confusion of women, slaves, and money as media of exchange is reasserted. This story neither ends the McCaslin line nor cancels out Lucas's role as archetype. It does not, significantly, end the novel. It emphasizes the temporal opening outward of the archetypal center through Roth's child of mixed blood come "back to home" (p. 362). The archetypal presence of Lucas does not stop time but proves it in its eternal repetitions; it tames accident into meaning. If the McCaslin myth is less comforting than the totemic system of Sam Fathers, it does not fail to speak to experience in order to mediate its inherent conflicts.

APOCALYPSE AND THE LOSS OF BEING: IKE McCASLIN

The two worlds that emerge through the cognitive strategies of these separate myths stand in tension throughout *Go Down, Moses*, but their importance to the reader of the novel lies not so much in their epistemological functioning as in the pattern of complex moral commitments that they illuminate. On this level distinctions are not easily made, and it is clearly inadequate to fall back on a simplistic moral thematics that juxtaposes the "innocent" prelapsarian world of Sam Fathers against the "fallen" world of the McCaslins, or the wilderness of natural piety against the culture of enslavement and exploitation. To do so is to be trapped by Ike's terminology, to reflect uncritically his romantic sentimentalism. Each of these two worlds makes demands on those who would belong. Sam's totemic myth preserves individual identity as "typicality" through its collective system of differentials; it is an orderly world grounded on the principles of meaningful, balanced conflict, but it can be entered only by sacrificing modern man's obsession with origins and ends, by relinquishing altogether our romantic reverence for uniqueness and originality. Sam's centerless world affects a negative and leveling tyranny by disallowing any significant hierarchy of values within the structure of its discrete parts. It denies even Sam's truly privileged stature just as it renders the hunt for old Ben a typical rather than an atypical moment in time. Conversely, the archetype-centered myth subjugates all who seek to belong by relegating them to mere imitations of the archetype, and with its premium on origins and originality it encourages a cult of "personality." Yet unlike the collective system of typicals in the centerless myth, the archetypal myth exists under the constant threat of dissolution from the pressure of surplus experientiality. The assertive, even violent, emergence of the centering personality sets the pattern for a constant revolution, a series of discontinuous, cataclysmic presencings of newly centered myths.

The opportunity for such a rebellion is offered to Roth Edmonds in "Delta Autumn"; through an act of love he could join the black and white, patrilineal and matrilineal McCaslin lines in a marriage that would exclude the heritage of enslavement and exploitation. Through the strength of the black woman, who could truly "have made a man of him" since she offers him a reunion with the patrilineal line of Carothers McCaslin, Roth might have accomplished what Ike never does. But the archetype-centered myth, open as it is to the challenge of temporality, proves its enduring qualities in "Delta Autumn" by absorbing both Roth and Ike into the subjugating terms of its orderliness. Roth repeats the sin of Carothers, and Ike humiliatingly repeats his earlier futile acts of atonement, once more attempting to buy off that sin. It is, perhaps, Ike who suffers most when confronted by the tragic failure of his life. The piercing truth of the black woman's accusation that he is most responsible for Roth's downfall, that his "repudiation" damned Roth to the McCaslin sin, reaches him despite his effort to explain it all away as an accident, "'because a box of groceries happened to fall out of a boat.'" The McCaslin myth traps him at this moment into an assertion of the very bigotry and racism that he sought to avoid. "He cried, not loud, in a voice of amazement, pity, and outrage: 'You're a nigger!'" (p. 361).

The weariness of tone in this pivotal story no doubt reflects Faulkner's sense of his own enslavement to the epistemological and moral limitations of his society; he allows his hero, Ike, to rebel only to fail to bring about the recentering of a new myth, and as a result there is a deepening of romantic individualism until it eventuates in an agonizing existential aloneness. But we would be too hasty if we condemned Faulkner for a pessimism that simply bows to the morality of exploitation; the very conflict between the two worlds, between the totemic and McCaslin myths, affirms a human historicity that encompasses more than any one cognitive system, more than any one myth. Although this does not guarantee a better world in the future, it at least makes possible the freedom to strive for such a world. Thus in the failure of his hero, a failure so often repeated in his novels, and in the long struggle of his career as a writer, we see the constant testing of man's myths, social systems, and moral orders in an effort to articulate to experience a structure of equality and human dignity.[70] If Faulkner implies that man has yet to attain such a world, it is less a resignation to man's impotence than a recognition of fact; the fragmentation of human society into a plurality of epistemological, moral, and political systems, many of which are enslaving and exploitative, reflects not Faulkner's failure to construct in this novel an exemplary, idealized aesthetic order, but his vivid articulation of the failure of misguided romantic humanism.

Having repudiated his heritage (not merely his inheritance), Ike chooses for himself the wilderness world of Sam Fathers to which he attributes moral superiority in its egalitarian structure. There Ike hopes to find that black/white distinctions, indeed, that all social and political differences are "indistinguishable" (p. 294) in a "communal anonymity of brotherhood" (p. 257). But Ike is unable to realize this dream, and his abortive efforts to do so result in an ironic exclusion from the brotherhood he so deeply believes in. His "initiations" in the forest are designed to help him reverse the inexorable process of moral maturing, to move instead from experience to innocence, age to youth, from the culture of enslavement to the world of natural piety. Roth's early perspective on Ike seems to argue that he had accomplished these ends: "born into his father's old age and himself born old and become steadily younger and younger until . . . he had acquired something of a young boy's high and selfless innocence" (p. 106). Ike's understanding of Sam's world, however, is imperfect; rather than a structure of indistinguishable and anonymous parts, it is a structure that elaborates differences. Its order is a result of the balancing of opposites, of conflict, so clearly manifest in the hunt, in the vital forces of life and death. The essential characteristic of this world is its voracious inclusivism, its power to embrace the extensiveness of experience without denying to any particular its individuality. Ike, of course, never views this world from within; his perspective, dominated by its natural temporality, distorts Sam's wilderness in what we might call overinterpretation. Ike's romantic high seriousness invests every particular moment, or, better, certain selected moments, with extraordinary meaning, fixes each moment against the onrush of time not in the collectivity of the embracing orderly structure but in uniqueness and exclusive apocalypticism. His effort to escape time, therefore, affirms it through his obsession with "last-dayism"; his consciousness is dominated by the fear of a wilderness shrinking before man's blind rush for progress. The natural world for him is filled with "momentary gods";[71] "truth" is not known logically or experientially but is intuited, known in the "heart" (p. 260). As a consequence Ike's life is a patchwork of discontinuous apocalyptic moments. The anonymous brotherhood eludes him, and his selfless innocence belies a destructive egotism rather than an assertion of communal belonging. Interestingly enough, Roth's opinion of Ike changes by "Delta Autumn"; he no longer sees him as an innocent young boy but as a foolish old man. Moreover, it is clear in this story that Ike's escape from the McCaslin heritage is only partial, that his initiations into innocence in "The Bear" were fatally disrupted by the insertion of section four. There Ike senses that unless the "fading ledgers" can be purged, replaced by a new myth (or an old but morally superior one), the McCaslin family will be condemned to repeat endlessly and meaninglessly the sins of their fathers. Even here, however, his solution is apocalyptic; he would "complete" the story elliptically told by the ledgers (p. 273) and pay off the inheritance that old Carothers willed to his black heirs. His efforts are futile for two reasons: he cannot locate them all (Tennie's Jim has disappeared) and, most crucially, in the very act of trying to complete the story he continues it. In "The Bear" and, with the haunting return of Tennie's Jim's descendants in the black woman and child of "Delta Autumn," he repeats his grandfather's effort to buy off the white man's guilt. Thus in the dispirited final years of his life the McCaslin myth traps him once more in a renunciation of his utopian dream and into a self-debasing racism. Ike is too much of a self-righteous individualist to submit himself to Lucas's superior, archetypal position; he wants to center his own myth, but in trying to do so he is exclusive rather than inclusive. He does not find mediation for the contradictions of his experience; he merely turns them away or reduces them to apocalyptic moments. Such a myth, of course, provides him with no identity through belonging; his fate, ironically, is precisely what he feels Lucas thinks of him, that he "reneged, cried calf-rope, sold [his] birthright, betrayed [his] blood" not for "peace but obliteration" (pp. 108–9).

The significant factor revealed through the character of Ike McCaslin is the enormously complex epistemological and moral confusion that results from his repudiation. Faulkner creates not only a representative modern character type but a setting, occasion, or world in a state of transition. The agony of his hero results not simply from being caught between two cultures, the one ancient and dying and the other modern and invincible, nor from the simple, though frightening, realization that time relentlessly alters the familiar face of empirical reality. Ike faces a dilemma much deeper and more puzzling, a muddling of epistemologies and moral values that isolates him from other men and neutralizes the effects of his moral commitments. The novel tells of his eighty-year pilgrimage of being only to arrive at the status of "Uncle" Ike; his name, an obvious parody of Sam "Fathers," also expresses the weakest of kinship links in the patrilineal McCaslin line, and Faulkner's mocking heroic epithet, "uncle to half a county but father to no one," reinforces the insignificance of his role in the family system and in the community. The confusion that torments him is best illustrated in the action of the fifth section of "The Bear," where he returns to visit Sam's grave and is surprised by a huge snake. He draws back both in fear and reverence uttering Sam's words, "'Chief . . . Grandfather'" (p. 330), but it is a blatantly ineffectual bit of plagiarism. Whereas Sam hailed his tribal totem in unconscious recognition of the deer's mythical mediating function, Ike substitutes an apocalyptic Christian symbol that belies his freedom from the enslaving yellow ledgers by evoking the image of his grandfather, Carothers McCaslin. The snake, "ancient and accursed" (pp. 329-30), is inappropriate to Sam's world; it carries with it Ike's obsession with original sin and man's "fall" into linear temporality, chronological history.

Ike's metaphors and analogies constantly return upon him with devastating effects. In "Delta Autumn," as he rides once more to the annual hunt, the repetitious and meaningless cycle of his life presses in upon him. He searches for one last analogy that will give proof to his existence, will give him an identity, but his choice is fatal. He notes that his beloved wilderness is disappearing year by year, and he thinks: "the territory in which game still existed [was] drawing inward as his life was drawing inward, until now he was the last of those who had once made the journey . . ." (pp. 335-36). The diminishing outward world reflects his inward being as the circular horizon of his sense of belonging contracts to the narrow midpoint of his own consciousness. Driven inward upon himself, alone in a world increasingly alien to him, he returns once more to his apocalyptic visions.

> Then suddenly he knew why he had never wanted to own any of it, arrest at least that much of what people called progress, measure his longevity at least against that much of its ultimate fate. It was because there was just exactly enough of it. He seemed to see the two of them —himself and the wilderness—as coevals, his own span as a hunter, a woodsman, not contemporary with his first breath but transmitted to him, assumed by him gladly, humbly, with joy and pride, from that old Major de Spain and that old Sam Fathers who had taught him to hunt, the two spans running out together, not toward oblivion, nothingness, but into a dimension free of both time and space where once more the untreed land warped and wrung to mathematical squares of rank cotton for the frantic old-world people to turn into shells to shoot one another, would find ample room for both—the names, the faces of the old men he had known and loved and for a little while outlived, moving again among the shades of tall unaxed trees and sightless brakes where the wild strong game ran forever before the tireless belling immortal hounds, falling and rising phoenix-like to the soundless guns. [P. 354]

The movement of the passage depicts a too easy transition in Ike's mind from the terrifying, discontinuous temporality of the "spans running out togeher" (that should logically end in oblivion, nothingness) to a denial of oblivion in the assertion of the apocalyptic, immortal world of soundless guns. The lesson of Sam's totem, which mediates the conflict of life and death, is here transformed into the metaphor of the phoenix, but the metaphor is a failure because, unlike Sam's totem, it cannot transform empirical reality into eternality, nor can it banish absence (obliteration) in the assertion of a magical presence. The long journey that the hunters make, longer every year, denies the apocalypse, and Faulkner jars his readers out of the metaphorical allure with the abrupt short sentence that follows this passage: "He had been asleep" (p. 354). Even the analogy of Ike's inner and outer worlds is destroyed a few moments later when one of the young hunters says, "'Uncle Ike . . . aint got any business in the woods this morning'" (p. 355).

Oblivion, nothingness, and obliteration have pursued Ike relentlessly, and now the very wilderness against which he has measured his own being is not only disappearing but has become alien to him. The reverence and respect that young Ike held for Sam Fathers is not perpetuated for Uncle Ike in the attitudes of the young hunters he instructs (p. 335), and Ike's apocalyptic dreams have proved no stay against time. The poverty of Ike's being results from a very narrow and romanticized version of the Cartesian *cogito ergo sum*. The words Faulkner attributes to Ike in the form of an indirect quotation, introduced in the long passage above by "he knew," purport an existence for Ike that follows from the very act of thinking itself, "from the issuance of any proposition whatever."[72] The entire dream passage functions as such a proposition (although it erodes into metaphor), and through its power as a performative act attributes being to the speaker in the form of a mind that knows. But it is a very narrow being at best, unmindful of the other, of the experiential reality that surrounds the thinker-speaker. It is a being without spatio-temporal presence (hence, the fall into failed metaphor), bloodless, fleshless and, because it asserts being only in the performative act, fatally impermanent, requiring assertion again and again. Tending toward a discontinuous sequence of apocalyptic moments, such a being is subjective, devoid of experiential content, and removed from the possibility of action or moral commitment.

In response to this morally empty life, Roth makes the first of two devastating comments to Ike in "Delta Autumn," asking him "'where have you been all the time you were dead?'" (p. 345). Yet it is the black woman, extending Roth's question, who forces us to see Ike's plight. "'Old man, . . . have you lived so long and forgotten so much that you don't remember anything you ever knew or felt or even heard about love?'" (p. 363). In the name of moral commitment Ike's repudiation turns out to be a repudiation of life and love, first with his wife (pp. 314-15) and thereafter with all mankind. He fails to project himself into life, to open himself up to a future, whether this be of mythical repetitions or historical progress, and he is condemend to merely dream of the days of "better men" (p. 345). The apocalyptic world of "anonymous communal brotherhood" eludes him to the very end, and he finds himself sending the black woman away proclaiming that the time is "not now" (p. 361). He gives her Roth's money and old General Compson's powder horn (pp.

362–63) as a token of her belonging and as an unspoken, half-realized admission of his own failure to complete the McCaslin myth. Ike has sought peace beyond the conflicts of experience and found only obliteration. Far from dead, the black woman and her child live on, as the McCaslin myth lives in them, with her strength in her love.

Ike's repudiation, reverberating throughout the family/culture, stands forth to demand moral judgment. One must not, however, judge motivations here, only implications. Lucas's emergence into archetype, the inverse result of Ike's retreat, preserves the conflicts that trap Roth and reveal Ike's prejudices. Ike's apocalypticism reasserts the desire for self-preservation, based on the negative actions of repression and exploitation, that marked the cultural icon. The ideal of purity (racial, sexual) ironically results in a restrictiveness that denies passion, procreation, love, and humanity. Thus Roth's fall is into promiscuity with its threat of chaos. Roth's chance for a truly revolutionary defiance of the family/culture myth, through marriage to the black woman, is forfeit under the terms of his own heritage, and he is not able to erase those terms. It is a revolutionary option Faulkner confronted frequently in his works, never without anxiety.

FORGING THE NOVEL: A GRAMMATICAL MODEL

At this point I hope the reader is at least predisposed to admit that myths enter literature in rather complex ways. To be sure, they provide fragments of meaning in the allusive surface of the work and are displaced into narrative structures, but often they are used in a more integral manner. The process is similar to what Jacques Derrida calls "deconstruction." This is neither the creation of a new myth nor the destruction of an old one; deconstruction, seen as a "literary strategy," involves simultaneous countermovements, distinct yet mutually dependent.[73]

The first of these movements is "demystification."[74] One primary effect of deconstruction is to undercut the tendency of mythical thought to assert itself in an aloofness from immediate empirical reality. The artist forces the objectified or "subsistent" mythical theme-structure to emerge in the living, experiential world, to "accommodate" itself to "reality."[75] Myth ceases to belong to the supernatural and the abstract or to purify itself as contentless, deep structure. The process draws myth down to earth, scandalously making it speak to individual human experience. Demystification, however, exists only in opposition to a countermovement on the empirical level. There, the merely familiar, habitual, unnoticed flow of experience is raised to the foreground of our perception; the familiar is "defamiliarized,"[76] made distinct or "strange" in an activity parallel to what Piaget calls "assimilation," with its set toward "repetition" and "typicality."[77] Both defamiliarization and demystification are positive movements, giving to the sequential, metonymic narrative its metaphoric tendencies and symoblic suggestiveness. Like the operation of Kant's aesthetic judgment, which is neither pure reason nor pure sense experience, the deconstruction of myth is neither the surrender to the infinite surplus of familiar experience nor to the surplus explanatory power of gnostic orderliness.

Faulkner's use of myth makes him an ideal representation of what Roland Barthes calls the "structural man," whose creative act is a double process like the one I have described: "decomposition" then "recomposition" or "dissection" and then "articulation."[78] But most crucially, deconstruction drives at the symbolic basis of mythical thought; it is a radicalization of myth in the sense of Paul Ricoeur's claim that: "symbols are more radical than myths. . . . Myths [are] a species of symbols, . . . symbols developed in the form of narrations and articulated in a time and space that cannot be coordinated with the time and space of history and geography. . . ."[79] Deconstruction, however, does not simply yield a discrete literary or aesthetic symbol that is merely suggestive of reality. Nor does demystification produce fragmentation: the scandal is not atheistic but is, at worst, agnostic. The act of radical articulation creates distinctness without alienating "unity" or "form." According to Barthes, form "is what keeps the contiguity of units from appearing as a pure effect of chance: the work of art is what man wrests from chance"; it is "a kind of battle against chance."[80] The artist's articulation raises the particular to distinctness, gives "meaning" to experience, and forces the merely empirical dimension of reality to emerge into formal presence.

The key word here, of course, is "meaning," and my fundamental assumption is that meaning arises only in the act of articulation where it shows itself as a composite of form and experiential content, and as the product of an individual voice. Perhaps a somewhat eccentric point of view, this reflects my conviction that it is better to see all abstract, contentless, logically consistent and anonymous discourse (whether this be philosophical thought or mythical deep structures) as meaningless until spoken to experience by a subject. With such an assumption a profound humanism is injected into the study of myth, literature, and philosophy, and the questions of the temporal and spatial, the historical and geographical dimensions of articulation are unavoidably raised. In his earlier work on myths Claude Lévi-Strauss seemed very much concerned with such an existential humanism, calling it "esprit"; for his effort he has been much criticized even by those who profess to be his disciples,[81] but surely what interests us about myths is the "human mind" as it "shows" itself in its particularity and social being.[82]

Articulation asserts meaning as both individuation and collectivity. The following syntagmatic chain depicts a familiar form of utterance, wherein the symbols *A* and *B* represent wholly meaningless slots that have, nevertheless, relational, logical, or grammatical functions:

(All) *A*'s are not *B*'s.

What particular signs we can substitute for *A* and *B* depends upon the interaction of three variables (rules simplified here to fit the present discussion): (1) the position of the slot in relation to other slots, (2) the culturally available items that form a class of permissible substitutions, and (3) the occasion, or spatio-temporal context, of the articulation, the by and to whom, for what, when, and where of the speech act. The process of selection and substitution, the paradigmatic function, is remarkably complex, having to satisfy a number of variables at one time.

Apropos of *Go Down, Moses* we might make the following selection/substitutions:

(All) bears are not men.

If the paradigmatic act satisfies all of the variables, is consistent with universal laws of ordering, cultural classification, and contextual intention, the sentence will be meaningful. Meaning, therefore, implies the idea of "sanction" (decoding, interpretation). Sanction is not mere recognition of what has been said before or even of what could have been said before; meaning is neither mere grammatical regularity nor Truth. The idea of Truth, of course, is problematic; Truth is neither a fact nor an idea nor a statement but a convoluted relationship of all three. The Truth of any statement of fact is contingent upon "agreement" under the concept of "the Known," or Knowledge. The truth value of a statement is its propositional function, the subsuming of the statement under a general law; but not all meaningful statements are true in this sense, for they may articulate what has not yet been codified into Knowledge, what for which there is no general proposition or even what may appear to contradict the Known (hence, a Falsehood).

Meaning, however, results from the sanctioning of the articulation on the specific occasion of its utterance. Thus, for the average American schoolchild the statement "Bears are not men" is meaningful and True, although perhaps trivial in its empirical referentiality. The opposite, "Bears are men," is more problematic. It is clearly False, but that determination seems to rest on a prior condition that allows us to say that it is meaningful before we even test it for Truth or Falsehood. Clearly, such a statement is not trivial, and the sanctioned meaningfulness rests firmly on the ground of the occasion of its utterance, on a sense of factuality that is very complex. For example, when Faulkner gives to Sam Fathers the slang phrase referring to old Ben, "'He's the man'" (p. 198), the hearers, both Ike and the readers, must be aware of the context (occasion) and culturally operative cognitive systems that are brought into play. To some extent the statement echoes the earlier story "A Justice," in which much of Sam's heritage is related; some significant details of this earlier story are contradicted in *Go Down, Moses*, and, in fact, the idyllic view that Ike has of Sam's Indian ancestry is very much denied by the violent struggles for power that are revealed in "A Justice" where the forest world has been already corrupted through property (slave and land) ownership. This information is withheld from Ike in *Go Down, Moses*; it was Quentin Compson who listened to Sam's stories in "A Justice." The phrase "He's the man," however, opens this past to us as it subverts Ike's misapprehension of its meaning. In part reflecting black slang referring to the slave owner, "the man," the designation more specifically indicates old Ikkemotubbe, whose name "Doom" was a corruption of the French *du homme*. Doom had adopted this name as a designation of power, magic, as an assertion of his intention to become chief. It is this heritage that Sam applies to old Ben, the concept of chief through violent power that carries with it both grudging respect and some distaste. For Ike the statement in its contradiction of the mutually exclusive categories of his language and systems of thought, and in its transcendence of empirical factuality, begins a series of comparisons that eventuate in a metaphorical apotheosis of Ben. First, Ben is the unique bear who has earned a man's name and is more than animal; then, moving toward transcendence, Ben is a bear-man, hence, more than man; and finally he is a sacred, godlike creature, truly taboo. Ike allows the slang phrase to impute a rich, apocalyptic meaningfulness to Ben that would be impossible for Sam Fathers, and here in this simple, almost unnoticed phrase, Faulkner hints at the vast, unconscious, and unbridgeable gulf that exists between the worlds of these two characters.

Such a radical act of articulation forces us to see, as Barthes claims, "not man endowed with meanings, but man fabricating meanings,"[83] and herein lies the primary function of "literary discourse," which calls attention to itself as a meaningful statement, and to the act of articulation (the artist and his experiential context) as well. We might say, then, that all discourse ranges between the realm of pure, discontinuous experience expressed in grunts of satisfaction or howls of repulsion on the one hand and the realm of pure Knowledge expressed in profound nods and winks of recognition on the other. Grunts and nods, of course, are not insignificant, but they are weak discourse, "formulaic" communication, and it is the ideal of a strong, immediate, communicative discourse that dominates literature. This impossible goal leads the literary artist to test both extremes in his act of articulation. He must raise his statement of particular experience to the level of communication, out of the private into the public domain, but he must not lapse into the collective system of recognizable propositions if he is to preserve the experiential meaningfulness of what he says. The collective system would damn him to plagiarism, to the loss of his voice, as well as the content of his statement, so that he says only what is sayable. The radical articulation of the writer, therefore, is neither anarchistic nor totalitarian, liberal nor conservative. Whether the act of deconstruction attacks myth, science, politics, or any other cultural structure of Knowledge, it preserves the possibility of structure in order to speak to experience. Similarly, it rescues experience from the dissipating outflow of energy in the flux of the elan vital, conserves energy as it isolates and foregrounds a fragment of familiar reality.

This concept of meaning perhaps plays havoc with our traditional sense of the term and should dislocate our most cherished critical assumptions about literature. In one respect it would seem to argue that all acts of articulation assert themselves as uniquely meaningful. Insofar as this would further destroy the shibboleth of literature's privileged meaningfulness, forever banish such distinctions as those between the inspired creative madness of the poet and the cool logical reasonableness of the scientist, between nonreferential, organic literary discourse and referential, prosaic logical discourse, I am inclined to accept the consequences. But the definition of "meaning" I offer may have these consequences only with qualifications. The idea that all acts of articulation are uniquely meaningful sounds too radically atomistic, and it must be remembered that every articulation is circumscribed by a complex contextuality that makes possible the very act of meaningful speaking. The attempt to define this contextuality is the most crucial function of this book.

The atomistic fallacy of meaningfulness seems to me to be the fate that relentlessly dogs the heels of recent speech act theory and reduces highly technical arguments to purposeless quibbles. I have used the term *articulation* to preserve at least some of the sense of "performative" utterance as developed by J. L. Austin,[84] but the utterance as act is meaningless in my sense when severed from a contextuality vastly more complex than either linguistic convention or explicitly expressible cultural rituals. If speech act theory is ever to be of use to literary critics (and Austin had no idea that it would be), it must be applied within a consideration of such a context. Even New Critical contextuality is not enough. It helps, of course, to read each individual statement in the context of a whole "work," but this ignores the fact that the work itself is nothing less than a complex statement within an even broader context. This is not to say that the work as text has no limits; rather I would argue that such limits result from the performative or articulated nature of its being. The writer (or speaker) may consider his performance "over," completed—but such an ending (even when apparent to the audience like the fall of the final curtain) never proscribes the reverberating meaningfulness that exceeds that limited textuality.

If this is so, and I hope to demonstrate that it is, several old "certainties" about literary meaningfulness vanish. Meaning is a function, here, not merely of what is said (of "these words in this order") but in a peculiar way of what is *not* said. Meaning always remains hidden behind the text—or partly so—in the realm of language's and culture's systematicities, conventions, rules, myths, and beliefs. Our traditional concern with textual integrity becomes a trivial issue,[85] though textuality, the "what" was actually uttered, remains as the focal point of meaning. Old theories of mimesis based on the referential nature of language must also be seen as subissues of larger questions concerning the referentiality of the text to broader systems of language, culture, and myth. We cannot even explore with contentment (if we ever did) the established issues of "point of view," for the reliability or unreliability of any fictional narrator/character remains clouded in the larger issue of the text's meaningfulness, in the dilemma of meaning dependent upon what is not said, on the silent term of meaning, the unuttered, unarticulated surplus of potential meaningfulness that belongs to linguistic/cultural systems.[86]

To partly explain this problem I would like to call upon one unusual example. In his discussion of the "performative" actions of the "shaman," Lévi-Strauss hints that the "magic" of the shaman's performance results from a kind of balance that he is able to strike between too much and too little meaning. "So called normal thought," he argues, "always suffers from a deficit of meaning, whereas so called pathological thought (in at least some of its manifestations) disposes of a plethora of meaning." Through the shaman's actions "an equilibrium is reached between what might be called supply and demand on the psychic level. . . ."[87] The "curative" or "magical" function of his performance comes in his adjustment of the two extremes, in his achieving a perfect fit between the myth/ritual's structural potential for meaning and the seemingly unexplained event (the experience of physical pain, a chance happening or seemingly supernatural action). That is, the shaman brings into balance the forces of accommodation and assimilation; he speaks infinitely potential systematicity to the infinite plenitude of experientiality. I would not equate the literary artist with the savage shaman in simplistic terms, nor call literary creativity "magic" (although to do so would be neither distorting nor new), but I would argue that the fullness of literary meaningfulness, its balancing of system against experience, implies that meaning exists not in the circumscribed text or completed performance, but in the balance of extratextual elements. Meaning is found in the unexpressed fullness of the systems that remain behind as the ground of articulation itself in what Derrida calls the "trace." My definition of "meaning" here differs from that proposed by E. D. Hirsch, Jr. For Hirsch the meaningfulness of any text is arrived at through a process of narrowing one's focus, through the cutting away of "potential" meanings until one arrives at the meaning of the "intrinsic genre" or the work itself.[88] My sense of meaningfulness, on the other hand, is radically inclusive; its very "validity" is that it is tentative, occasional, and essentially incomplete. At its best (I do not shrink from the value term), in our greatest literary works, meaning cannot be narrowly circumscribed, for it is neither normative nor pathological. It is both.

Some will object that such meaningfulness is too vague, elusive, even chimerical. Indeed it is, but not to the extent that it opens literature to impressionistic criticism; the text *does not* mean whatever any individual reader wants it to mean. The reverse is true, for my sense of meaningfulness militates against impressionism; a text means within its context and in relation to its occasion. Moreover, it thrusts beyond this historical relativism in its performative nature, by engaging the reader in the experientiality of its dynamic structure. The act of articulation is in essence a violence against both system and experience; it enlivens the former and tames the latter. Thus the paradigmatic function I have emphasized above is activated by a voice whose articulation is an assertion of being (or Heidegger's "being-there") against the anonymity of normative systems (linquistic or cultural) and against the indistinguishable flux of experiential plenitude. To select words, concepts, to force them into meaningless slots in a syntagmatic chain, is to speak being meaningfully. But this is heroic, and artistic, only when the act, the selection and substitution, refuses to reduce particular items (words, concepts) to stereotypical deadening roles in the systematic structure and refuses to fracture the system into a plethora of atomistic parts, into the plenitude of nonsystematic experience. To resign ourselves to either extreme, to either the "beyond" of "nods and winks" or the "beyond" of "grunts and cries," would be to fall into "silence," into nonbeing, and to die. We would surrender to the noise of plenitude's buzz and hum or to the noise of the system's static.

It must be plainly noted, of course, that the activity I have designated as "articulation to experience" does not assert a simple referentiality in language usage, the idea of a one-way relation between a word and a thing in the world. Articulation to experience is an experiential event in its own right; its referentiality is comprised of the arrangements of things in the world and cultural/personal attitudes toward those arrangements (an idea discussed more fully in part 2 as "states of affairs"). Meaning is not referential but attitudinal (what Kenneth Burke in a most Kantian moment once called "the dancing of an attitude"), and it can be presented in three forms: (1) what an experience *can* mean, (2) what an experience *is likely* to mean, and (3) what an experience *does* mean. The first has to do with the logical limits of meaningful information available for communication. These limits are, practically speaking, infinite, and thus an experience *can* mean anything. That is to say, the articulation of an experience *can* convey information for what seems to be unlimited purposes; this expresses the function of language as total signifying system, as *langage*, the all-inclusive potential for meaningful articulation. The second presentation of meaning (the *is likely*) represents the cultural limits or designated limits of meaningfulness, or *langue*. This is the ghostlike system that defines, and is defined by, the elastic horizons of culture or subculture. All meanings are not always available in all systems of communication (cultures). This is the level of statistical predictability, but must not ignore the third level (the *does* mean) that calls attention to the individual act of articulation at a specified time and place, under the pressure of an occasion. This third level, or *parole*, evidences the struggle for identity and being in the world; to be known for one's words strikes against the cultural limitations of what may or may not be meaningfully articulated, and it can do so because of the unlimited potential or *langage* (which has been only conventionally repressed by cultural *langue*). *Langage* is a threat to *langue* as unrepressed desire is a threat to social order, but *langage* is also a threat to *parole*, for identity and being are cultural concepts. One comes to be, to have identity, only in culture, in *langue*, and this is the conspiracy of *langue* and *parole* against *langage*, against the infinitely potent meaningfulness that is timeless, placeless, anonymous, and meaningless.[89]

Because of this complexity we can say with Umberto Eco that "every human experience . . . can be translated into terms of verbal language, while the contrary is not true."[90] This he calls the concept of effability, but the term *translated* here covers a polymorphic activity ranging from the categorizing of particulars under general concepts to the expression of passionate desire for something. That an experience *can* be expressed meaningfully by exercising the potentiality of *langage* has nothing to do with whether or not the expression is adquate to existential fact; yet adequation is a function of the level of *langue*, expressing the idea that culturally predictable meanings are always adequate to experience since a culture permits only conventional meaningfulness (and by implication only conventional experientiality) to be expressed. This sense of adequacy may at times seem inadequate, which leads to the artistic struggle for the right word and the frustration at not finding it available, at the need to make the old word fit the seemingly new experience. Where desire for individuation is blocked by cultural adequation there is created the driving force of lack or need. At this point we move from what Eco calls a "*rule-governed creativity*" (the adequation of *langue*) to a "*rule-changing creativity*"[91] (a conspiracy of *parole* and *langage* against *langue*). This is the opening up of unrestricted commerce and communication and the introduction of the idea of "intentionality" (towardness) into the idea of closed systematicity. The conspiracy is a powerful tool; it is the echo of anarchy and natural desire that must be repressed, and it is the scene, the situation, and occasion of art. Again from Eco, "It is indeed difficult to avoid the conclusion that a work of art *communicates too much* and therefore *does not communicate at all*, simply existing as a magic spell that is radically impermeable to all semiotic approach."[92] Here we have again the idea of too much meaning, which blurs the outlines of what an articulation *does* mean, but this is the essence of literary art.

It must be understood that this schema of relationships between *langage, langue*, and *parole* implies no hierarchy and does not define mutually exclusive categories. The function of *langue* is chimerical: to exclude (repress) *langage* (as anarchistic) and to show *langage* within itself. Thus there is no inside/outside distinction to be made here, for *parole* too excludes/shows both *langue* and *langage*, and *langage* is the very possibility of both *langue* and *parole*. To the extent that *langue* evidences (cultural) limits (limits of Truth), *langue* is a machine for producing meaningful truths, but the machine is blind to its own potential for untruths, blind to its own problematical status. Moreover, it is not technically correct to say that revolution comes from within the closed cultural system of such a *langue*, for it is the conspiracy of *parole* and *langage*, within and beyond *langue*, that gives rise to a countermovement, a new problematical structure.[93] Any *langue*, as presented here, tends toward the status of an ideology or dogma; its very tendency to delimit Truth precludes the generation of a new ideology wholly from within the old. Change, revolution, and history, therefore, assume the form of a series of discontinuous eruptions.[94] The more repressive any *langue* (ideology) becomes, the more the otherness within and outside it shows itself as the possibility for a wholly new problematical structure.

The complexity of these chimerical relationships also precludes the traditional view of literature as comprised of a special language outside normative language, as radically unlike normative language. Literature is the act of articulation that makes perfect use of language's capabilities, and, as neither normal nor pathological, exhibits language to its fullest. Here, it seems to me, is a definition of literature's privileged status more exalted than any yet proposed. No longer superior to either language or experience, not free from language's systematicities nor the infinite variety of lived experience, literature profoundly deconstructs what has been said as well as what might be said through the dynamics of demystification and defamiliarization.

It is possible, in this oscillation between demystification and defamiliarization, to measure historical periods according to their relative cultural stability. Moreover, this sense of cultural movement has a precise structural parallel in the way that systems of literary criticism react to new works. As Claudio Guillén says, "Systems will tend, generally speaking, to absorb change and assimilate innovation. . . . In this connection, the roles of critic and reader are important. Most critics . . . view a new work 'through' a system. . . . The critical intelligence 'assimilates' and 'accommodates' nearly in the sense that the psychologist Jean Piaget gives to these terms."[95] The radical act of articulation threatens to disrupt the stasis by speaking the unspeakable, yet there are two sides to the temporality implied in the duality of deconstruction. One, at its extreme, is illusory since it captures change within the limits of permissibility; the emphasis is on defamiliarization, on the assimilation of experience to a communicable form. The best model for such change is found in contemporary linguistics, where alterations in the surface structure of language are controlled by "transformational-generative" rules. An extension of Saussure's "synchronic" linguistics, such a system emphasizes the static nature of its internal motion, for all apparent variations are "permitted" by the basic code else they are adjudged ungrammatical and, perhaps, meaningless. The existence of transformational movements and their essential regularity has been firmly demonstrated by Noam Chomsky, but a nagging question remains: why, under what impetus, do they occur? The laws explain how they operate but not why they operate. The answer is relatively simple and introduces us to the other temporality I have been at pains to describe. Transforms occur when an individual speaker at a specific time and place attempts to speak the general (generative) structure to particular experience. Here we reintroduce Saussure's diachronic dimension to language and emphasize the activity of demystification, the accommodation of system to reality.

The essential characteristics of the synchronic linguistic model have been brilliantly applied by Michel Foucault in his analysis of seventeenth- and eighteenth-century cognitive systems (in the fields of biology, monetary exchange, and theories of signification). He describes in *The Order of Things* fixed, synchronic taxonomic structures that arose within their specified historical contexts and were solidified into Knowledge; that is, the structures have an operational validity in a given spatio-temporal milieu. Within their carefully defined limits the structuring powers of the systems permit certain regularizable speakings to experience, but as Foucault describes them, they do not necessarily derive from a universal core of thought nor do they arise out of previous structures. Moreover, the decay or decline of these seventeenth- and eighteenth-century systems takes place only under what we must see as a cataclysmic event. The emergence of new classificatory systems in the nineteenth century cannot be explained by an evolutionary movement, but only in terms of what Foucault repeatedly calls the "discovery of man," a radically revolutionary shift in human thinking.[96] As a historian of ideas Foucault gives us here a "general history," what Claudio Guillén defines as a "succession of totalities," or what Foucault himself calls a "series of series."[97]

The cataclysmic nature of the transition between discrete totalities, however, cannot be so easily ignored; the discovery of man surely betokens a reorganization of thinking that justifies extraordinary claims on the magnitude of Kant's "second Copernican revolution," and such is the very stuff of which history is composed. In part, a new mode of organizing implies a new awareness; old structures are fractured, even replaced, by radical articulations to experience, by speaking the unspeakable. The result is a new way of saying things and the constitution of a new reality, not necessarily better or more accurate, but, from inside the system, more immediately meaningful. The parallels in the languages of myth and literature should be obvious; at the base of any form of discourse, and any structure of Knowledge, is man's impulse toward an experiential world, toward "life." As Ernst Cassirer says, with acknowledgement to Humboldt, "man puts language between himself and the nature which inwardly and outwardly acts upon him; . . . he surrounds himself with a world of words in order to assimilate and elaborate the world of objects, and this is equally true of the configurations of the mythical and aesthetic fantasy."[98] The stability of discrete systems is always threatened by the recalcitrance and inexhaustability of human experience; with the act of assimilation comes also that of accommodation—even to the point of a cataclysmic rejection of the old structure.

The self-reflexive temporality of synchronic structures, the illusory sense of change within the permissible limits of transformational laws reflects, perhaps, one basic human fact: man's urge toward order, stasis, and the conservation of energy. The understanding of such an urge, particularly in its linguistic manifestation, spells the end of traditional linear, continuous history; for the literary historians it may provide a better means of getting at those elusive units we call "literary periods."[99] But the experiential dimension of man's everyday life and its tendency toward discrete particularity are equally important, and it is here that literature, rather than the linguist's finite generative grammars, might be the most significant model. The creation of a literary work is an act of presencing that proposes that work as an experiential object, but the act remains always a proposition, existing somewhere below the collective, all-consuming egalitarianism of the structure of Knowledge and above the flux and blur of sense experience. Literature fragments and vitalizes society, not anarchistically, not by plunging us into chaos, but by repeating once more man's desire to make meaningful the world he senses around him. Literary history is, therefore, not linear continuity but the energy of continuous emergence, and such a history cannot ignore the personal elements of vision and style without at the same time denying collective order itself. As Émile Benveniste argues, it is by virtue of "the polarity of I:you," the polarity of "I" and all "others," that "the individual and society are not at all contradictory terms, but rather complementary terms."[100]

Furthermore, the author's vision is a correlative of such literary categories as "style" and "structure." In *Go Down, Moses* Faulkner comes face to face with the mutually dependent polarity of the two temporalities that I have been at pains to describe above: one reflecting illusory movement within the culturally delimited model of a transformational system, or *langue*, the other a radically expansive and open-ended expression that seeks to speak the unspeakable, or *parole*. The former, of course, manifests the conspiracy of *langue* and *parole* against *langage*; it spreads out the culturally sanctioned confrontation with experience as if across the surface of the page, giving the illusion of linear movement while it disguises the deep structure of the unarticulated (disguises the repressive laws of cultural limitations). The latter, which manifests the conspiracy of *langage* and *parole* against *langue*, breaks through the surface to dwell on the endless potentiality of what is not articulated, thus risking exposure and violation of the repressed. This warfare of conspirators and double agents (notice the dual function of *parole*) is most easily illustrated in a work like *Go Down, Moses* by focusing on the grosser levels of structure, on plot, but we need to reconsider the term *plot* in ways unlike the traditional Aristotelian definitions of a causally arranged sequence of events reflecting the artist's "imitation" of the "actions of men."[101] Plot is this and much more; fundamentally it is a juxtaposition of meaningful articulations to experience. To return to the syntagmatic/paradigmatic grammatical model above: plot is a certain relational sequence of selected incidents along a temporal axis. The axis is temporal not only when it is causal, when it imitates chronology, but also because it must be read sequentially. Plot has coherence, but not necessarily logical progression, and the coherence of a literary narrative is simply another term for meaningful articulation.

The plotting of *Go Down, Moses* demands our recognition of the discrete character of the stories, for it is the struggle of these units to break free of traditional narrative restrictions, to defy even the sequential motion of reading, that makes plot crucial to the sense of history Faulkner wants to present. So it is with the story "Was," which institutes in the reader's mind an ill-defined time-set understandable only in terms of the novel as a whole. The story is a complete unit, composed of its own arrangement of incidents, yet it belongs to a broader framework hinted at in the somewhat cryptic naming of the hero, Ike McCaslin, whose life is recapitulated in the first paragraph. The fact that the first story belongs to *a* history (Ike's) reveals Faulkner's narrative strategy and illustrates what I would like to call the first law of plot structure: *that no narrative can be allowed to undercut the immediacy and independence of the incidents that comprise the narrative as a coherent whole*. The parts are always more than the whole in the sense that the presence of an individual incident implies that there is more than what is being presented, that the making distinct of the individual experience necessarily results in a loss or blurring of contiguous details. It is here that we get the fullest sense of irrelevant texture, but this surplus also points up the surplus power of the total narrative structure, the excess of explanatory capacity that suggests that the whole could contain more than it does. To speak of one of these surpluses is to speak of the other. The novelist's task, unlike that of the historian, for example, is to allow the rich particularity of the moment full sway in its battle against the totalizing powers of systematicity. The historian, confronting a multiplicity of details and perspectives, must always resist the explosiveness of the particular event; he chooses always within the prescribed limits of his structural assumptions, according to the discursive principles of his own half-perceived cultural schema. The novelist risks the danger of allowing his typified experiences to assert a life of their own and is faced with the disruptiveness of something like Ike's apocalyptic vision, which fractures coherence into a discontinuous series of discrete, "supermeaningful" moments.

Literary and historical narratives differ insofar as each demands a certain, peculiar "attitudinal leaning" from its reader. This has nothing to do with truth functions, but it does involve a distinction between explanatory and nonexplanatory systems.[102] We might say again that historical narrative aspires (hopelessly) to the condition of myth. The historian selects from the myriad possibilities of events (or texts) a subset of such events (or texts) that "stands for" the whole.[103] It must seem to the reader (in a kind of optical illusion) that the narrative, based on the free transformation of the subset through endless permutations and repetitions, is adequate in its explanatory force to the period covered. This necessitates that the historian efface his personal voice so that it appears he is spoken by his myth/system rather than that the narrative is spoken by him. The historian's ideal is to be absorbed in the anonymity of his discursive system, to project the center of his narrative structure outside himself as other and assure his own absence from it.

The literary artist reverses the historian's drive toward self-effacement by insistently asserting his presence. But he does not do so by characterizing himself as narrator—as the express or implied "I" of his story; as Barthes claims "the one *who speaks* (in the narrative) is not the one *who writes* (in real life) and the one *who writes* is not the one *who is*."[104] The matter of authorial voice or presence is vastly more complex than our traditional questions about point of view led us to believe.[105] The author's presence is marked by his treatment of the narrative as "meaningful assertion" and not as explanatory system. The explanatory force of the historian's text, which subordinates the majority of particularities to the transformational unfolding, is corrupted by the literary artist's unpredictable expansion of particularities. That is to say, literary narrative seeks not to explain but to render meaningful. The reader is drawn into this engagement, into the questioning of meaningfulness, because the explanatory force of the narrative has been pushed aside—leaving in its place a pluralistic, dynamic text as meaning-event.

This is simply the sense we all share that literary narrative is freer than historical narrative, in its allowing the moment to distort the whole, but it is an illusory freedom at best. Barthes, speaking of narrative in general, characterizes neatly what I would call literary narrative in particular. "Form in narrative is marked essentially by two governing forces: the dispersion of signs throughout the story and the insertion of unpredictable expansion among them. These expansions appear as opportunities for freedom; nevertheless, it is in the nature of narrative to absorb such 'discrepancies' as a part of its language."[106] This would seem to take away with one hand what is being offered by the other, but such is the problematics of the case. A balance is struck between the "discrepancies" and the regularizing flow of the whole in literary narrative, and this balance deflects us away from the explanatory function toward the meaning function. Literary narrative is full of gaps; to raise certain moments to disruptive prominence relegates others to an irrelevant background. Meaning resides tenuously in these gaps, both within and outside the moment, both within and outside the text as a compound of moments, as the imaginary locus of the balance between particularity and system.

The pattern of narrative writing that I suggest above has a remarkably wide currency in contemporary literary theory. There is no space here for an inclusive discussion of the study of "narratology," but several parallels might help clarify the central issues of my argument, issues not always treated with the same attitude by all commentators on narrative form. The pattern of linear flow and disruption can be expressed as the interplay of the syntagmatic and paradigmatic functions, of the metonymic and metaphoric poles, or simply as the idea of narrative digression.

However, digression, like the "unpredictable expansions" cited by Barthes, must be seen as rule-bound freedom; it is, perhaps, more like the assertion of the idea of freedom, a sanctioning of the narrator's right to give the lie to normative ideology. The concept is at least as old as Homer, embodied in the character of Odysseus, whose prodigious talent for deception (lying) is closely allied with his unquestioned abilities as storyteller. Digression, as I want to use the term, is the revelation of the possibility of the "lie," which is precisely the problem with literature that so worried Plato: its power to meaningfully "say that which is not." Digression reveals that the surface ordering of a sanctioned meaningfulness (like the historian's explanatory systematicity) is the repression of free play, the repression of the promiscuous interlinking of all possible meanings, of infinite meaningfulness (which bears the threat of nonmeaning and death).

There is much to indicate that excessive and self-conscious use of digression, which calls attention to a need/desire for order, reflects the artist's sense of a fragmented world; this lends support to the efforts of theorists like Georg Lukács and Julia Kristeva to define the novel as the art form of modern fragmented social consciousness.[107] On the other hand, the degree to which such digressions seem to be playfully indulged by an audience, as Odysseus's stories are applauded and urged on by his listeners, may reflect a social stability or sense of belonging and cultural identity of a high degree. If we were to follow this set of ideas it would be necessary to devise a distinction between digression as rebellion against repression and digression in the service of repression (social order),[108] but my interests are simply in the revelation of the pattern.

Roland Barthes has been mentioned already in this connection, but a closer look at his suggestive reading of a short story by Balzac in *S/Z* provides us with the clearest example of the narrative of linear flow and disruptive digression. Barthes's approach consists in positing five "codes," or lexical elements, that uncover various narrative patterns. Of the five codes two are clearly linear and three are disruptive, or, as Jonathan Culler points out, two reflect Émile Benveniste's concept of distributional functioning and three reflect Benveniste's concept of integral functioning.[109] Barthes's "proairetic code," with its focus on the sense of plot as "sequence," and his "hermeneutic code," with its emphasis on the formulating of questions and delaying of answers, are oriented toward linearity. The remaining three codes are: the "semic," which concerns signifiers that "create characters, ambiances, shapes"; the "symbolic," which is very close to the traditional sense of "sign functioning," providing "a vast symbolic structure" for "many substitutions"; and the "cultural," which marks a referentiality in the text to culturally sanctioned "knowledge or wisdom"; these three codes tend toward the disruption of linearity, toward the endlessly expansive digression on character (in the romantic-organic sense), on the overcoding of sign-function patterns that permits endless choices and substitutions, and on the opening of literary textuality to cultural (even mythic?) contextuality.[110]

In *S/Z* Barthes emphasizes the act of reading and rereading; he emphasizes the multifunctioned nature of the text, but he does not emphasize the interplay of linearity and digression in quite the way I have presented it. Such a syntagmatic/paradigmatic interplay has been proposed by Tzvetan Todorov as the basis of narrative structure, and a recent study of narrative by Harold Toliver discovers similar patterns of interplay between horizontal and vertical motion.[111] A. J. Greimas has also constructed a grammatical model of narrative dynamics that resembles a scaled-down version of the famous Proppian dramatic approach to the narrative structures of Russian folktales.[112] The insistent linearity of Propp's thirty-one syntagmatic functions called forth, as a corrective, some greater emphasis on the paradigmatic function from both Greimas and Todorov.[113] To be sure, the Proppian analysis with its diachronic, dramatic bias has come to be directly opposed to the synchronic, homological analysis of (mythical) narratives developed by Lévi-Strauss;[114] together they represent the poles of a tension in narrative structure. It is, I would suggest, in the discursive unfolding of Barthes's practical analysis in *S/Z* that we can best see the mediation of these two views, even if that is not Barthes's primary concern.

As always, we are better able to examine this interplay through critical analysis than through abstract argumentation, and thus it has been one of the goals of this first essay to show that this pattern is the crucial organizational device of *Go Down, Moses*.

Nowhere, moreover, is it more clearly at work than in the seemingly inexplicable and disruptive insertion of the story "Pantaloon in Black" into the pattern of thematically related stories of the McCaslin family. This may be the best of all the individual stories; it is surely the most intense and economical in form and expression. Most commentators on *Go Down, Moses* have either ignored its relation to the rest of the novel or have connected it thematically, but few have accepted Faulkner's ironic claim that it was included merely to give his readers their money's worth.[115] There is nonetheless some truth to this claim, for the story is an excellent example of the not-so-irrelevant detail of narrative form. Here Faulkner is at his descriptive best, as in the passage telling of the black hero Rider's struggle to lift a huge log.

> He had done it before—taken a log from the truck onto his hands, balanced, and turned with it and tossed it down the skidway, but never with a stick of this size, so that in a complete cessation of all sound save the pulse of the exhaust and the light free-running whine of the disengaged saw since every eye there, even that of the white foreman, was upon him, he nudged the log to the edge of the truck-frame and squatted and set his palms against the underside of it. For a time there was no movement at all. It was as if the unrational and inanimate wood had invested, mesmerised the man with some of its own primal inertia. Then a voice said quietly: "He got hit. Hit's off de truck," and they saw the crack and gap of air, watching the infinitesimal straightening of the braced legs until the knees locked, the movement mounting infinitesimally through the belly's insuck, the arch of the chest, the neck cords, lifting the lip from the white clench of the teeth in passing, drawing the whole head backward and only the bloodshot fixity of the eyes impervious to it, moving on up the arms and the straightening elbows until the balanced log was higher than his head. "Only he aint gonter turn wid dat un," the same voice said. "And when he try to put hit back on de truck, hit gonter kill him." But none of them moved. Then—there was no gathering of supreme effort—the log seemed to leap suddenly backward over his head of its own volition, spinning, crashing and thundering down the incline; he turned and stepped over the slanting track in one stride and walked through them as they gave way and went on across the clearing toward the woods even though the foreman called after him: "Rider!" and again: "You, Rider!" [Pp. 145-6]

Faulkner dwells on the scene with such rapt fascination that it alone threatens to break free of the narrative flow. For an unmeasurable moment all motion is stopped, lingered over by Faulkner's play with words, concentrated into stillness yet containing the potential of a mighty eruption of energy. But the narrative, the force of temporality, pushes in again, opened by the short, breathless and quiet comments of an onlooker, whereupon the scene rushes to its conclusion.

A scene so powerful begs for interpretation. What does it tell us of the hero, Rider? Is it merely a demonstration of his strength? Does it express in physical action Rider's tormented drive for self-destruction, his agony at the unexplained death of his wife, Mannie? Does it depict the awful laughter of some deranged god who allows Rider to triumph here even though the grief-torn black man wants to fail, to have the agonizing breath of life crushed out of him? Is it a parable on existence, on the eternal struggle between the forces of life and death where Faulkner tips the balance ever so slightly in favor of the former? Perhaps the passage says all of these in varying degrees, but none exhausts its rich experiential value. The descriptive force draws the reader into the struggle, causes our breaths to suck in as Rider strains against the tree. It is, moreover, a quality that pervades the entire story and calls for our participation in the vitality of human experience without the effort of explanation. It is a virtuoso performance on the part of author and character that does not depend on the other stories for its effect; so far as we know, the time and place of the action is not specified and Rider's relation to the McCaslins or Sam Fathers is not given in the text.[116] More or less instinctively we place it in Yoknapatawpha County, Mississippi, and roughly at the time of "Delta Autumn," and we acknowledge the thematic congruence it has with the other stories of race relations. But little of this has any direct bearing on its affective strength.

Let me return for a moment to the passage of Rider's struggle quoted above. It concludes with the voice of the foreman twice naming the character, "Rider." That in itself may be somewhat surprising—because Rider is addressed by name and not by a racially pejorative term such as "boy." This is not to put words in Faulkner's mouth; the force of the passage, stronger than any other in the story, is to confer on Rider an identity so sharply defined that it resists reduction to racial stereotypes. The passage, then, is descriptive of Rider's actions while it also performs for the reader a singular act of characterization. It takes on the feel of what we traditionally call poetry through the author's play with language. "Poetry" implies that an unusual attention has been given to words and structure themselves; every element of the poem's form is crucial, fixed, contextual. A poem is "these words in this order" and permits no alteration. To label this passage "play" or "poetry," however, is not enough, for what is at issue in the formula "these words in this order" is the degree of motivation revealed in the language, and Faulkner's poetic play in this passage demonstrates a shift in emphasis from relatively arbitrary selectivity to an intensely motivated performance.

The terms *arbitrary* and *motivated* I have somewhat roughly borrowed from Saussure, whose famous dictum on the arbitrariness of the linguistic sign could have produced a theory of language as a multitude of discrete elements, a lexical chaos, if not restricted by some rule. Thus it is through the concept of "relative arbitrariness" that Saussure introduces into language study the idea of "system." The structure of *langue* has only a limited arbitrariness because of "associative and syntagmatic" forces that bind signs together into "bundles." For example, the Latin term *inimicus* is not absolutely arbitrary for it bears the trace of an elaborate class of signs through its elements, *in* and *amicus*.[117] *Inimicus*, then, is very highly motivated through its syntagmatic bindings; the whole class lies unexpressed behind the expressed term.

To be sure, Saussure's thoughts on arbitrariness are ambiguous. Primarily concerned with the arbitrary relation between signs (words) and things in the world, Saussure seems also to see it is a factor in the internal relationship of the sign itself, as in the arbitrary relationship between signifier and signified, between acoustical image (sound) and thought content (concept).[118] It is, however, the business of *langue* to repress the anarchistic force of the arbitrary (or *langage*). On the level of *langue* the relation between signifier and signified must be rendered "necessary"[119] or "motivated."

Within the system of less arbitrary or motivated meaningfulness we must also take notice of the function of *parole*, of the act of choice. The term *motivation* here begins to take on a deeper significance. The motivating force of *langue* is relative to general classes of substitutable items and the rules for their selection. It is the function of *parole*, sometimes in conjunction with the freedom (arbitrariness) of *langage*, to render the articulated poetic utterance with a much more intense sense of motivation—not the motivation of class substitutions but of particularities of experience. Ironically, at this level it is impossible to say whether the poetic utterance is radically motivated or radically arbitrary; it is a matter of perspective, a double vision that glances at the poetic passage simultaneously from inside cultural limitations (*langue*) and from outside such limitations (*langage*). What is revealed in this double vision is intentionality, not the actual thoughts of the author but the fact of his activity of choice, the fact of his articulation to particular, irreducible experience.

We are trapped once more in the obscurities of distinctions of degree, or, I would prefer, by the endless adjustments of an integral system. There is, therefore, nothing absolutely unmotivated about any particular act of articulation; hence Faulkner's description of Rider's efforts to lift the log can only be spoken of as more or less arbitrary. The key to understanding the passage comes to us only in the act of calling attention to motivation. That choices were made is obvious. But Faulkner moves from broad views of the scene in the hustle and bustle of the camp to the more specific details of the lifting of the log, to even further specificity in the infinitesimal details of arching chest and clenched teeth. The effect is to break the general descriptive scene down into smaller and smaller units, and to emphasize more and more the arbitrary nature of the author's choices—or at least to emphasize the vastness of details available for his choice. Most important, however, is a countermovement that arises necessarily from this breaking down. The pace of the scene seems to slow even as the details multiply; overwhelmed by particularities the reader begins to search for an orderly focus. At the point where such a focus should come, however, at the moment of balanced tension with the log held aloft, the reader is forestalled by the disrupting voice of an anonymous onlooker (who speaks breathlessly for us?): "'Only he aint gonter turn wid dat un.'" A turn will come, but at this unmeasurable moment of pause we find in the language of the passage a disturbing absence, a lack of a focal center that contains the opposing forces within itself, the absence of a true metaphor to unite the multiplicity of metonymic particularities.

We get instead only the relatively impersonal third person pronoun "he"; yet the pronoun shifter calls our attention to what is missing: to the unexpressed motivation for the descriptive passage, and the tension of such a gap or absence is intolerable. The pause suddenly breaks open and the passage rushes to a conclusion; then, and only then, do we find the metaphor that we sought, but we find it outside the descriptive articulation itself. This belated fulfillment is very significant, for the focal metaphor could not be named in the passage without being reduced to the status of the other details, without becoming merely one metonymic detail among the others. Left unexpressed, it retains a fullness of meaning even in its absence, and we cannot avoid recalling here, by way of contrast, the weak metaphor of the phoenix dreamed by Ike as a banishing of all absence (time) through its magical presence. The container for the tensions of the passage, the unity for the seemingly endless details, can only be said afterwards in the name "Rider," into which name rush all the expressed and unexpressed details of the scene as a whole. Ike's phoenix metaphor does not work as an effort to deny absence; the naming of Rider as metaphor does not deny but recognizes the affective force of absence. Saying the name, of course, consigns all that explicitly and inexplicitly went before to absence, but the battle has been won.[120] The name "Rider" has become radically motivated, allowing us to see motivation ambiguously as a matter of both character development and literary articulation. If it is true, as Eugenio Donato argues, that our Western culture has grown more and more obsessed with the idea that proper names are privileged signs that confer identity,[121] the rush of the chaotic and relatively arbitrary details of the passage into the name, the replacing of the pronoun with "Rider," lends an intensity of identity to this particular character, confers on him an "authenticity," that nothing in the remainder of the story can efface.[122]

Such authenticity, of course, is an illusion of linguistic utterance, not because Rider is a fictional character but because the idea of authenticity itself is illusory. The disruptive force of Rider's metaphoric naming functions as a paradigm for all assertions of being, for the winning of experiential presence out of the anonymity of structural absence. This, too, is a philosophical and critical idea with a broadly romantic history. The idea of a privileged moment of being, of the arresting moment, the emergence of metaphor, is no more than a sense of "wonder"[123] or "apocalypse,"[124] two characteristics already attributed to Ike's romantic turn of mind. Parallels can be found ranging from Kant's definition of the "sublime" to Cassirer's description of "momentary gods" or "mana-experiences," to Joyce's religious/aesthetic "epiphanies," to Eliseo Vivas's "rapt intransitive attention."[125] Ezra Pound idealized the poetic moment in the "vortex," Wallace Stevens in the crystalline "fiction," and T. S. Eliot in the "still point." Confining himself to the level of style, Barthes has spoken of the "perverse" pleasure we receive from such a disruptive opening in the text, a kind of orgasmic rapture, experiential but unspeakable.[126] Deep within us Jung located the "archetype" of a timeless, racial heritage, and Freud, perhaps most suggestively of all, defined the experience of disjunctive temporality as the "uncanny," the moment of the strange that is not strange in the midst of the familiar.[127] Freud is particularly significant here because his sense of the uncanny can be read in a way that drives out the romantic argument that these moments are literally "unique," unrepeatable, and even ineffable. The essence of the Freudian uncanny is its recurrent patterning, its revelation of a repressed absent meaningfulness, yet it is never free of the aura of wonder, of the two much meaningfulness of metaphor, or of the paradox of the familiar (half-remembered) defamiliarized.

Thus we see that Rider's defamiliarization, though a singular act of *parole* that cannot be erased, calls attention to the very act of linguistic (and impersonal) substitution that allows us to put the "name" in the place of the pronoun. We are aware of the choices that not only relegate "he" to the stockpile of unused signs, but also negate culturally determined racial stereotypes such as "boy." That awareness does not come to us at the wondrous moment of Rider's naming but only in the course of the story itself; it comes with our growing awareness of Rider as a disruptive force infused into a cultural system of dehumanizing stereotypes. It is a profound comment on the rigidity of society that at the same time, in the textual violence of Rider's naming paralleled by the violence of his self-destructive actions, makes us witnesses to the power and self-destructive violence of metaphor itself. Faulkner's articulation to experience, therefore, speaks the tensions of revolution or impending change. It is not prophecy so much as recognition again, here in this seemingly irrelevant story, of the internal tensions of the southern culture that we also see in the self-destructive repudiation made by Ike McCaslin and in the archetypal emergence of Lucas Beauchamp. Failure to confront this internal pressure for change, of course, will result in the dreaded invasion of the North; the corruption from within will unleash a corruption from without, the same corruption that Ike half perceives in the disappearance of the forest and openly fears in his discovery of the written ledgers.

The addition of the white deputy sheriff's monologue serves as a crucial counter-voice, as another failed interpretation. The deputy never engages Rider's story at the level of experience; he does not, as one critic notes, "recognize humanity when he sees it."[128] The stupid insensitivity of his remarks angers us not just because they are racist, but because they also rob Rider of a unique, experiential being that we, as readers, have already granted him under the compulsion of Faulkner's language. The deepest level of interpretation—the radical level of articulated meaningfulness—defies the detached voice of a disengaged observer-analyst armed only with stereotypes and abstractions. The deputy's language fails him, for on the propositional level Rider's suffering, and his essential being, is silent. The reader feels the story come alive with meaningfulness as Faulkner draws us in through the "gestural" nature of his language, and the story's title calls attention to this dimension of literary discourse by reminding us of the conventions of mime performance where communication through physical movement challenges the hegemony of mere words. It demands dramatic participation, a hermeneutic engagement, that is not available on the level of conceptual or abstract Knowledge.

Here again we affirm the provincialism of articulated cognitive structures; the failed interpretation of the white deputy recapitulates the failure of Ike McCaslin to reinterpret, for his own romantic purposes, the totemic world of Sam Fathers. Myths are, then, nontransferable, and Faulkner, dealing with several myths in his novel, must not allow the readers to confuse them as his characters often do. Close attention to Faulkner's novel, to its pattern of failed interpretations, should warn the reader and professional critic alike that it is not *a* structure but the *potentiality* of structure that is universal: the distinction is a crucial one. The linguist's dream of describing a finite generative grammar that is universal,[129] yet permits infinite variations in its manifestations, cannot be solidified into a sense of universal sameness in all human expressions. It is the meaningfulness of literary articulation that is proof against such a theory. Yet much of modern criticism, influenced by this very linguistic model of universal structure, has denied literature this function.

The result has been an overemphasis of the conservative forces of the structuring process. In the alliance of T. S. Eliot and Northrop Frye the dominance of "tradition" or the "dream world" of literary myth overshadows the "individual talent" or the uniqueness of the "displaced" monad.[130] More recently John Barth has extolled the virtues of Jorge Luis Borges to define literary creativity as a kind of plagiarism, Robert Scholes, chary of the word "conservative," has defined what he calls the "illiberal imagination."[131] As a corrective for the exaggerated emphasis on progressivism in twentieth-century philosophy, the trend is admirable, but it risks the opposite extreme by rejecting all philosophies of change and branding all versions of existential humanism as irrationalism.[132] There is in this conservatism an irrational fear of irrationalism and the expression of a nostalgic yearning for simpler and temporally self-reflexive primitivism. The old adage that all literature is about literature assumes a new and restrictive focus; for Borges the world of discourse (which is *the* world) is a vast library catalogued and ordered wherein one discovers the source of all possible utterances. It is an exhaustive system of permissible transforms reflecting, as John Barth says, every novelist's desire to rewrite *Don Quixote*.[133] The fact that all fictions repeat other fictions to some extent, however, does not necessarily argue for Borges's closed library. Even for the conservative Eliot, faith, universal stability, and Knowledge, the tradition of literature and Christianity, all had to be won in the articulation of his *Four Quartets*, in the speaking to experience through his very personal voice.

In *Go Down, Moses* Faulkner sets for himself no such task as Eliot chose in *Four Quartets*. To prove the functional validity of a universal schema, to show its meaningfulness, is alien to his vision where different worlds exist side by side in the same narrative. Thus, if one cannot return to the embracing wilderness of Sam Fathers, one is not necessarily condemned to the dissipation of energies in a chaotic world that defies meaningfulness. If anything, Faulkner depicts a world of surplus meaningfulness where general systems and discrete experiences abound. Lucas, Ike, and Sam are not part of one world but of a multiplex world, full of interactions and conflicts that threaten them all with the terrifying specter of discontinuity. Yet the narrative encompasses this diversity, not by regularizing it into a series of permissible transforms, but by allowing history to express itself in an elaborate pattern of emergences, each of which holds for its space against the violence of mere temporality. For Lucas and Sam the myths succeed in raising experience to meaningfulness even though neither exhausts empirical reality. On the other hand, Ike's apocalypticism evidences the most spectacular failure of all, for he drags discrete experience out of temporality by fixing it in a timeless, mystical sacredness. Ironically, this thrusts him back into the discontinuousness of temporality; because he cannot live in time, cannot bring meaningfulness into presence in a "world" that "worlds," his apocalyptic imagination, his egotism, fails to create for him the stability of being he so desires.

Ike's overinterpretations are nowhere more clear than in his response to the fading McCaslin ledgers; these dusty volumes become for him a personal Bible, a holy book.

> To him it was as though the ledgers in their scarred cracked leather bindings were being lifted down one by one in their fading sequence and spread open on the desk or perhaps upon some apocryphal Bench or even Altar or perhaps the Throne itself for a last perusal and contemplation and refreshment of the All-knowledgeable before the yellowed pages and the brown thin ink in which was recorded the injustice and a little at least of its amelioration and restitution faded back forever into the anonymous communal original dust. [P. 261]

The ledgers are his Old Testament, the history of the McCaslins like the history of the Israelites and their captors. Old Carothers's sin is the primal sin of Adam, and Ike's Egypt is the South "cursed" by God (p. 298). This holy book, with its dialogue between the gospellers Buck and Buddy, infringes upon the mythical world of Sam Fathers, forcing Ike to see the wilderness as a new Eden and Sam as a new Adam.

In a very crucial way Ike's ledgers represent his enslavement by the written word. The inexorable logic of this text has the force of history, of metonymy, which in its orderliness strives for the condition of myth. We must not be fooled by Faulkner's teasing presentation of the information in section four of "The Bear"; the ruthless simplicity of Buck's and Buddy's dialogue is not a designedly elliptical presentation. It is a purified form of script, which notes events only insofar as they follow the cultural schema of the authors. The terror of these chronicles for Ike is in part this very starkness, the relentless movement of the pattern from which he finds no escape. Unable to alter the course of this text, he fears that soon his name will be the focus of its progress, that his hand will be drawn into the dialogue, into a continuation of the history he abhors. The result is Ike's dread of time, which the ledgers have reduced to chronology; he is a slave to prose unable to transform it into an autobiographical narrative, unwilling to bow to Lucas's mythicizing of the family history, but stained by it so that he cannot enter Sam's collective myth, which is spoken, not written, by the univocal voice of Sam and Sam's ever-present ancestors.

Most significantly, however, Ike's exaggerated interpretation reflects his own sense of a deep personal guilt; it is the manifestation of his romantic consciousness, similar to what Paul Ricoeur says is man's assertion of himself as "tribunal" of himself thereby bringing about his "alienation" from mankind. In Ike we observe not only "self-righteousness" but also the "curse attached thereto." Here the supreme "sin consists . . . in the vain attempt to justify oneself."[134] As a result Ike comes to live on the fringes of society, not unlike the man-child Boon who belongs neither to the wilderness nor to culture, and whose end is presented to us as madness.

But Ike's position is instructively different from Boon's. Ike's guilt/fear of the family ledgers expresses his entrapment by the McCaslin genealogical myth, what we must call his subservience to it and to the cultural patterning (authoritarian, patriarchal, and racist) that it reveals. Such a pattern is undeniably Oedipal as it measures belonging (to race or family) by means of subservience (political or personal) to the master race of the (fore)-fathers. Regardless of his histrionic rebellion/repudiation, Ike is never able to break free from this myth; to do so would be too frightening a revolt, and perhaps Ike's failure unveils Faulkner's own drawing back. Faulkner gives us, in his characters of racially mixed heritage, several openings toward a truly revolutionary cultural action, yet these characters never express a truly alternative culture. Lucas is absorbed into the genealogical myth, very much by his own choice, in order to function as its archetype. The child of Roth Edmonds and the black woman of "Delta Autumn" is literally ejected from the South, sent away by Ike himself. And Boon, whose time-innocence and arrested Oedipal development makes him the most promising anti-Oedipal figure in the novel, suffers a fate familiar to all of Faulkner's readers; he is condemned to madness, to an antisocial status where his breaking of the pattern no longer threatens the pattern itself.[135]

Thus Ike's solution to his dilemma is inevitably apocalyptic; he would write an ending to the ledgers, to the narrative text that is his (family and cultural) life, but his problem with endings has its inverse in the problematics of beginnings.[136] He would have the renunciation of his heritage carry with it the renunciation of patrimony, even though this leaves him alone, able to assert himself as an "original original" only in a weak emulation of Christ. Time becomes his enemy, and he is submerged in a surplus of apocalyptic meaningfulness that is endlessly repeatable. Edward Said describes Stendhal's romantic hero Julien Sorel in terms that seem also to fit Ike.

> Such a character is hungry for the distinctions of more and more originality. His time is no longer the possession of the community, nor of the family man, but is rather an illicit dream of projected fulfillment whose high subjective purpose at the end is radically underminded at the beginning by refusals, the sacrifices, the renunciations, and the selfishness on which it is based. A life so lived is less an orderly biography than a series of collisions and compromises . . . ; this new private affair—especially when it becomes compulsive—substitutes irresponsible celibacy for fruitful marriage.[137]

It is very significant, indeed, that Ike neither begins (he is merely introduced in "Was") nor ends the novel, for the detailed experiential reality of Faulkner's fictional province is too much for his apocalyptic imagination. Thus the title story of the novel, the last story of the collection, defies his sense of endings; this story is what R. P. Adams calls "a contextual expansion of what has gone before,"[138] and it puts Ike outside the burgeoning life that Faulkner describes. Molly Beauchamp's choral lament dominates the final narrative segment as an expression of her grief over the execution of her grandson, Samuel Worsham Beauchamp, for the murder of a Chicago policeman. Significantly, it takes on the terms of Ike's confusion of the Bible and the McCaslin family history; Molly's song, too, associates the black McCaslins with the captive Israelites and the white McCaslins with the oppressing Egyptians. "'Roth Edmonds sold him. . . . Sold my Benjamin. Sold him in Egypt. Sold him to Pharaoh. Sold him to Pharoah and now he dead'" (p. 380). Roth of course, had no direct responsibility for Sam's death, but the song re-evokes the slave market morality established in "Was" as the system of exchange that supports the McCaslin myth, the exact terms that Lucas utilized in his assertion of mythical-archetypal presence.

The traditional spiritual from which the story's title comes is a prayer for deliverance from bondage, for a new Moses, while it is also a defiant assertion of the slave's sense of belonging to a "chosen" people. Here too the chanting of Molly and the other blacks reflects in its participatory function a sense of collective being that closes out others—most particularly Gavin Stevens and his world of practical concerns (pp. 380–81). Gavin is the last of the novel's long list of failed interpreters stretching all the way back to Buck and Buddy McCaslin who fail to understand why the violated slave, Eunice, "drowned herself" (p. 267). Gavin's efforts to keep the story of her grandson's death from Molly are not merely futile but unnecessary, for Molly's world encloses Samuel within its own mythical terms. Her reaction, which ignores the "facts," becomes, then, not so much an act of foregiveness as an assertion of her own perfectly adequate rationale; for Gavin it is a puzzling dilemma that seems to say Molly "*doesn't care how he died*" (p. 383). But that is only partly true. Molly's acceptance reflects what Ricoeur calls a sense of "the 'reality' of sin—one might even say the ontological dimension of sin which must be contrasted with the 'subjectivity' of the consciousness of guilt."[139] The final story, therefore, also closes out Ike, whose subjective guilt condemns him not only to fail in his pilgrimage of being, to fail to find the promised land, but even, unlike Moses, to glimpse it. To borrow once more from Ricoeur, Ike remains perpetually at the crises moment of human consciousness "after which myth and history are disassociated. Mythical time can no longer be co-ordinated with the time of events that are 'historical' . . . mythical space can no longer be co-ordinated with the places of our geography."[140] Ike can neither move forward into history nor backward into the old myth; tortured by what Mircea Eliade called "ontological thirst,"[141] he finds himself, to paraphrase Lucas Beauchamp, excluded from the true benefits of belonging yet not free from the genealogical myth's heavy burden of responsibility.

ON METAPHOR AND METONYMY: A STYLISTIC ANALYSIS OF "NOW" AND "THEN"

Faulkner's style, distinctive, daring, and powerfully affective, has often been discussed in relation to the recurrent theme of time in his novels, and there is an exemplary stylistic device of this kind in the repetition of the words "now" and "then" that contributes forcefully to the impact of *Go Down, Moses*. The former term (indicating a priviledged presentness that is also closely associated with the term "still," and thus indicates an absence of sound and motion as well as a continuous presentness) and the repetitive patterning of the latter (a parataxis emphasizing a disjuncture between two successive points in time) are frequently used to counteract one another. The long descriptive paragraph quoted above where Rider lifts a heavy log from the lumber truck depends upon this balancing of movement and sound against stillness and quiet. The paragraph begins with two "thens" and introduces us to the busy, loud commotion of the millyard. The images raise the picture of random, though purposeful, movement, something like beehive or anthill activity. "Then the trucks were rolling again. Then he could stop needing to invent to himself reasons for his breathing, until after a while he began to believe he had forgot about breathing since now he could not hear himself above the steady thunder of the rolling logs . . ." (p. 145). But, as we have seen, Rider cannot forget, cannot diffuse his agonized being in the furious activity of sound and motion. The rolling logs reach a temporary end and he prepares to test his strength against the last one, doing what "he had done before . . . but never with a stick of this size. . . ." His effort not only seems to stop all motion but even to still the thunderous noise. "For a time there was no movement at all. It was as if the unrational and inanimate wood had invested, mesmerised the man with some of its primal inertia." The primal inertia brings us to a moment of equilibrium, and Rider stands in the center of everyone's attention, "in a complete cessation of all sound save the pulse of the exhaust and the light free-running whine of the disengaged saw. . . ." The struggle between the opposed forces, however, is not really a total lack of motion as the pulse of the engine and whine of the saw show; here the descriptive force of Faulkner's style reveals the massive concentration of pulsing, straining, vital energy that may explosively erupt at any moment. There is, as well, no real pause in the forward movement of the prose. We have only the illusion of a pause created by the insertion of a simple short sentence, "For a time there was no movement at all," between a long, rambling sentence telling of exhausts, trucks, saws, and the crowd watching Rider and the contemplative restful "as if" sentence, which mesmerizes the reader with its abstract speculation about primal inertia.

The equilibrium of forces, therefore, cannot be long maintained, and the stillness and quiet of the vibrating moment are broken by the inexorable onrush of the narrative. Both sound and movement are reintroduced suddenly, but softly, in another "then" clause: "Then a voice said quietly: 'He got hit.'" The hushed, disembodied voice, seeming to feel that it voilates the sacredness of the moment, is also prophetic, for it opens the way to movement once more: "The movement mounting infinitesimally through the belly's insuck." At first the progress is halting, "until the knees lock," and "until the balanced log was higher than his head," pausing again while "none of them moved," and finally erupting, only to be interrupted one last time by a negative phrase offset with dashes, but that cannot hold back the flow of temporality. "Then—there was no gathering of supreme effort—the log seemed to leap suddenly backward over his head of its own volition, spinning, crashing and thundering down the incline. . . ." The "then" clause violently reintroduces through the active verb "leap" and the triple present participles the busy movement and "thundering" noise that opened the paragraph.

There is a sense, as we have seen in the naming of Rider, that metaphor is no more than a name we give to the idea of conserving vital energy in equilibrium. It is an absence that makes possible a presence, a unity that violently breaks itself apart. Here the metaphoric function of language rises to "stillness" and "nowness" out of and against the pull of metonymy, and in this tenuous assertion of presence, metaphor shows itself to be the stylistic expression of the philosophical idea of a centering archetype. Similarly, the emergence of Lucas Beauchamp finds its affective power through the interplay of metaphor and metonymy; it is this that gives Lucas's archetypal presence its crucial prototypical function, establishing through the play of language the extensive explanatory power of the McCaslin genealogical myth.

On the day of ritual confrontation with Zack, Lucas, the direct male descendant of old Carothers, appropriately waits for the woman-born McCaslin to come to him. "Then the light disappeared. He began to say quietly, aloud: 'Now, Now. He will have to have time to walk over here.' He continued to say it long after he knew the other had had time to walk back and forth between the two houses ten times over" (p. 51). Zack does not come, and Lucas's waiting for the sacred, archetypal "now" falls victim to the passing of time. "Then he knew that the other was not even waiting, and it was as if he stood already in the bedroom itself, above the slow respirations of sleep, the undefended and oblivious throat, the naked razor already in his hand" (p. 51). Jarred from his passive waiting, Lucas thrusts the "now" into a vision of the future; he must make that future a present; and when he does so, it will be as if he had already performed the ritual sacrifice (p. 52), an exercise of his "mythical memory." Yet the momentousness of that timeless "now" continues to elude him. "He was waiting for daylight. He could not have said why. He squatted against a tree halfway between the carriage gate and the white man's house, motionless as the windless obscurity itself while the constellations wheeled and the whipporwills choired faster and faster and ceased and the first cocks crowed and the false dawn came and faded and the birds began and the night was over" (p. 52). Only halfway toward the future "now," the universe whirls in mad, accelerating motion around him, but he has not yet earned the right to center the wheeling stars, to emerge from obscurity into archetypal presence. The syntagmatic pull of the sentence jerks us forward in tiny fragments of blurred events linked only by a chain of "ands."

When he enters the inner sanctum of Zack's bedroom all is again silenced, but this is only the prelude to the "now." The relentless series of "thens" continues. "Then he found the eyes of the face on the pillow looking quietly up at him and he knew then why he had to wait until daylight" (p. 52). He has come not to murder in darkness the man who stole his wife but for a ritualistic confrontation. He throws away his razor to equalize the oppositions, but Zack does not at first accept the challenge; "still the other didn't move" (p. 53). Lucas knows instinctively what Ike never learns from Sam, that by possessing one thing other you possess them both. His emergence into being, the establishing of his identity, necessitates the active participation of "the other," Zack. The scene wavers for a while between the two men. Zack enters the contest by retrieving his pistol from the drawer, but as he does so Lucas is momentarily stilled: "still Lucas didn't move" (p. 54). Lucas attempts to provoke Zack into holding the gun while he rushes him, but Zack, too, knows the rules of equilibrated confrontation and tosses the gun on the bed between them. Suddenly, the to-and-fro play bursts into simultaneous action; a series of "then" clauses cascades around us. "Then Lucas was beside the bed. He didn't remember moving at all. He was kneeling, their hands gripped, facing across the bed and the pistol" (p. 55). Locked in confrontation they kneel in reverence to the moment. "Then he cried, and not to the white man and the white man knew it; he saw the whites of the negro's eyes rush suddenly with red like the eyes of bayed animal—a bear [!], a fox [the trickster] . . . *I was wrong*, the white man thought. *I have gone too far*" (p. 55). "Then they did not move save their forearms, their gripped hands turning gradually until the white man's hand was pressed back—downward on the pistol. Motionless, locked, incapable of moving . . ." (pp. 55-56). Physically motionless, Lucas fills the moment with an extraordinary recapitulation of the events preceding it, almost as if he must be certain that the ritualistic procedures have been properly observed. "'I give you your chance,' Lucas said. 'Then you laid here asleep with your door unlocked and give me mine. Then I throwed the razor away and give it back. And then you throwed it back to me'" (p. 56). The sacred "now" has not yet come, the to-and-fro movement still dominates, but the time of the past few hours has been concentrated into the seconds of this speech, into another very rapid sequence of "thens." The moment, therefore, begins to draw the past and present into itself so that even in its finite, discrete, metaphoric timelessness it will be expansive and inclusive. The conflict is more than the confrontation of Zack and Lucas, or of two men, or of the "I" and the "other." Its context becomes that of the McCaslin history transformed by the power of language into the universal, identity-conferring conflict between master and slave, and not that conflict only in the sociological sense of southern history, but in the phenomenological sense of Hegel. The "I" and the "other" come to be only within the historical context, and this context, if we recall Benveniste's insistently triadic model, takes shape only in the confrontation of the "I" and the "other."[142]

Significantly, it is Zack, the "master," who must actively confer identity on Lucas, who must acknowledge the "now." "The white man sprang, hurling himself across the bed, grasping at the pistol and the hand which held it. Lucas sprang too; they met over the center of the bed where Lucas clasped the other with his left arm almost like an embrace and jammed the pistol against the white man's side and pulled the trigger and flung the white man from him all in one motion, hearing as he did so the light, dry, incredibly loud click of the miss-fire" (p. 57). The rapid actions are here accelerated into what is almost simultaneity, centered over the bed in an embrace and concentrated into an instant of sound in the metaphoric click. Clearly a narrative foreshadowing of the statue-like culmination of the conflict between Boon-Lion and old Ben presented later in the novel, the reduction of time to a spatial point gives to the moment a ritualistic presence. But there is a crucial difference: the conflict of the hunt is typical and will be repeated again and again in actuality, whereas the symbolic marriage of opposites here will never actually occur again; it is the opening of an absence, the making of space for an archetype that is "summary" or functions only as prototype to be imitated. Even here, of course, the metonymic pressures of the prose defy a true stopping of time; the concentration of motion into the click is achieved by a stylistic illusion, first in the not wholly convincing claim that all of this happened in one motion, and more effectively through the violent hiatus in the narrative that follows this passage. There is, after the "miss-fire," an open space on the page, a graphic stillness or absence, which announces a radical time shift out of the flashback sequence. Before being plunged back into the world of time, where images of revolving seasons pass quickly before our eyes, we are suspended in the blankness where a metaphor *should be*, in an absence where the magic word goes unwritten yet, like certain arresting sounds that even when no longer heard seem to linger in the mind, which word silently holds our attention. After this moment a metaphor *is* written, in the "cartridge" from the miss-fire, but the metaphor's graphic presence takes its force from the absence that made a place for it in the text.

When we confront the metaphor as written, therefore, we cannot forget that the scene of symbolic marriage between Zack and Lucas grows out of a tradition of exploitation and eternalizes it. The master/slave relationship of Zack and Lucas undergoes a violent reversal in the struggle. The dominant white partner Zack is provoked into action only to be suddenly forced to undergo the passive marraige role of the female—as the woman-born McCaslin. The reversal is crucial if Lucas's archetypical presence is to contain the essential conflicts of the McCaslin heritage, and Lucas gains not only an identity here but also a position of unquestionable (male) dominance, exploiting Zack for his own satisfaction (it is Lucas who fires the pistol) then roughly flinging him aside. This action reveals the power of the archetype, which continues to exercise its repressive force over the other descendants of Carothers McCaslin, over Roth and Ike, for belonging necessitates an acceptance of the conflicts and, hence, an acceptance of Lucas. Lucas, therefore, carries with him not only the past but extends the forces of the McCaslin myth into the future. He is the keeper of the McCaslin "icon": "the live cartridge, not even stained, not corroded, the mark of the firing-pin dented sharp and deep into the unexploded cap—the dull little brass cylinder less long than a match, not much larger than a pencil, not much heavier, yet large enough to contain two lives" (p. 58).

Out of the world of merely familiar items, pencils and matches, this small cartridge has been infused not merely with two lives but with a family/social heritage. The bullet, so common an item in this novel filled with the violent but ritualistic world of hunting, has been defamiliarized into metaphor. Unexploded, its conserves the energy of conflict unspent, concentrating into itself the polysemantic, multi-experiential world of the McCaslins and Faulkner's South, closing out the totemic world of Sam Fathers. It is the radical symbol of another mythical world, a world of repression, exploitation, racial conflict, and self-destructive idealism, all manifest in the narrative of Ike's family, which speaks to a dead god, not the god of Christian myth nor the deer totem of Sam's tribe, but to old Carothers. Appropriately, Lucas himself acknowledges this deity: "'*I needed him and he came and spoke for me*'" (p. 58). The symbolic cartridge, articulated in the click, asserts the power, limited but essential, of metaphor to do battle against the metonymy of prose and the randomness of change, but as it does so it extracts from those who would belong to the myth of the McCaslin family commitments that are harsh. These commitments Isaac McCaslin is unwilling to make, although in his retreat he fails to find a better world comprised of better men. Perhaps, too, we must see the world of Sam Fathers as in its own way equally harsh, for it makes demands to which Ike, alien to its mythical terms, cannot accede, although he is willing. Caught between these two worlds, he is a man without a history, feebly projecting his personal apocalyptic visions on experiences that defy his thrust toward order and stasis. So, then, he becomes a paradigm of the modern, ahistorical, and uncommitted existential man, but although Faulkner's vision[143] of true historical meaningfulness escapes Ike, it does not escape the reader. Faulkner's novel is, certainly, neither history nor myth, yet it strives to give us an immediate experience of the force of each working its way through our daily lives. It is a vision of history to which only the capabilities of a literary language are adequate.

Part Two

The Centrality of Language

The centrality of language in the interpretation of literature may at first appear to be obvious. It is not. Language is the medium of creative expression, but what sort of medium? It lacks the corporeal solidity of the sculptor's marble and the sensual purity of the musician's sound waves. Modern aestheticians, following the lead of nineteenth-century philosophers, have tended to argue that language paradoxically partakes of both the corporeality of stone and the incorporeality of sound, but this is a metaphorical way of speaking indicating only that language, as a medium for artistic expression, should be defined by its own characteristics.

A THEORY OF LITERARY LANGUAGE

A major contribution to the theory of language as a medium for creative expression was developed in the 1930s and 1940s by the American New Critics.[1] Parallel, though not always identical, attitudes were also presented by the Russian Formalists,[2] the Prague Linguistic Circle,[3] and the French promoters of *explication de texte*.[4] Yet the New Criticism provides the most available and instructive model on which we may begin our analysis of the problems of language and its artistic uses. Metaphorically, the New Critics argued that language is a vital medium—living, not dead. In the creative process language, by its own peculiar characteristics, contributes to the making of the poem. It is not a mere vehicle or form into which one pours content or meaning.

The source of this doctrine lies in nineteenth-century romantic aesthetics.[5] Coleridge's long response to Wordsworth in the *Biographia Literaria* revolved essentially on the point that language is an integral part of the poem. The form of poetic language, particularly its meter, is its distinguishing characteristic, and Coleridge claimed, "I write in meter, because I am about to use a language different from that of prose."[6] Actually, he means that he is going to use language differently than does the prose writer, and this leads to his emphasis on meter. The rhythmic qualities of poetic language do not merely embellish the poem's content; they are the vital characteristics of the poem itself—its life. They reflect the energy of aesthetic creativity and beyond that the creative vitality of natural life, the *natura naturans*. Thus, for Coleridge, poetry is tied to the creative life of the universe, is an echo of the creative spirit of God, and is qualitatively unlike the mere prosaic use of language.

The difference between poetry and prose in this theory, I would emphasize, is *how* the writer uses language, for Coleridge argues that "a poem contains the same elements as a prose composition; the difference therefore must consist in a different combination of them, in consequence of a different object being proposed."[7] This different combination is not so mechanical as it sounds; it is not merely the working over of a dead medium or a clever use of words. The poet revitalizes language; he restores it to its essentially creative function of infusing life into lifeless objects, of creating wholly new combinations springing from new and individual intuitions. "[The poet] diffuses a tone and spirit of unity, that blends and (as it were) *fuses*, each [part] into each, by that synthetic and magical power, to which I would exclusively appropriate the name of Imagination."[8] It is the imagination that fuses form and content into the organically self-sufficient poem. All the rest is mere fancy, the mechanical use of language as already fixed and definite, the production of prose.[9] This essentially Kantian idea leads to the theory of the poem or symbol as a dynamic object to be contemplated for its own sake, with "disinterested interest." The New Critical formalism that follows from this tradition assigns to poetry a unique status in being, but it, too, was not a theory of static form and always implied the affective dimension that involved the reader in the dynamism of the aesthetic object itself.

After Coleridge's rather eloquent defense, it has never been easy to break down the barriers between poetry and prose.[10] Among the later romantics, Verlaine summarized this doctrine for the French Symbolists by extolling the "art poetique." He disparaged other uses of language claiming "tout le reste est litterature." Henri Bergson argued that the prosaic use of language is symptomatic of man's separation from the vital flux of life. Language had, in its general use, fallen to the level of "fixities and definites" that could not express reality. Bergson urged that we turn away from this "counter" language toward a truly poetic, or metaphoric, expression that is more nearly in tune with the vital energy of reality—with the *natura naturans*.[11] Benedetto Croce, and his disciple R. G. Collingwood, went so far as to collapse the mode of expression (language) into the act of perception itself, calling the entire process "intuition" and grounding it in man's epistemological capacities.[12]

At this point, however, the exact nature of poetic language seems to disappear into the mystery of human consciousness. Croce's radical idealism reduces the creative function of language to a wholly internal operation of the mind. This necessitates another order of language, a prosaic order, to externalize the internal perceptions, and for the literary critic this raises the question: Where is the poem? Internal or external? The New Critics, although influenced by romantic idealism, never went this far. They admitted that the creative use of language was the defining characteristic of the artistic imagination, but poetic language was not wholly internal. It had an external form, an ontic status.[13] As Colerdige argued, the poem contains the same elements as prose but combines them in different ways for different purposes.

The New Critical approach to poetic language was not without opposition. With its debt to idealism it came under the direct attack of logical positivism for its tendency to lapse into metaphysical speculation. For mathematicians and logicians like Bertrand Russell and Gottlob Frege language was a system for logical communication, and an imperfect system at that. As a result, they sought to develop a language that would be logically valid, that would avoid what Gilbert Ryle later called the "systematically misleading expressions" of normal language usage.[14] Philosophy's first order of business was to build an adequate philosophical language based on logico-mathematical structures (which were themselves fundamentally linguistic).

Questions of aesthetics were ignored or generally pushed aside as wholly subjective, even mystical.

There was opposition as well from traditional historians of language like F. W. Bateson. Repeatedly Bateson argued that "To discover [the meanings of words in the poem] we have to ask what they meant to their author and his original readers."[15] For Bateson the culturally determined meanings of words delimited their meaning-functions in the context of the poem; and, with this emphasis on historical relativism, Bateson sought to return literary criticism to its old scholarly tradition. Rejecting the New Criticism and the claim that poetic language is the product of a peculiar, creative use of language, Bateson argued that the proper interpretation of a poem is historical. The distinction between poetry and prose—the New Critical distinction in "kind"—he could not accept.

This has been, from the beginning, the central problem of radical New Critical aesthetics: to explain the relationship between historically determined language (prose) and the unique poetic object wrought out of this language. Often the New Critics made the distinction so severe that no relationship could be described; poetry and prose appeared to be opposed. Croce warned against this very absolutism when he rejected the prose-poetry dichotomy developed by Hegel. He attacked Hegel for seeing all "distincts" as "opposites"; the Hegelian triadic dialectic, he claimed, tends to make anything that is distinct appear to be opposed. Croce's idealism led him to emphasize the unifying element of human consciousness; distincts operate in matters of degree—where one may be part of another though the second is not identical with or part of the first. "Poetry can exist without prose (although it does not exlude it), but prose can never exist without poetry; art does not include philosophy, but philosophy directly includes art."[16]

With this a very practical question emerges. In the study of "poetic" language, do we begin with the poetic use of language seen as the generating principle of all other language uses (as Croce's theory implies), or with the general system of language within which the peculiar poetic use can be defined as a deviation (as the positivists argue)? These two views have effectively separated the disciplines of literary criticism and linguistics, for the literary critic takes the first option defining poetry as a unique and originating use of language, whereas the linguist takes the second option defining poetry as a special, even aberrant, use of normal language functions.

The New Critics were firmly in the first tradition. This arose largely from their promotion of the organicist doctrine and their stand on the related question of the form-content dichotomy. They saw the poem as a discrete and timeless object, meaningful in its own right as an individual and irreducible act of speech. The essence of poetry was metaphor. I. A. Richards argued that the language of poetry is "non-referential"; that is, there is no separable "content" for which the word-structure of the poem functions as a "sign."[17] But for prose, the form-content dichotomy is its defining characteristic; prose seeks to convey information, and words function as "signs" pointing to an unambiguous content. The nature of prose is linear and metonymic because its structure sets up logical relationships between words, and between their contents.

The form-content dichotomy, in its many ramifications, is finally part of a more general and pervasive philosophical dilemma: the result of Cartesian rationalism and the mind-body dualism. The New Critics could reject the separation of form and content because Coleridge defined poetry for them by defining the characteristic operation of mind that produces it: the imagination. This is the implication of his claim that the poet and his poem are the same. Poetry is neither thought encased in language nor the Crocean externalization of the artist's intuition. Poetic language "fuses" thought and form, giving the poem its own peculiar ontic status. Language, at least in its poetic usage, has a unique and exalted function, for it is intimately involved in the actual process of human consciousness. It is not merely a conventional system of signs (Bergsonian "counters") for the communication of preformed perceptions of the world. Poetry is part of the activity of comprehension, inseparable from the operations of the faculty of understanding itself. It is in poetry, in the poetic act of mind, that the gap between inner and outer worlds is bridged. The objects of poetic imagination become the immediate and present objects of aesthetic experience. Inevitably, therefore, New Critical aesthetics, with its basis in Kantian idealism, becomes entangled in psychology and epistemology, and language in this theory must be seen as both dynamic form and static substance.

For the more radical followers of Coleridge, this active dimension of poetic discourse provides the basis for a distinction between the creative and the instrumental uses of language. Creative language is more than the instrument for carrying messages through a system of neurological impulses, from one mind to another mind, but how much more? Creative language usage emphasizes the process of forming messages, calls attention to that process and thereby activates a special kind of awareness in both speaker and hearer, an awareness not only of the message as message but also of the context or occasion of its formation and transmission, of characteristics such as motivation, will, and intention. The importance of this dimension of linguistic activity has even been noticed by Jacques Derrida, whose philosophy of language is militantly anti-idealistic, anti-creative. Form is, for Derrida, "force"; the poetic utterance is a strategy of words expressing the effort of the artist to express.[18] There is no reason why Derrida should not extend this idea of force to the more traditional sense of poetic language as creative, as grounds for the utterance of individual (we might call them original) ideas (or perceptions). Unfortunately, he is more inclined to exert his energy toward the debunking of the ideas of originality and privileged poetic perception.[19] Nevertheless, it is my contention that Derrida does not stumble upon the idea of force without reason; in fact, I will go further: the sending of messages of any kind *necessitates* some such idea and thereby provides us with an insight into a startling kind of communication, the blending of the very processes of thinking in two separate minds.

To reduce language to mere instrumentality, to a system of signs functioning as content-carrying vehicles, is to deny the possibility of this form of true communication. Rather than drawing author and reader together the instrumentalist function distances them—and distances both, by the process of abstraction, from the world. Derrida's temperament leads him, not without anxiety, in this direction, into what might almost be called the worldlessness of words. On the other hand, poetry, as its most eloquent apologists claim, mediates this distance and draws closer together the author's world as he knew it and the reader's world as he is coming to know it. Poetry gives life to the world, to its dead objects, by involving the author, the reader, and the world in the act of creative perception. It is this unique power that Poulet describes when he says that literature deals with objects, but objects that are "subjectified." "In short, since everything [described in a literary text] has become part of my mind, thanks to the intervention of language, the opposition between the subject and its objects has been considerably attenuated. And thus the greatest advantage of literature is that I am persuaded by it that I am freed from my usual sense of incompatibility between my consciousness and its objects."[20]

AN OUTLINE OF PROCEDURE

This is, admittedly, a romantic, a phenomenological, and perhaps an illusory, solution to the mind-body problem, but it rests squarely on a theory of language that, if it can be developed, provides interesting solutions to many of the problems faced by linguists and literary critics alike. I will outline here briefly the course to be followed in my progress toward the construction of a theory of literary hermeneutics. In the succeeding sections I propose to focus on the poetry-prose dichotomy as a convenient heuristic device. The precise division between them is not likely to be so radical as the New Critics seemed to claim; but we may find them to be distinct even if they are not opposed. The central question of the form-content dichotomy will also be redefined and will be useful in raising certain essential points for discussion. If Coleridge is correct and poetry differs from prose because it proposes for itself different ends, and poetry is structured by the peculair power of the imagination to achieve these ends, then three basic and traditional areas of interest to literary criticism emerge: (1) We must explain the so-called creative act of structuring that gives form and existence to the poem and the relationship of this act to the poet's own individual perception of reality, to his "world;" (2) We must explain the nature of the poem's structure as poem; and (3) Finally, we must explain the effects of this structure on the reader. That is, we must explain the "act of interpretation" as it is involved in the process of understanding.

In my effort to arrive at these explanations, I will be concerned with the relationship of the poet's individual expressive act (*parole*) and the linguistic system within which he works (*langue*). I will consider also the relationship between the poem as an individual expression and the general linguistic system that envelops the reader. This inevitably leads me to the historical problem of the relation between the general systems of language of the author and reader, for I may safely assume that the farther author and reader are separated across space and time the more difficulties one encounters in comparing the general language systems of each. Thus, we are finally confronted with the most crucial of all aesthetic questions: How does the poet communicate with his reader through the medium of the poem across vast periods of time? Is such communication possible?

THE PHILOSOPHY OF LANGUAGE: WITTGENSTEIN

"What is language?" This question has been asked and answered so often, and from so many perspectives, that it is difficult to know where to begin. In general, we may say that language comprehends a system of meaningful utterances utilized for the communication of thoughts and feelings between particular speakers (writers) and particular listeners (readers). Language, because it is both written and spoken, tends to bifurcate itself, and this problematic duality will need to be treated at some length below, but for the moment we must focus on more general issues. If language, written and spoken, is "systematic," one might begin a discussion of it by analyzing the system into basic rules that govern its operation as a whole. This approach is traditional, but it is often misleading. Of the many efforts to do this, few of them agree upon the basic nature or scope of the system that is being studied. They have produced a multiplicity of rules, many of which are contradictory. Thus a second level of analysis has arisen that might be labeled "metalinguistics," the attempt to go behind the superficial manifestations of the language system to the very core of man's linguistic capacities. Linguists and philosophers of language have searched for a descriptive schema of language by studying the mental operations that seem to be most intimately involved in language usage. The nature of language has become embedded in the study of man's cognitive capacities, a more abstract or philosophical endeavor that focuses on questions that we might generally designate as "humanistic." It is necessary to distinguish between this philosophical study and another level of language analysis that I will refer to as "stylistics"; the latter presupposes the former, for it is the general functioning of language as an act of mind that defines the limits of stylistic meaningfulness. Style will be the primary subject of part 3.

For our present discussion, we can find a most instructive example of the problematics of the relationship between language and cognition in the early philosophy of Ludwig Wittgenstein. Wittgenstein belongs, at least in this early phase, in the camp of the logical positivists. He thereby seems to be removed from my interest in the aesthetic dimension of language, but even when he is nearest the positivism of Russell and Frege, Wittgenstein is not wholly unmindful of the broader implications of his own logico-mathematical theory. There is the hint of both phenomenalism and idealism in his philosophy, and this provides a convenient opening for my development of a general literary theory that extends beyond Wittgenstein's own goals.

Max Black characterizes Wittgenstein's affinity for logical positivism in a way that provides an escape from the narrow strictures imposed by Russell.

> Distrusting the ambiguity and formlessness of ordinary language, [Russell and Frege] had hoped for a symbolism that would perfectly reflect logical form. Although Wittgenstein also demands "a sign-language that is governed by logical grammar" (*Tractatus*, 3.325a) he thinks that ordinary language, just as we know it, is "in perfect logical order" (5.556a). So the ideography is for him merely an instrument in the search for the essence of representation that is present in all languages and in all symbolisms.[21]

The distinction is crucial; for it does not split apart man's logical capacities from language as we know it, but rather welds the two together by claiming that the logical, cognitive operations of the human mind and the underlying structure of language in general are the same. Hence to study one is to study the other; to understand the logical form of language is to understand the cognitive capabilities and limitations of man. The theory, even at this level, has a definite Kantian dimension.

Wittgenstein begins his study of language, in the *Tractatus*, at what he considers its most basic level: the relationship between words and things. This is, of course, a complex relationship and an important one for literary theory, for it reactivates one of the oldest principles of aesthetics, the doctrine of *mimesis*. How language relates to reality is the focal problem, for example, of Plato's *Sophist*, where it is part of a larger metaphysical question that must explain the relationship between a world of (false) appearances and the realm of (Real) Ideal Forms.[22] Plato's attention here is specifically on false statements, on the use of language to "say that which is not." By saying the "unreal" the sophist (or poet) utters false representations; but saying the "unreal" is saying some-*thing*, and thus the "unreal" paradoxically is both real and unreal. It is a false picture of reality, an imitation that is a mere semblance, a phantasma, both like and unlike reality.[23]

The metaphysical problems here are less interesting to a modern reader than the extraordinary idea that falsehood always has about it the aura of truth, for to "say that which is not" implies: (1) that falsehood is a species of truth, and (2) enormous power in the hands of a clever "user" of language. The former proposition is at once Platonic and anti-Platonic and must be elaborated. To "say that which is not" is necessarily to misuse reality (Truth). Plato's example is as follows: a true statement, "Theaetetus sits," is composed of a name, "Theaetetus," which has reference to an identifiable being, to a perceptible fact, and of a separate term, "sits," which refers to an identifiable state of affairs, "sitting," which is also a separate perceivable fact. In addition, the state of affairs, "sitting," is a specific case of an Ideal Form, "Sitting," from which the specific case derives its meaning. There is a similar relationship to be established between Theaetetus as being and the Ideal form of Being, although this is more of a Heideggerian concept than a Platonic one. On the other hand, a false statement, "Theaetetus flies," is also composed of two terms, the same name with the same reference functions as the name in the true statement, and the term "flies," which corresponds to a state of affairs, "flying," which is a specific case of an Ideal Form, "Flying," from which the specific case derives its meaning. The false statement is as meaningful as the true statement. The false statement is logically composed of separate and meaningful terms, and even if we ignore Plato's transcendental Idealism and argue that the false statement is composed of terms that are meaningful in many different contexts, we are left to say, as is Plato, that "falseness" or "that which is not" is some-*thing* that distorts or is "different" from that which "is."[24]

"Difference" here has to do with the relationship between separate and meaningful terms; we might say that the true statement is composed of a logical ordering of terms that defines or "pictures" a possible relationship of things in the world. The false statement, conversely, is composed of a logical ordering that pictures an impossible state of affairs in the world. Both statements are logically meaningful. As a result, we must distinguish between two kinds of meaning, what Frege called *Sinn* and *Bedeutung*; the former or "sense" reflects logical meaningfulness irrespective of empirical verification; the latter is "referential" meaningfulness that "indicates" (points toward) actual things or states of affairs in the world.[25] The sophist and the poet, for Plato, have the power to misuse reality by falsely picturing the world in meaningful statements. This is, in Platonic philosophy, a misuse of Knowledge and is the basis for Plato's general distrust of language. But the examples imply the necessity of a world of empirical fact as a ground for the idea of truth and falsehood, a ground that traces all verbal propositions through the realm of empirical fact, "that which is (not)," to the level of the Ideal, "that which can(not) be." Meaning and truth (*Sinn* and *Bedeutung*) are different matters that meet in the function of *mimesis*. One can imitate the world truly or falsely, but in both there is imitation.

This unique feature of language allows Aristotle to focus on imitation without regard to questions of Truth. Aristotelian *mimesis* posits an analogy of form between work and world that allows for "probable impossibilities," or logical presentation of "that which is not."[26] The mimetic theory after Aristotle was generally corrupted into a much narrower doctrine, simplistically into a naive realism under the rule of *ut pictura poesis*, and, finally, by displacement, into the doctrine of "imitate the ancients" for, as Pope proclaimed, "Homer and nature are the same." In these corruptions a barrier is raised between language and world (subject and object) and all of the Platonic/Aristotelian complexity is lost. The necessary mutuality of *Sinn* and *Bedeutung* is destroyed, and it is not until Kant's "Copernican revolution," that a new and revitalized relationship between language and world emerged.

Wittgenstein's opening propositions in the *Tractatus* are part of this post-Kantian reawakening; clearly no simple restatement of the narrow doctrine of *ut pictura poesis*, his "picture theory" revitalizes the Platonic problematics of "saying that which is (not)" by affirming Frege's *Sinn* and *Bedeutung* interplay.

> The proposition is a picture of reality.
> The proposition is a model of reality as we think it is. [*Tractatus*, 4.01][27]

Here he is not far from Ernst Cassirer, who describes the basic structure of Kantian idealism in the following passage.

> The metaphysical opposition between subjectivity and objectivity is replaced by . . . transcendental correlation. In Kant the object, as "object in experience," is not something outside of and apart from cognition; on the contrary it is only "made possible," determined and constituted by the categories of cognition. Similarly, the subjectivity of language no longer appears as a barrier that prevents us from apprehending objective being but rather as a means of forming, of "objectifying" sensory impressions. Like cognition, language does not merely "copy" a given object; it rather embodies a spiritual attitude which is always a crucial factor in our perception of the objective. Since the naive-realistic approach lives and moves among objects, it takes too little account of this subjectivity; it does not readily conceive of a subjectivity which transforms the objective world, not accidentally or arbitrarily but in accordance with inner laws, so that the apparent object itself becomes only a subjective concept, yet a concept with a fully justified claim to universal validity.[28]

Because Wittgenstein's picture theory forms the basis for his more comprehensive idea that the essential structure of language is identical with the innate structuring capacities of cogntion, he can claim that logical thought gives objective validity to our world *via* the medium of language. Moreover, in *Tractatus*, 3.221 he makes a most important distinction between "asserting" and "speaking of" objects. "A proposition can only say *how* a thing is, not what it is," and the "how" is, not wholly unlike Cassirer's constitutive perception, neither the presentation of an object nor the copy of an object, but rather a rendering of objects in the world.

Once this claim has been made we can no longer see Wittgenstein's theory as proposing a naive epistemological realism. His argument that "In the picture and the pictured there must be something identical in order that one can be a picture of the other at all" (*Tractatus*, 2.161) should be read in the light of his earlier statement that the "form" of a linguistic picturing is no more than "the possibility that things are combined with one another as are the elements of the picture (*Tractatus*, 2.151). This implies an important distinction between mere "naming" (where one word refers to one thing) and "picturing" (which gives us not things but combinations, not objects but states of affairs).[29] Clearly, then, we can distinguish between language as *Sinn*, meaning as logical relationship, and language as *Bedeutung*, meaning as naming. Naming, nevertheless, is a necessary basis for the higher level function of cognition in picturing, and Wittgenstein's failure to develop this idea is perhaps the weakest portion of the *Tractatus*. He merely assumes (as his own Kantian a priori) that a formal correspondence exists between language as a logical structure and the world as states of affairs; his approach narrows to "instrumentalism" as he proposes to analyze only what he calls "complex propositions," the more sophisticated utterances that are composed of "elementary propositions." The latter may derive from a primal system of words as names, but this is, as Max Black claims, no more than a "metaphysical inference."[30]

So limiting himself, Wittgenstein sets out to demonstrate that within the system of language there is a logical order. It is this logical structure that enables language to *give us our world* as states of affairs, but the logical basis of language is "hidden" (*Tractatus*, 4.002) as is the formal relationship between "elementary propositions," "names," and the world of objects. Because of this, Wittgenstein's study of language is bracketed between extremes, between the general, but hidden, logical structure (which in the *Tractatus* is solidified into an "essentialist" philosophy, into the positing of a single, unified essential core for all language usage) and the fundamental basis of picturing seen as naming. In the *Philosophical Investigations* Wittgenstein further restricts his focus by seemingly abandoning both the picture theory and the essentialism of the *Tractatus*; in this later work he argues that the structure of language is nothing more than a series of communal ratifications, a specific set of "games."[31] By moving further into instrumentalism Wittgenstein escapes some of the more pressing problems of the *Tractatus*.

But the early and late approaches are not wholly incompatible. Wittgenstein's later study of language games, of systems within systems established by communal ratification, need not force us to see language again as a barrier between the subject and the objective world, as a denial of some form of picturing. If games are in any way situational, if they are controls placed on group actions, they must also be seen as controls, communally ratified, placed on, and thus involving, individual experience. Just as language games militate against, and repress, "private languages," they also order and control private contact with reality. The boundaries between individual and communal expression, private and communal experience are necessarily vague and allow each extreme to encroach upon the other; there is no communal experience that does not imply individual participation. Following the same logic, there cannot be any propositional arrangement of particular things into states of affairs without the implication of a concomitant level of picturing or naming that situates the particulars to be so arranged. Language, therefore, is ambiguously both a barrier between us and reality and a means of bridging the gap, and it is both communal and individual.

Similarly, Wittgenstein's later theory does not necessarily deny the hidden functioning of language's logical structure. We must remember the argument of the *Tractatus* that puts that structure beyond the powers of descriptive language use. To talk about the hidden structure would be tautological, for it would necessitate the use of language to describe the essence of language. "To be able to represent the logical form, we should have to be able to put ourselves with the propositions outside logic . . ." (*Tractatus*, 4.12). And since "*the limits of my language* mean the limits of my world" (*Tractatus*, 5.6), this would mean that to discuss the essential logic of language one would have to transcend the limits of one's own world.

> That which expresses *itself* in language, we cannot express by language.
>
> The propositions *show* the logical form of reality.
>
> They exhibit it. [*Tractatus*, 4.121]
>
> What *can* be shown *cannot* be said. [*Tractatus*, 4.1212]

It is not unjustifiable, I think, to see this as no more than an argument to bracket questions of essentialism even as Aristotle bracketed questions of Truth by narrowing Plato's concept of imitation. Wittgenstein does not in his later philosophy abandon his search for logical structures even though he does abandon his early focus on essentialism.

Reading the *Tractatus* and the *Philosophical Investigations* together allows us to draw from the differences between the two texts certain inferences about the nature of language. Between the functions of (hidden) logical meaningfulness and referential naming, language is a complex structure of many structures. It ranges between solipsism, as broadly defined in the *Tractatus*, and the discontinuous series of communal games described in the *Philosophical Investigations*, and it is this range of possibilities that Richard Kuhns uses to give Wittgenstein a curious but interesting link with the phenomenologists.[32] Wittgenstein's claim that "*the limits of my language* mean the limits of my world" involves him in a revitalized and neo-Kantian sense of solipsism, and here he is not all that far from the phenomenology of Husserl.

> In fact what solipsism *means* is quite correct, only it cannot be said, but it *shows* itself.
>
> That the world is *my* world, shows itself in the fact that the limits of language (the language which I understand) mean the limits of *my* world. [*Tractatus*, 5.52]

We are confronted here with the phenomenological problem of explaining how the personal, inner or private, world of the individual user of language relates to the broader, outer, social or cultural context—the collective or communal world. Wittgenstein's solipsism sounds too much like romantic egoism. Yet we should note Jean Piaget's observation that this solipsism is actually an extension of logical positivism that was dominated by the desire "to reduce mathematics and logic to linguistics and the entire life of the mind of speech."[33] In many ways this is the reverse of Kantian idealism, which wanted to reduce speech to the basic operations of the mind, and we should, therefore, be struck by the similarity of goals. When Wittgenstein defines solipsism, it is impossible to tell whether it is radically idealistic or positivistic.

> Solipsism strictly carried out coincides with pure realism.
>
> The "I" in solipsism shrinks to an extensionless point [one could

> as easily say it expands to an infinite circumference] and there remains the reality co-ordinated with it.
>
> The philosophical "I" is . . . the limit—not a part of the world. [*Tractatus*, 5.64]

Thus we have in Wittgenstein's philosophy a series of oscillations between several sets of poles: between views of language as logical order and as naming; between solipsistic idealism and positivistic (picture theory) realism; between transcendentalism and instrumentalism. None of these sets is quite congruent one with another, and each seems logically to involve all of the others. At this point Kuhns provides us with an insight that leads to a better understanding of Wittgenstein's complex theory. He suggests a most instructive comparison of Wittgenstein with the French Symbolists. "Valéry's idea that a poem is a machine for producing poetic states is analogous to Wittgenstein's idea that logic is a machine for making sense, that there exists a structure which is the structure of possible meanings."[34] Wittgenstein's concept of *logische Raum* (the logical space of language) is analogous to the Symbolists' idea "that the internal, self-referring 'poetic form' defined the linguistic world."[35] The relationship between an individual text (utterance) and the hidden logical structure of all language is also not unlike the Platonic relationship of shadow-image, "phantasma," to Ideal Form (also hidden), only Wittgenstein is more certain of a correspondence between the two and thereby trivializes Plato's transcendental problematics. The individual text is never *about* the logic of *logische Raum* but *shows* it. The *Tractatus* itself is not about the logical form of linguistic propositions, but it is a form that shows logical form. Wittgenstein's "zettelistic" method of writing ("the inscribing of propositions on slips of paper" to be later arranged into a text) makes "any order . . . a possible order where a text is concerned, and therefore whatever order is established can stand for any order,"[36] or for order in general, as long as what is expressed are probable states of affairs. Every proposition, indeed every utterance, presupposes the totality of all utterances, presupposes the "world" without saying anything about it.[37] A writer's (solipsistic) world, his individual picturing of states of affairs, is his world even as it silently shows worlds that are not his yet to which he belongs. We may speak of a system of dependencies. The individual's world, asserted in a Saussurian *parole*, stands for and within the communally ratified world of Saussurian *langue*, which in turn stands for and within the hidden logical form of *logische Raum* (seen as the world/space of logical possibilities, as language in its most encompassing form, which we have designated by the term *langage*).

Form, in any of these manifestations or inferences, can never be static and can never be seen as either wholly inner (private) or wholly outer (communal). Comparing Mallarmé's *Un coup de des* with the *Tractatus*, Kuhns says, "the movement of the poem on the page is the movement of thought in the speaker and reader; the text is an imitation of itself."[38] This involves the reader in a demanding "act of interpretation," an active engagement with text and world (in its multiple inferences). The means of ordering the text produces meaning, stands for the writer's world and the reader's world, and for the potential world that binds writer and reader in a very complex kind of dialogue. Paralleling Wittgenstein once more with the Symbolists, speaking particularly of Valéry, Kuhns argues: "His poetry might be thought of as an incantation, a linguistic evocation of the self, bringing it into its reality from the edges of the world where it resides. The self comes out of negation and nothingness . . . and lives, if at all, in the poetry created by its violent fight against the negativity of existence."[39] Language begins to take on a life of its own, and the concept bears striking resemblance to the ideas of Wilhelm von Humboldt who in good romantic fashion proclaimed that language "is something persistent and in every instant transitory. Even its maintenance by writing is only an incomplete, mummified preservation, necessary if one is again to render perceptible the living speech concerned. In itself language is not work (*ergon*) but an activity (*energia*)."[40] Humboldt's priority of speech over writing and his romantic subjectivism will ultimately prove to be more problematic than he suspected, but his emphasis on the "transitory persistence" of language is of crucial importance when seen in connection with his insistence that language is motion and not fixed structure. Once more we confront the echoes of Coleridge's dynamic *natura naturans* as well as Derrida's "force."

I can now make a series of preliminary observations about the nature of language based on Wittgenstein's claim that a language system has a logical structure which defines the limits of our world.

1. Language as total verbal system (*langage*) refers to that hidden, logical system that comprehends all of the possibilities for meaningful utterances; within that system are codified (through use) worlds within worlds, both individual and communal. The term *system* here is no more than the potential for order because it is hidden and is not a thing that can be described. *Langage* is that surplus of cognitive power that I described in part 1.
2. The individual writer creates a text within this system of systems, but the text does not tell us *what* the world is but *how* it is.
3. Within the logical sysem of *langage* language usage is dynamic expression; *langage* is *energia* not *ergon*. *Energia* must not be seen as an expression of the subject; it is the gift of *langage*.
4. As *energia, langage* must be seen as a process that gives meaning to our experience. It acts upon the listener or reader as a kind of incantation, involving that person in an act of interpretation.
5. By *means* of the structure of the text our world takes on meaning. It can be argued that *langage* gives us our world, our place of being and dwelling, by means of its "energy" of knowing.
6. Language usage, consequently, is a way of knowing, and the study of *langage* belongs to the discipline of epistemology.
7. Below the logical structure of *langage*, in the realm of the constitutive function of consciousness (naming) *langage* itself cannot venture; for *langage* cannot discuss its own origins; it may only *show* us its nature.
8. Conversely, *langage* also cannot transcend itself to describe its own hidden structure.
9. This leads Wittgenstein to conclude that "Logic is transcendental" (*Tractatus*, 6.13).
10. Furthermore, as with the French Symbolists, Wittgenstein's theory of language eventuates in the mystical, for ethics and aesthetics are also transcendental (*Tractatus*, 6.421). "There is indeed the inexpressible. . . . This shows itself; it is mystical" (*Tractatus*, 6.522).

Wittgenstein ends the *Tractatus* at this point, having moved from the lower limits of *langage* (the level at which he must posit a necessary relationship between words or "elementary propositions" and real things) to the upper limits of *langage* (where the logical form of *langage* transcends *langage* itself). True to his own philosophy he stops there by declaring: "Whereof one cannot speak, thereof one must be silent" (*Tractatus*, 7), although we may now see that the text of the *Tractatus* itself stands for, albeit silently, that hidden ordering that is the logical basis of *langage* and the potential for all propositional statements seen as picturing states of affairs. Language (in its most familiar usage) is, therefore, always characterized by a powerful drive toward the real, not as a condition for the verification of meaningfulness but as (reminiscent of Plato) the ground of the logic of all propositional knowledge of the world (the meeting place of *Sinn* and *Bedeutung* in *mimesis*). For Plato, the sophist's black art is his creation of a meaningful illusion, made possible by the malleability of language and the inconstancy of the world of appearances. Wittgenstein trivializes Plato's transcendental problematics, but the lure of the empirical remains a necessary projection, for the possibility of logical meaningfulness in the utterance of propositions as states of affairs implies the concomitant function of referential meaningfulness. States of affairs are propositions about the world, and "The World is all that is the case," according to Wittgenstein. Even the proposition seen as tautology, which needs no empirical justification with regard to its logical meaningfulness (its grammatical "truth"),[41] cannot ignore its thrust toward the world as referential meaningfulness subject to empirical grounding.

THE PHILOSOPHY OF LANGUAGE: CASSIRER

If in the *Tractatus* Wittgenstein limits the scope of his philosophical analysis of language and cognition, Ernst Cassirer admits of no such limitation. Fundamentally agreeing with Wittgenstein that language systems have a logical basis, Cassirer emphasizes (in contradistinction to the general "creativity" of Wittgenstein's "show" theory) the peculiar "creative" dimension of *poetic* language. For literary theory this is crucial, but the two men, taken together, give us an expanded sense of poetry and language that finally provides us with a much deeper insight into problems of literary interpretation.

Cassirer is avowedly Kantian and a student of Humboldtian linguistics. For Cassirer (as for the logical positivists and for Cassirer's New Critical followers) there is a meaningful distinction between the language of poetry and the language of philosophy or science. But this distinction is *not* absolute. It is derived from Cassirer's sense (based on Kantian faculty psychology) that we may distinguish between "*aesthetic* universality" and "the 'objective validity' which belongs to our logical and scientific judgments."[42] The former describes our peculiarly aesthetic involvement with creative works, a Kantian "disinterested interest" in the object of aesthetic contemplation —an involvement with its form or structure for its own sake. The latter belongs to our world of operational values (to philosophy or science) whose objects are "used" and even "consumed" but not contemplated. Both eventuate in a particular version of truth. For aesthetics it is an "understanding" of things in themselves; for science it is a "theoretical description or explanation," a propositional or conventional truth that expresses "Knowledge."[43] Not unlike Wittgenstein, Cassirer has outlined here a distinction between "showing" and "saying" (between the "how" a thing is and the "what" it is). The truly creative dimension of language for both men is that of showing.

At this point Cassirer and Wittgenstein sharply diverge. Wittgenstein's Augustinian sense of language as logical order, as *langage*, leads him to see all language systems as potentially creative (giving us our world) on the level of logical structure. This, of course, necessitates his a priori assumption of a "picture" function. The aesthetic dimension of language he pushes into mysticism, and beyond the logic of *langage*. Cassirer's theory somewhat rearranges these relations. The logical structure of language, for Cassirer, belongs to the sophisticated development of language usage that reflects man's conceptualizing urges toward his world. It is a system of classifications that aims toward the accurate explanation of life, as, for example, in conceptual classifications like the pair: edible/inedible. For Cassirer, as for Wittgenstein, this is in its own way creative; but as it creates a rational world, a world of causes and effects and hence a world of temporal or linear relationships, it grows away from the immediate, atemporal, intuitive creativitiy of the aesthetic uses of language. At the level where Wittgenstein merely posits the necessity of a referential or naming function for language, Cassirer founds his theory of language's "constitutive" intuition. Clearly both men realize the force of language reaching toward the world of things; but whereas Wittgenstein concerns himself (in both his early and late writings) with states of affairs, the relations between things pictured in language, Cassirer concerns himself with things themselves, with, as he says, objects in experience.

The difference is a reflection of Cassirer's idealism as opposed to the positivism and instrumentalism of Wittgenstein. Cassirer sees the aesthetic use of language as a more rudimentary creativity that is the basis of language in general—its psychological and historical genesis. One might say that for Wittgenstein "logic is prior to all experience,"[44] whereas for Cassirer priority is given to man's originary experiences, to the very foundations of human consciousness. Unlike Wittgenstein, then, Cassirer attempts to lay bare the very origins of language before explaining man's more sophisticated linguistic skills. The connection between these two levels is clear. The scientific use of language grows out of man's primitive consciousness as he strives to posit "the limits of things," and "this is accomplished as man's activity becomes internally organized, and his conception of Being acquires a correspondingly clear and definite pattern."[45] Prior to this conceptualization of Being, man's cognition of his world consists of what Cassirer calls "mythical thought." This primitive activity of mind manifests itself in the forms of "mythical invention" that "reflect, not the objective character of *things*, but the forms of human practices."[46] That is to say, the forms that mythical invention takes do not conceptualize Being into patterns of things, do not describe or explain; rather the forms reflect the process of human cognition itself, the dynamic interrelation of man's consciousness and his world. Not unlike the theory of Bronislav Malinowski, Cassirer sees language as originating in a magical realm of functioning. The relationship between word and thing is, therefore "productive" rather than merely referential; to speak *to* reality (the world) is a mode of bringing the world into presence.[47] For Wittgenstein "things" in the world apparently come into presence only in the operation of their being arranged into states of affairs,[48] yet we must ask if Wittgenstein and Cassirer are really very far apart in this particular concern with the power of language to call forth and situate man in his world?

The epistemological origin of consciousness and language is what Cassirer calls a "violent act of individuation." Apparently this falls into two stages. The first is the most basic act of self-awareness, the separation of the perceiving subject from the undifferentiated flux of objective Being, a negative act of existential consciousness. The second is characterized by the assertion of the subjective will upon the separate world of objective Being, breaking the undifferentiated flux into categories and particulars, grouping reality into logically meaningful patterns. This twofold process seems to find an analogy in the developmentalist theory of Jean Piaget outlining the two fundamental structuring activities of every individual's epistemological growth. The first, which Piaget calls "simple abstraction," describes how the mind derives knowledge from the object itself; the second, "reflective abstraction," is knowledge that results from the perceiver's action upon objects, from his sense of abstract relations among objects. These two modes of abstraction have, for Piaget, both a logical and a temporal relationship: simple abstraction is a primary function of the most rudimentary level of human consciousness, man's primitive (infantile) awareness of himself as a separate entity in the manifold. "Reflective abstraction" is a secondary function that builds upon this primitive awareness by arranging objects of the outer world into logical systems, states of affairs.[49] This reflective function asserts the individual's control over the world, or, perhaps with reference to Freud, at least it marks man's desire for such mastery.[50]

For Cassirer, although not quite so directly for Piaget, language is integrally a part of this consciousness and partakes of these two stages; we can, therefore, extend Cassirer's insights to make the following distinctions. The first stage of language is a form of mythical thought constructed on the I-thou relationship: the first person pronoun is opposed to a series of individual and discontinuous proper nouns that function as names for things. But these names are not empty signs. In the primitive consciousness they are conceived as an identity of word and object; they are, in the purest sense, metaphors because they assert a transcendental correspondence between the perceiving subject and the outer or perceived world. They assert a magical "at-oneness" even as they necessarily affirm the newly awakened self-consciousness that divides self and other. The primitive consciousness of self is, as we said, negative; but the metaphoric dimension of language is, for Cassirer, both negative and positive in that its assertion of transcendental at-oneness must contain also a self-conscious awareness of a fundamental apartness, a "lack," which motivates such an articulate reaching out toward the world. Cassirer's debt to Romantic language philosophy, and particularly to Humboldt, is most clearly revealed in the primacy he gives to the function of the "shifters" "I" and "you." They are treated as very primitive, cognitively originating, elements of all language. This concept has been challenged by modern linguists whose primary concerns have drifted away from the romantic fascination with the origins of human consciousness,[51] but such is the thrust of Cassirer's philosophy. He argues that the birth of consciousness and the origins of verbal systems of communication are one and the same. "Mythic ideation and primitive verbal conception [have as a function] a process of almost violent separation and individuation. Only when this intense individuation has been consummated, when the immediate intuition has been focused and . . . reduced to a single point, does the linguistic form emerge, and the word or the momentary god is created."[52]

The second stage of language is dominated by man's will, for it reveals logical relationships between the previously unrelated proper nouns. It works by a process of abstraction to categorize man's infinitely expansive individual perceptions. Thus language begins to take on a metonymic quality where elements are grouped according to types, and the relationship between these grouped elements is one of part to whole. The elaboration of a logical grammar emphasizes the part/whole relationship by transforming the immediacy and singularity of metaphor into the sequentiality (or linearity) and multiplicity of metonymy. On this level—the level of logical grammar—it is easier to perceive the relation between language and cognition. It is the study of this level that forms the limits of Wittgenstein's analysis of language and, Cassirer claims, led John Stuart Mill to assert "that grammar is the most elementary part of logic because it is the beginning of the analysis of the thinking process. According to Mill the principles and rules of grammar are the means by which the forms of language are made to correspond to the universal forms of thought."[53]

On the secondary level of consciousness and language usage man transforms the primary opposition of self and other into the more sophisticated opposition between particularities (the fragmented parts of objective Being). Here man begins to make the primal cognitive separations that Lévi-Strauss, in his study of mythical thought, calls "binary oppositions," distinctions like night and day (which Cassirer cites) or raw and cooked (the most familiar example used by Lévi-Strauss). On the primary level Cassirer sees mythical thought and language as "two diverse shoots from the same parent stem,"[54] and apparently Lévi-Strauss would concur. But Cassirer temporalizes the theory as Lévi-Strauss does not, in order to seek the source of the "parent stem" in an originary act of human consciousness. This returns language theory once more to the essentialist camp, and Cassirer's posited "essence" lies in the genetic foundations of human thought, a primitive thought that is subject to development as well as sophistication. Wittgenstein's and Lévi-Strauss's "essentialism" is, contradictorily, a "metaphysical inference" positing a full-blown logical structure for language systems.

At this point it is necessary to pause in order to consider a rather crucial distinction between Cassirer's idealism and the positivsm of Wittgenstein (along with its near kin in Lévi-Strauss's structuralism). Cassirer's theory, like Piaget's, is developmentalist; it emphasizes the evolution of complex, logical language systems out of rudimentary, primitive cognitive awareness. Wittgenstein, who deliberately cuts himself off from genetic speculations, treats language as a systematic whole, complete in itself and not as a development from some more basic origins.[55] The latter theory parallels specifically Lévi-Strauss's sense that man's emergence into culture, and into consciousness, was marked by a cataclysmic appearance of a cognitive structure (and, consequently, a full-blown linguistic structure) that was whole and complete at the moment of its birth. Of course, this structure exists in any one man or any single culture only in potentia; it defines a surplus of explanatory power that is the "ghost" of perfect knowledge. As such, it is what Jacques Derrida called a "centerless" system,[56] describable only through the approximation of abstract models (such as those posited by Noam Chomsky for language) and not limited by a single, "visible" explanatory law.

The evolutionary theories of Cassirer and Piaget and the static structure theories of Wittgenstein and Lévi-Strauss are in direct conflict, but all are predicated on rather general hypotheses. The immediate results for a theory of literary interpretation are that the idealist emphasizes the unique, individual, "original" source of language usage in defining poetry, whereas the positivist emphasizes the general, systematic, and collective structure that defines language as a totality. We are returned here to the debate between the literary critics who see poetry as the "father" of instrumental language and the linguists who see poetry as an aberration of general, normal language usage. I am convinced, however, that a theoretical reconciliation of these two opposed and heavily armed camps is possible. The oppositions here must not be seen as mutally exclusive even though the lure of polemics has led the combatants to state their positions *as if* nothing were possible but either/or commitments. The debate between critics and linguists, geneticists and structuralists, idealists and positivists reflects a crucial tension in language itself, a tension between logical system and individual utterance, *langage* and *parole*, and, consequently, between prose and poetry. Significantly, Cassirer's developmentalism does not indicate that the rudimentary linguistic origins of language and thought have been wholly eclipsed by the sophisticated cultural or scientific structures that developed from them. Thus poetry is always possible—within or in opposition to the system. Despite the developmentalist hierarchy in Piaget's description of simple and reflective abstraction, the relationship between the two is not only temporal; it is also and importantly logical—each necessitating the other. So, too, Lévi-Strauss's emphasis on general, collective structures has never denied the force of the individual who lives consciously and unconsciously within the system. As I outlined in part 1, the collective myth structure, thinking its way into the minds of men who live within its province, does not eradicate the fundamental individuality of the members of that culture, nor even negate the privileged individualism of the myth singer. It is the singer who "shows" the myth. The primary result of this tension between system and individual is to redefine our concept of cultural, linguistic, and literary history, to emphasize the interplay of forces that conserve the energy of the individual will in the holistic system while risking in this conservatism the ever-present possibility of revolution that would restructure the collective system in order to respond to different awarenesses or to delimit a different meaningful reality.

Cassirer, then, adds another dimension to Wittgenstein's proposition: "The limits of my language mean the limits of my world." The general creativity of language as a system gives way to the privileged creativity of poetry that exists within the system but is not wholly determined by it. Which came first, the unique poetic expression or the hidden logic of the full-blown system, is a question that we need not answer. In his haste to deconstruct the ontotheological bias of Western metaphysics toward "poetic expression" (what he generalizes under the term, *speech*), Derrida teaches us that the question of primacy is always and everywhere problematic. Derrida's torturous analysis of Rousseau's essay on the "origin" of language convinces us that speech cannot precede the logic of systematic discourse (which he generalizes under the term *writing*). "Writing precedes and follows speech, it comprehends it."[57] In effect, Derrida confirms my broad reading of Wittgenstein. If "writing," seen as a hidden logical system, as *logische Raum* or *langage*, as potential for arrangement of states of affairs, defies description or explanation because it encompasses (transcends) all such description and explanation, then any utterance is, as Derrida says, a "trace" of the totality of all other utterances past and future; any text stands for all texts. "The trace itself," as potential for order, as spacing, "does not exist."[58] Yet its logic is not effaced by articulation, nor, I would argue against Derrida, by the thrust of an articulation toward the expression of experience. The logic of the system that always remains hidden is displaced into utterances of states of affairs, into arrangements of particulars that *have* presence, if only in those arrangements. Moreover, this relationship between writing (*langage*) and speech (*parole*) must not be seen as a simple contest for power, as simple dialectics. If writing "comprehends" speech, it does so only as it "shows" itself in speech. Writing does not come into existence through speech any more than speech dies under the diffusive nonbeing of writing, although Derrida is certainly convincing in his argument that Western humanism has frequently employed a life versus death or being versus nonbeing metaphorics to describe the interplay of speech and writing.

It is possible, therefore, that Jean Piaget's model of epistemological development, wherein he claims that ontology recapitulates phylogeny, that the development of the individual is a paradigm for the development of the race, is also a model for linguistic history, but Piaget's concept of the eternal tension between particular and system, the struggle for "equilibrium" between what he calls "assimilation" and "accommodation," is much more significant. It is better, I submit, to assume that man has always been possessed by his structures but not determined by them. But if the collective structure is not determinative it is necessary; it is the ground of human culture, of "belonging"; it is the context of communication, and it also guarantees to man an individual freedom. The two extremes define our "collective individuality," the structure that is expressed by difference and not sameness. Thus we can be satisfied with neither radical romantic, existentialist individualism nor with classical, universal orderliness.

Language has enormous capabilities. It can be explained neither by speculating merely on its primitive origins nor by positing only Wittgenstein's *logische Raum*. To be sure, Cassirer, through his concept of symbolic thought, attempts to define language as somehow both of these extremes. Language, like myth, is at one level an expression of man's rudimentary awareness: "at this point, the word which denotes . . . thought content is not mere conventional symbol [or sign], but is merged with its object in an indissoluble unity."[59] The poetic function of language so defined is fundamentally human, and even though Cassirer explains it in terms of a primitive emergence (man's unsophisticated sense of mysterious "powers" surrounding him, of "momentary gods"), it is an abiding form of consciousness in all men. Such a function springs from and points up the general structure of language capabilities in man. Communication is predicated upon the existence of a linguistic structure shared by both speakers and hearers. Language as a whole, therefore, must encompass both of these extremes, ranging between the particular, personal response to discrete and familiar experience and the whole, collective system of perfect Knowledge, between a "surplus of experience" and the "surplus of explanatory structure." When Cassirer defines the limits of language, he is far more expansive than was Wittgenstein in his ever-narrowing instrumentalism, and Cassirer here puts little emphasis on the idea of developmentalism.

> Language moves in the middle kingdom between the "indefinite" and the "infinite"; it transforms the indeterminate into a determinate idea, and then holds it within the sphere of finite determinations. So there are "ineffables" of different order, one of which represents the lower limit of verbal expression, the other the upper limit; but between these bounds, which are drawn by the very nature of verbal expression, language can move with perfect freedom, and exhibit all the wealth and concrete exemplification of its creative power.[60]

Between the extremes lies the realm of meaningful discourse, in the mutual relationship of defamiliarization (seen as constitutive intuition) and demystification (seen as activation of the potentials of *langage*); the articulation of meaning fixes the indefinite within the "sphere of finite determinations," holds the extremes in a tensional or balanced relationship and marks the limits of literature in its metaphor/metonym functions. The tension between these functions defines the distinction between pure poetry and pure prose, but this raises severe problems in the area of literary criticism. For the philosopher who wishes, like Cassirer, to describe the aesthetic dimension of language this problem can be defined in two ways: (1) he cannot transcend language in order to speak of language itself, and (2) he must use the metonymic tendencies of prose to describe the metaphoric tendencies of poetry.[61] Thus the philosopher and the literary critic frequently find themselves breaking out of the limitations of prose and into the realm of poetry. This is most certainly the fate of Wittgenstein in the *Tractatus* and is the basis for Richard Kuhns's association of Wittgenstein's "zettelistic" method of composition with the poetic theory of French Symbolists like Valéry. So much more problematic is the fate of the literary critic whose task becomes that of achieving a balance between the prosaic reduction of the poem to metonymy (the New Critical "heresy of paraphrase"[62]) and the poetic transformation of his prose analysis into metaphor (where criticism becomes a poem about a poem). It is truly problematic because we cannot assign privileged status to either poetry or prose; they are not different languages but different functions of language. More importantly, the dynamic tension between the two (between metaphor and metonym, assimilation and accommodation, defamiliarization and demystification) "shows" us that we cannot have one without the other; for example, to defamiliarize experience is at once to demystify conceptual understanding. The philosopher, whose thrust is toward the latter, is forever constrained by the necessities of logic, the need to demystify his system by speaking it to indeterminate experience. The poet, who risks absorption into the indeterminate, must draw defamiliarized experience outward toward the determinate idea. Great philosophy, therefore, is always somewhat poetic, whereas great poetry is to some degree philosophical. Moreover, to speak of a distinction, even merely a functional one, between poetry (metaphor) and prose (metonymy) is a conceptualizing reduction of a relationship that in itself can only "show" itself.

With these insights it is necessary to revise the preliminary propositions about language that I listed at the end of the discussion of Wittgenstein.

1. The term *langage* refers to the system of utterances that gives us the world of both our individual and communal experience. The term *system* indicates a potential for order rather than an existential shape and, therefore, as system *langage* cannot be explained or described. *Langage* embodies worlds within worlds, utterances that do not tell us *what* the world is but *how* it is.
2. The metaphoric use of *langage* is represented by the poetic tendency of literature; it is the immediate, atemporal engagement of subjective experience, emphasizing the act of articulation or the paradigmatic function of language as the expression of meaningfulness. The metonymic use of *langage* is represented by the prosaic tendency of literature; it asserts the relationship between objects in a logical series thereby emphasizing the syntagmatic function of language as logical (grammatical) meaningfulness.

3. The two uses of language are distinct but not antithetical. They characterize the difference between poetry and prose, a tensional relationship that is the basis for all utterances and defines the limits of *langage* (as *logische Raum*) and, therefore, man's capacity for signification. Poetry and prose, however, must be thought of as functions and not objects. The term *poetry* is closely allied with what traditionally has been called the "creative" function of language, but there is, as I have stated above, reason to say that in prose there is a specific kind of creativity seen as Wittgenstein's manipulation of "states of affairs" with its attendant metonymic presencing of things. The issue here is that poetry as creativity uses the potentialities of *langage* (as *logische Raum*) in order to defy and reform those culturally ratified linguistic systems (Wittgenstein's "games" or, more broadly, Saussure's *langue*) that have become static or repressive. This is possible because metaphor always lurks within metonymy, because simple abstraction is the "logical" basis of reflective abstraction, because if *langage* is to give us the relations of our world it must also give us the particulars of relationship.
4. All language functions as a dynamic medium of expression, as *energia*, not *ergon*, but in poetry and prose there is a functional distinction between the metaphoric and metonymic uses.
5. As *energia*, *langage* gives meaning to our experiences. *Energia* is the gift of *langage* to man, the gift of a dwelling place, of belonging, to all humankind. In literature the metaphor/metonym tensions reproduce the drive toward the flux of familiar experience, the strange or typical.
6. As *energia*, *langage* acts on the attention of the listener or reader, involving him in an act of interpretation.
7. Language, consequently, is a way of knowing, and the study of *langage* belongs to the discipline of epistemology.
8. Within the system of *langage* metaphor and metonymy exist in a tensional relationship. Neither metaphor nor metonymy may adequately explain one another; each may only "show" its nature.
9. There are, therefore, limits beyond which metonymic prose and metaphoric poetry cannot go, but that need not be seen

as severe restrictions on the freeplay of *langage* as a dynamic system.

10. *Langage* as a system can neither describe its own origins nor its hidden structure. These, however, "show" themselves through usage, through the interplay of individual articulations (*parole*) and culturally ratified subsystems (*langue*).

THE METHODOLOGY OF LINGUISTICS: CHOMSKY

Having come this far in the development of a philosophy of language it is necessary to do some backtracking—even at the risk of being repetitious. My focus will shift accordingly, and in this section I will turn to the formal study of language known as linguistics, specifically to methodological problems arising from the study of language.[63] My focal figure will be the very influential Noam Chomsky who echoes both the essentialist and instrumentalist tendencies of Wittgenstein. Chomsky is a self-declared rationalist, an opponent of transcendental idealism in linguistic studies, and in many ways dominated by a positivistic temperament. But if these are more or less characteristic of his general philosophy, there are variations on these tendencies that are instructive and necessary to the development of his methodology.

If I may begin my study of Chomsky in medias res, perhaps the single, most important observation to be made concerns his division of language into two broad categories: "deep" and "surface" structures. Roughly speaking he bases this distinction on his belief that "language has an inner and outer aspect. A sentence can be studied from the point of view of how it expresses a thought or from the point of view of its physical shape, that is, from the point of view of either semantic interpretation or phonetic interpretation." These two aspects are related on the level of structure.

> The former [deep structure] is the underlying abstract structure that determines its semantic interpretation; the latter [surface structure] is the superficial organization of units which determines the phonetic interpretation and which relates to the physical form of the actual utterance, its perceived or intended form. . . . Deep and surface structures need not be identical. The underlying organization of a

> sentence relevant to semantic interpretation is not necessarily revealed by the actual arrangements and phrasing of given components.[64]

Yet if the connection between the two is not "necessary," then how can we study "deep structure"; what is its value to linguistics?

This problem is crucial to the development of a methodology of language study, for that methodology must reflect the nature of language itself. Chomsky here is being careful to remain faithful to the Cartesian rationalism that he defines as the basis for his own linguistic theory. He wants to avoid the trap of neo-idealistic aestheticism, like that of Croce, which collapses language into the inner operations of the mind, surface structure into deep structure. Thus he holds firmly to Cartesian dualism, which keeps separate the inner mental processes and the outer sensuous manifestations of those processes in language. This leads him to flirt dangerously near a form-content dichotomy that, ironically, is much like that of Croce. The external physical form of language serves as mere clothes for an inner semantic concept—or for meaning.

The mind-body dualism of Descartes is problematic here. John Lyons, in his study of Chomsky, refers to a radio interview in which the linguist simply dismissed the mind-body dualism as an illusory dilemma; yet this answer is unsatisfactory. As Lyons says, Chomsky is sufficiently within the "mentalist" school of Descartes to believe that the internal operations of the mind are at least partly free from the determining influence of either external or physiological stimuli. "On the other hand, he differs from Descartes and most philosophers who would normally be called 'mentalists' in that he does not subscribe to the ultimate irreducibility of the distinction between 'body' and 'mind.'[65] This wavering dualism is troublesome for his linguistic theory when he asserts that there is some relation—but not a relation of identity—between deep semantic and surface phonological structures. The methodology of linguistic analysis that he develops depends upon the use of the outer "physical forms" of language to determine the inner "abstract structure" of meaning. Moreover, if the relationship of inner and outer structures is vague or only intermittent, Chomsky cuts himself off from the profound communicative dimension of language that is so crucial to his linguistic theory. Speaking on this matter, he borrows from Humboldt, reflecting both Cassirer and Wittgenstein, a definition of a "dialogistic" relationship between speaker (writer) and hearer (reader) that defies the absolutism of a mind-body dualism. "The received signs activate within the listener a corresponding link in his system of concepts . . . causing a corresponding, but not identical, concept to emerge."[66] "Dialogue" here sounds more mechanical than what Cassirer proposed, and the term *corresponding* is appropriately more conservative, but the relationship between the physical form of the language and the deep structure of thought must be a "necessary" one even to achieve "correspondence."

I have belabored this point in order to take issue with Chomsky's own characterization of his linguistic theory as a development of Cartesian rationalism. For his methodology to work—and to support his faith in Humboldt—he might better describe himself as a Kantian rationalist; the possibility of transcending the subject-object (or mind-body) dualism is essential to his deep structure-surface structure theory. This is not an unjustified suggestion, since Chomsky himself traces Cartesian philosophy directly through Kant to romantics like Humboldt.[67] The enemy, it would seem, is not post-Kantian romanticism but nineteenth-century British empiricism with its "passive mind" philosophy.

Chomsky, therefore, brings in a covert idealism by arguing for an attempt, like that of the Port-Royal school, to discover a *grammaire generale*, a general grammar. "The discovery of universal principles would provide a partial explanation for the facts of particular languages in so far as these could be shown to be simply specific instances of the general features of language structure formulated in the 'grammaire generale.' Beyond this, the universal features themselves might be explained on the basis of general assumptions about human mental processes or the contingencies of language use. . . ."[68] The methodology described here is "inductive," positivistic or scientific. The discovery of the general grammar is made by a process of simple abstraction from particular instances—or "facts." But we should note that the explanatory power of the general grammar is limited, partial; it works only where specific instances of language usage can be clearly shown to derive from the general grammar. Since the general grammar is itself abstracted from specific instances, its explanatory power is tautological.

To escape this vicious circle, Chomsky pushes beyond the general grammar to an even higher—a metalinguistic—level of abstraction. He posits the possibility of an explanatory power based on "general assumptions about human mental processes"; these assumptions give us not merely a general grammar but a universal grammar. In order to avoid becoming tangled in purely descriptive linguistics—the tautological limitations of the abstract general grammar—Chomsky is forced, by his own methodology, to a Kantian metaphysical assumption, to an essentialism not unlike Wittgenstein's. He must, therefore, affirm as strongly as both Wittgenstein and Cassirer the intimate relationship between language and cognition. And against the empiricist tradition he does defend the "active mind theory" of the romantics and its implications for the dynamic quality of language usage itself. He drives all the way into the epistemological basis of language. "In approaching the question of language acquisition and linguistic universals in this way, Cartesian linguistics reflects the concern of seventeenth-century rationalistic psychology with the contribution of mind to human knowledge."[69]

Once the leap into essentialism has been made, Chomsky articulates a general justification of his theory. He borrows from Charles Peirce the argument that human knowledge is not simply a random development. Quoting Peirce he argues that "the history of early sciences shows that something approximating a correct theory was discovered with remarkable ease and rapidity, on the basis of highly inadequate data, as soon as certain problems were faced. . . . " By analogy, Chomsky applies this insight to his theory of language acquisition. "*A fortiori*, the chances are even more overwhelming against the true theory of each language ever having come into the head of every four-year-old child." Reviving the rationalist argument from first causes, he concludes that a universal grammar is "necessary." "Knowledge of a language—a grammar—can be acquired only by an organism that is 'preset' with a severe restriction on the form of grammar. This innate restriction is a precondition, in the Kantian sense, for a linguistic experience. . . ."[70]

The original, hesitating step into essentialism has now been rigidified into a universal law that is a "severe restriction" on both cognition and the structure of grammar—that determines the forms of thought and linguistic expression and makes language learning and communication possible. "It is because of the virtual identity of this underlying system in speaker and hearer that communication can take place, the sharing of an underlying generative system being traced, ultimately, to the uniformity of human nature."[71] At this point, Chomsky has moved very near the structuralist essentialism of Lévi-Strauss's innate reason.

The relationship between deep and surface structure that I cited at the beginning of this section can now be more tightly drawn. This relationship depends on certain "transformational rules" that are potentially discoverable through analysis of the specific, physical, utterances of native language users. They differ from language to language,[72] but the principle of transformation itself is universal. It is the active process of language generation that is grounded in the innate powers of human cognition—indeed, is determined by them. Although there are no empirically determinable limitations on the number of individual linguistic utterances that might be formulated, there is a severe restriction on the grammatical form of such utterances. Chomsky's search is for a finite grammar that will explain an infinite (or apparently infinite) number of individual speech acts.

Chomsky has, in his battle against an abstract Cartesian dualism, attempted to bridge the gap between the inner, or private, world and the outer, or communal, world, and the relationship between deep and surface structure is instructively problematic. If deep structure is the expression of a thought, if it is described as "the underlying abstract structure that determines . . . semantic interpretation," it seems bound to the subjective world of the individual mind, what we might describe as the speaker's "intention to mean." Deep structure is, we remember, also nonidentical with surface structure seen as the "phonic" or "physical shape" of an utterance that Chomsky calls its "intended form"—what is clearly the outer, or communicative, dimension of language. Nevertheless, the inner is also the outer insofar as a correspondence exists between them. More crucially, the outer is also the inner in the identity of those universal rules of grammar, in the uniformity of the generative system. It is this tangle of possibilities that leads Chomsky to trivialize the problematics of Cartesian dualism despite his struggle with that philosophy.

There is, we should now note, no room in Chomsky's theory for a traditional poetry/prose distinction. The determinative nature of the universal grammar rules all linguistic utterances. If a use of language is meaningful to a native speaker, it apparently must fall under the universal grammar. Unlike Wittgenstein, Chomsky refrains from pushing the aesthetic outside normal language usage; he refuses to give it, as Wittgenstein does, an exalted, transcendental value. Nor does he see language, as does Cassirer, as the product of the primitive transcendental consciousness, as a fundamentally poetic act of mind. Chomsky's "universal grammar" or innate reason reflects his concern with the "hidden" logical system of generative potentiality posited as a logical necessity and inductively derived. Consequently, Chomsky develops a more detailed conception of how the logical system of *langage* gives us, as Wittgenstein argued, the limits of our world.

But Chomsky's Cartesian problematics offers much more than this if we risk extending the theory in the light of my previous discussions. The interchangeable nature of inner and outer worlds and the different orders of "intentionality" associated with deep and surface structures introduce a complex language system that is not reducible to either mere transcedental systematicity nor mere constitutive intuition. In his concept of universal grammar Chomsky emerges as a theorist of cognitive structures parallel to Lévi-Strauss. Together (although Chomsky's sense of innate reason seems more rigid than Lévi-Strauss's logic of binary oppositions) they have described the ideal of a systematic and wholly adequate (more than adequate!) structure of Knowledge. The completeness or holistic nature of the system would appear to restrict any possibility of "change" or "history" or "creativity."[73] The regularity of the system tends to close out temporality by explaining change as mere transformation. Yet, following a lead from Derrida, the system must be thought of as a nonentity, as in potentia, as unrealized.

Also, transformational rules do not, one must suspect, move by themselves; for just as Wittgenstein's logic, which gives us states of affairs, necessitates an active articulation toward particulars in order to arrange the particulars into states, a system of transformations shows itself as a system only through the intentions of men to produce meaning, to speak the inner thoughts via the outer, communal structure. This intentionality, furthermore, is circumscribed by conditions that are themselves both of the world and of the human mind, and we might return here again to the wisdom of Aristotle's concept of tragedy for an instructive example. It is the actions of men in the world (particularities or historical events) rendered through the intentional act of the tragedian (a performative act of communication externalized in the spectacle of stage production) into a form of universal validity, into probable impossibilities (the logic of things that cannot be experienced) that defines the limits of the art of imitation. But these limits are broad. Imitation is far from copying, for that which is imitated is subject to the constituitive intuition of man's mind, as the image of an image, or as true or false imitation. Nor is this an individual or private activity, for the shared cultural logic of probable orders has, as Lévi-Strauss argues, always already thought its way into men's minds, even into the local structures of their languages (*langue*) as potential for order.

The surplus adequacy of Lévi-Strauss's myth-logic, of Chomsky's universal grammar, of Wittgenstein's *logische Raum*, even of Derrida's "writing," necessitates intentionality and the empirical realm of individual activity. The vastness, comprehensiveness, and incorporeal nature of the logic of potentials, of probable states of affairs, does not merely leave room for the particular; it requires particular incidents of expressiveness, requires corporeality, in order to show itself in the first place. Without consciousness, without the inner that is both a dwelling place for and a tool of the outer, the distinction between self and world, between mind and things, between the world as chaos and as order, cannot be made; the questioning nature of these states cannot even be raised. On the other hand, to ask the question brings this whole problematic world into being. Perhaps this is why Derrida, the most demanding critic of the Western bias toward the inner, himself despairs of escaping its claim to privilege.[74] It is, he confesses, a need; we may call it a "passion" that is, if nothing else is, definitive of Man.

It is in this context of need, of an emptiness at the soul of man, that we must interpret the term *intentionality*. To intend meaning is productive, an expression of desire extending beyond the individual, as the transformation of materials into products. Very much like the relation between deep structure thoughts and their surface, phonic structures, intentionality is an articulation of an inner emptiness (seen as a given potential for movement) that attempts to fill the void by expressing it, in a physical form, to an-other. At the same time this is an opening of the inner to the invasion of the outer as the promise of plenitude, as, in fact, *energia*. That which is beyond us, which is not the same as us, is also an absence within us, what Derrida calls the "trace." To speak of an "absence" that "is" within us places us again in the Platonic dilemma of saying "that which is not."

This somewhat tangled set of relationships, true to the idea of *langage* as hidden logic, can best show itself in a series of paradigms. Consequently, I shall briefly outline one such structure in the following section. It is a multivalent model, however, that implies several others.

A PSYCHOANALYTIC MODEL

One of the major traditions in post-Freudian psychoanalytic theory has concerned itself with the primacy of "ego development." This is a multifaceted movement, filled with internal polemics, but the general focus on ego strategies for dealing with the world (society) brings the problematics of inner/outer interplay into the foreground as the principal concern of this tradition. For the most part, the ego psychologists have emphasized the process of individual adaptation to social demands, and this has produced both a theory and a therapy of the status quo.[75] The argument against this movement charges that "ego adaptation" serves the interests of society's power structure by exploiting individual needs in the name of some sort of social "cure." For example, commercial marketing procedures are designed to both create (false) needs and provide products for the satisfaction of those needs. But this creation of need is more insidious than it may at first appear, for the need to "consume" products is a negative displacement of deeper psychic energies of creativity or production. What the commercial establishment does, in fact, is intensify the sense of inner lacking by diverting energies (drives, desires) to socially acceptable ends. This Freud saw as "repression." The displacement of created need onto the level of conscious or preconscious human activity (material consumption) collapses inner and outer by superimposing collective need (social self-preservation or commerce) onto individual desire. In particular, advanced industrial society protects itself from entropic disintegration through self-generated overconsumption, giving this the name of "progress." The difficulty is that such progress depends upon a shifting inequality within the system in order to create the drive of need and justify overproduction; it can be argued that unemployment, inflation and ecological waste are the inevitable by-products.

My purpose here is not primarily to draw forth a moral or political argument; rather, I am proposing a simplified model that expresses the means whereby the psychology of ego adaptation becomes a tool of social repression. The breakdown on one level of the gap between inner and outer worlds produces a false sense of equilibrium, of psychic well-being. This cure is expressed as a sense of wholeness, completeness, or, most suggestively, as *togetherness* (a term displaced from its sense of social integration to serve as a metaphor for individual, inner, mental health). Ego adaptation therapy tends, in its many popularized versions, to serve the ends of social stability by creating pockets of "acceptable," and also commercial, "deviant" behavior. Art has traditionally been considered such an area of permissive self-indulgence, but a more familiar form of social permissiveness can be found in the equally ancient function of the carnival. The carnival, viewed as a privileged time and place, serves as a sanctioned release of socially destructive energies, as an orgiastic *Walpurgisnacht* where "everything goes." It is also an event easily (perhaps inevitably) adapted to economic ends, and it serves as an analogy for all the privileged times and places of a host of so-called primal scream therapies. Perhaps a more sophisticated version, ego adaptation theory has established a similar form of privileged time and place for psychoanalytic treatment. In the analytic session the psychoanalyst plays the role of objective, nonjudgmental listener and thereby creates an atmosphere of permissiveness that seems to allow the release of socially destructive drives in a harmless way. This is, however, merely a displacement and not a cure. Such sessions are endlessly repetitive; they are, in fact, repressive and economically exploitative.

Recently, a revisionist Freudianism has faced this ego-adaptation theory squarely, but not simply by charging that the adaptationists have misinterpreted the master.[76] In fact, the argument takes quite another direction. The adaptationists are seen as "repressive" agents who divert us away from the true depth of Freud's theory; they are, therefore, more Freudian than they know. The attack moves generally in the following pattern:

1. Freud's texts revealed (showed) the unconscious as hidden, as a primal lack at the soul of man.
2. The ego adaptationists have substituted Freud's texts themselves, as writing, for the unconscious that the texts merely showed.
3. This substitution is the same as a repressive displacement, for it allows the act of interpretation of texts to take the place of a more threatening confrontation with the unconscious that the texts only show.
4. Freud's "talking cure" (the analytic session) becomes an endless act of self-interpretation that displaces or represses the unconscious.

To write about or interpret Freud's texts allows us to repress what his texts show as the lack or absence of the unconscious; to speak about our personal needs with an objective analyst allows us to repress those needs in the illusion that repetitive self-expression satisfies those needs.

The very fact of repetitiveness belies the "cure," and the exploitativeness of the analytic session belies the "objectivity" of the analyst. Displacement serves the interests of socioeconomic self-preservation, confining psychoanalysis largely to the affluent, upper middle class and providing this class with a paradigm, in the model of Oedipal authoritarianism, for its own general self-preservation as power elite. The "talking cure," it is clear, depends upon the power of language (more accurately, *langage*) to generate endless expressions, on the surplus of signifying capacity, on what Derrida would call language's power to "defer" fulfillment.[77] Thus language, as a structure of Saussurian differentiation whose overriding logic is hidden, never expresses fully, in any individual text or utterance, that hiddenness. Yet because of this Freud's texts cannot be interpreted in order to domesticate the unconscious into a onesided form of Oedipal lacking. Language, seen as wholeness-defering *langage*, is both plenitude and lacking, *gives* us both a world of logical order, satisfaction, well-being and a world of desiring and emptiness. In this way *langage* is always the locus of the encroachment of the outer on the inner, possessed of both the power toward domestication, social homogenization, repression and the power of showing the depths of individual, socially destructive desire.

Derrida's remarkable analysis of Husserl's phenomenology provides us with a vivid example of this encroachment through its focus on the special status of the first person pronoun *I*. The signifier *I* has an ambiguous functioning in language usage, an "ideal" status, although not a romantic "idealistic" status like that assumed by Cassirer or Humboldt. When a speaker says "I" he expresses to himself his intuition of his own unique, immediate selfhood, an irreducible self-identity or self-presentation. But the same "I" as signifier has quite a different functioning for the hearer; it indicates for the hearer the "otherness" of the speaker's self-intuition. It indicates a presence that is absent to the hearer. We must define the function of the signifier *I*, therefore, as "ideal," as more than any one of these functions and thus comprehending both: the one inner-directed, the other expressing absolute outwardness. The signifier *I* has a status wholly apart from any consideration of subject or object.[78] Thus Derrida can say, "hearing oneself speak is not the inwardness of an inside that is closed upon itself; it is the irreducible openness in the inside; it is the eye and the world within speech."[79] Derrida's aim is to decenter man's consciousness of the world, to argue that the outer world's encroachment on the inner world demystifies the primacy of the romantic constitutive intuition, the "privilege" of speech, and even the claims of phenomenology to be the irreducible basis of the philosophy of knowledge. But by damaging phenomenology at the heart of its reductive methodology in order to pry open the inner world, Derrida has not abolished the inner world entirely. Nor is it clear that he wants to do so, for his technique, borrowed from Heidegger, of writing *sous rature*, of inscribing a privileged term ("Being," or "essence," or "presence," or "I," or "is") and then crossing it out, does not, in fact, erase so much as it indicates the ~~essential~~ absence of the term's privileged signification. The term, then, must be written in order to be crossed out, it must be seen (be present) as a *necessary* trace of an always deferred (absent) meaningfulness. There is, as Heidegger would argue, a necessary falling away from every appearing that marks the degeneration of being, or presence, or ego into the "other-than."[80] Derrida, in this discussion of Husserl, sets aside the simple dialectic of inner and outer seen as a struggle for superiority and argues for the vision of an inevitable encroachment of one world on the other. Unless we read Derrida this way his concept of freeplay is reduced to a meaningless "interplay of presence and absence."[81]

We are justified here in defining a radically new concept of intentionality: as the expression of an inner desire that is a given of our outer world. Language's inner/outer interplay "shows" us self and other not as competitors but as mirror images of one another.[82] Each "shows" the other, and this emergence of self into and out of the cultural context makes possible both an existential self-awareness and the motivating force of historical change. The vision of the literary artist, self-reflexive and acculturated throughout, is manifest in his intention to mean; vision and meaning are "occasional," showing themselves at the historical moment of inward will to speak but also showing the trace of always-deferred fulfillment.

For literary studies this is a profound nondualism, one that Gerald Bruns has recently confronted with admirable boldness. Quoting Paul Ricoeur, Bruns situates man as apart from and yet a part of his world, as defined by the interdependent yet conflicting impulses of assimilation to the cultural/linguistic system and the effort to accommodate that system to individual experience. "Man's adoption of language is in general a way of making him absent to things by intending them with 'empty' intentions, and correlatively, of making things present through the very emptiness of signs."[83] Ricoeur's correlation here, recalling Heidegger's emphasis on man's being in the world, leads Bruns to propose a dialectical relationship between Derrida's demystified metaphysics of presence (the nonprivilege of "speech") and his metaphysical antimetaphysics of absence (the comprehensive differentiality of "writing").[84] But I would suggest that a dialectic is not quite enough. A dialectic describes only the motive of intentionality, the *why* of a thrust, which has ambiguous psychological implications, toward an outer reality. The act of intentionality in its use of "empty intentions" drives a wedge between the self and the other in order to confirm the noncontingent integrity of the self. Yet it also makes reference to the other as object of desire in experience, as potential for fulfillment, as the other of myself, thereby affirming the self's contingent "belonging" to the world. Is this, then, far from Cassirer's conception of metaphor, or from the general, romantic idea of metaphor as ineffable, as beyond writing, "absent," fleetingly "suggested" through poetic articulation? Language, as *langage*, comprehends the possibility for intentionality even as it shows itself through intentionality. *Langage* is the context for dialogue, for imitation and constitutive intuition, for culturally ratified *langue* and individual *parole*. *Langage* is the hidden space of *logische Raum* that fragments into both solipsism and realism, allowing for the transformation of the one into the other, for an extension of Wittgenstein's baffling tautological proposition:

> Solipsism strictly carried out coincides with pure realism. The "I" in solipsism shrinks to an extensionless point and there remains the reality co-ordinate with it.
>
> The philosophical "I" is . . . the limit not a part of the world. [*Tractatus*, 5.64]

The "philosophical 'I'," of course, is not the same as the "I in solipsism." The "philosophical 'I'" is the Derridian "I" that must be seen as both inner and outer; it is the "ideal" that comprehends both the "solipsistic I" and, if you will, the "realistic I"; it is the possibility of inner/outer, the possibility of that intentionality that shows itself as the illusion of dialectics.

No longer the romantic self-conscious Being, present to itself in the expression of the "I," the first person pronoun nevertheless has about it the lingering ("longing") trace of romantic idealism. "I" refers not to a person but, according to Émile Benveniste, "je se réfère a l'acte de discours individuel où il est prononcé."[85] Thus, subjectivity arises in the act of discourse as the product of the ideality of the pronoun "I," which marks the here and now of the utterance. "Le discours provique l'emergence de la subjectivité."[86] That emergence, predicated on the functioning of the "I" as both personal and communal, as endlessly repeatable, opens the space for what we call "intentionality" or what John Searle sees as a "speech act." Speaking directly of Derrida's theory of the endless iterability of language, Searle correctly speculates that such "freeplay" necessitates "the particular forms of intentionality that are characteristic of speech acts."[87] Searle fails to develop this idea and seems to misread badly Derrida's, admittedly somewhat obscure, appropriation of "speech act theory."[88] There is no real communication between the two. But the importance of intentionality as will (desire) to articulate, and hence as emergence of the self in and through discourse (communication, communion, community) cannot be denied even as Derrida struggles to deconstruct every last vestige of romantic "presence."

The multifunctioning of the pronoun *I* permits the emergence of the "self," moreover, not only in the familiar romantic guise of self-conscious subjectivity but also in a variety of other masks. If I may call attention once more to the discussion of Faulkner's *Go Down, Moses* in part 1, the three principal characters of that novel all may be seen as "emergent" subjects (as "I's") whose various characteristics reflect quite different cultural/linguistic functionings. The traditional romantic "I" is the "I" of Ike McCaslin, the reflection of egoistical, self-conscious, and nostalgic yearnings for a primitive I/thou dichotomy and its promise of apocalyptic transcendence. The Derridian "I" is the "I" of Lucas Beauchamp, the expression of self as both individual and archetype (familial/communal), as both center and circumference. Lastly, the "I" of Sam Fathers we may call Lévi-Straussian as it derives personal "identity" through "typicality," through belonging. This latter emergence is directly opposed to the egoistical "I" of Ike McCaslin and is perhaps better written as a "we."

The significance of these three "figures" (characters, signifiers) lies in our overall reading of the novel, a reading that goes beyond the simplistically historical observation that Faulkner is writing about the passing away of one culture and the emergence of another. History is more cataclysmic than that. The three characters described above, furthermore, do not represent Faulkner's effort to think like an Indian (Sam), or like a black slave (Lucas). They are all expressions of Faulkner's culture, traces of three sets of defining human relationships (Ike's pattern of dominance and withdrawal, Lucas's inversion of the master/slave roles, Sam's immersion in an idyllic/pragmatic "nature") that subsist in Faulkner's South long after the disappearance *in fact* of slavery and the frontier. It is accurate to say that *Go Down, Moses* tells the story of the death of one culture and the birth of another; there is a chronology, a history, in the plot or narrative structure. But at the juncture of the three "I's" we see a very different order of time and history, not a chronology that erases its past, rather one that bears traces of that past. The key, therefore, is an interaction of cultures through the interaction of characters, and this interaction forms an interface that shows an opening for a revolutionary rupture in the historical chronology. What emerges is necessarily unexpressed; it is neither the sum of these worlds (they are irreducible to one another) nor the displacement of a weaker culture by a stronger, more progressive, one through which "time" is defined. This unarticulated context of the novel opens outward in order that we may discern the limits of Faulkner's problematical white southern world, a somewhat confusing and confused society driven by economic necessity and religious guilt. The contradictions of this culture are terrifying for its members, who, like Faulkner, have been forced into a position of critical self-consciousness. Ideals of egalitarian brotherhood, it seems, must be generated out of the materials of racial repression, that is, out of the interweaving of incest and miscegenation, but this is no less than a wilful act of cultural and personal self-destruction. Faulkner's history, therefore, contains no easy transitions; it is revolutionary, disruptive, and, finally, virtually inconceivable, for it posits a *new* cultural (linguistic, cognitive) structure, a *new* set of human relationships radically unlike all of those the traces of which show through the characters of Sam, Lucas, and Ike.

Clearly this reaffirms the crucial importance of the very act of self-emerging, of intentionality, that takes place in and for the sake of culture. The assertion of "I-presence" reveals the potentials of collective cultural identity both in the sense of belonging to a determinate system (a potential loss of self) and in the sense of critically, revolutionarily, deconstructing that system and the "self" it defined. Derrida's demystification of "presence" may, therefore, inevitably return us to the western metaphysical tradition it was designed to explode. If we no longer puzzle about the origins of man's "poetic" self-consciousness, nor about the "priority" of speech over writing, poetry over prose, it is because these traditional questions have been rewritten. If the essentialism of Wittgenstein's *logische Raum* or Chomsky's universal grammar, and the essential irreality of Derrida's trace, can only "show" themselves, we must wonder as does Derrida, about the "force" (what we once called "origin") of this showing. This question of motivation, perhaps of individual will, we now call "intentionality," seen as a form of displacement directed toward some end, some-*thing*. The encroachment of outer on inner, the mirroring one of the other, does not collapse the two, any more than Saussure's *langue* and *parole* may be collapsed, into inarticulateness, silence. The separation of inner and outer, self and culture, presupposes the entire, hidden system of differentiation in a way that an individual speech act presupposes Derrida's system of "writing." It is, in fact, Derrida who shows us this, as his highly articulate critical texts (like Wittgenstein's *Tractatus*) stand for (stand forth, stand before) that hidden system. At this juncture Cassirer enters again, at the point where we can say that particular texts show themselves as articulations of the moment, as the presentation of an experience that may well melt away into deferred fulfillment, but that nevertheless "activates" the system, divides inner and outer, and manifests the richness (if fleetingness) of experience of time and place, of history. Cassirer calls this a violent act of individuation (metaphor). Heidegger calls it "speaking being." Vico metaphorically concentrates it into the thunderclap, and a modern interpreter of Vico, Edward Said, labels this a "beginning intention."[89]

THE POSSIBILITY OF HISTORY: PIAGET

It is to the problem of history, the diachronic dimension of man's cognitive capacities, that Jean Piaget addresses himself, and it is Piaget who most clearly of all recent students of language ties linguistics to epistemology. In this very general sense he furthers the tradition of linking language to those operations of mind that give us our world. He does not, as does Cassirer, speculate about a primal or innate origin of man's capacities for logical thought. He apparently rejects the various essentialist attitudes of Cassirer, Chomsky, and Wittgenstein, preferring to argue that there are several logical systems, not just one, and that a universal or innate core for these systems is little more than idle speculation. This releases him from the confining stasis of Chomsky's theory (as well as from that of Lévi-Strauss) and allows him to argue for what he calls a "developmentalist" theory of human knowledge.

Piaget rejects the idea defended by logical positivists that logic is fundamentally a kind of language. "The position in general is that logical and mathematical reality is derived from language. Logic and mathematics are nothing but specialized linguistic structures. [But] if . . . we find logical structures in the coordinations of actions in small children even before the development of language, we are not in a position to say that these logical structures are derived from language."[90] Illustrating his claims with laboratory-controlled studies of the development of reasoning power in children, Piaget concludes that "intelligence precedes language," both "ontogenetically" in each individual child and, a fortiori, "phylogentically" in the human race.[91]

The theory that logical capacity precedes the development of linguistic skills seems to counter Cassirer's argument that language emerges along with man's most primitive cognitive development—as a product of his violent act of individuation. But Piaget, in fact, does not specifically refute Cassirer, nor does he devote much time to what he calls "unnecessary" speculation about the primal source of human consciousness. There is no clear evidence, as we shall see, that Piaget's theory is in all ways incompatible with that of Cassirer. Piaget does, however, directly reject Chomsky's position (just the opposite of logical positivism) that "language is based on logic, on reason," and that this reason is innate. "I deny that these structures are innate. I think that we have been able to see [in laboratory observations] that they are the result of development. Hence the hypothesis that they are innate is . . . unnecessary."[92] Piaget's developmentalism in this sense helps us situate the concept of language as a total system, helps us place the "givenness" of *langage* as the horizon of man's being but as in no way really "innate."

There are, we should recall, two stages in Piaget's developmentalist theory: "simple abstraction" and "reflective abstraction." The first is remarkably close (although not the same as) Cassirer's sense of the dawning of primitive consciousness, the violent act of existential awareness based essentially on a dialectics of struggle between a "self" and an "other." "Reflective abstraction," also reminiscent of Cassirer, is a sophisticated development of the first stage, which exercises a kind of control over the outer world by grouping objects into logically meaningful categories (states of affairs). Moreover, for Piaget there are "many different logics, and not just a single logic." "Any one Logic . . . is too weak, but all the Logics taken together are too rich to enable logic to form a single value basis for knowledge."[93] One might say that there is an individual logic for each experiential system, each way of confronting the world; but this would lead to a form of solipsism, and Piaget finds himself very much in Wittgenstein's dilemma of showing that one logic and many logics necessitate one another just as "my" language/world presupposes "our" language/world. By rejecting the innate reason of Chomsky and Lévi-Strauss, Piaget hopes to gain the possibility of real novelty in the evolution of the individual's (and Man's) capacity for knowing. Moreover, without making the relationship between language and cognitive development as intimate as does Cassirer, Piaget opens the door for individual, creative activity. Knowing, he claims, is active (though unlike Cassirer he means that it is "operational" or "instrumental"). "Knowing an object does not mean copying it—it means acting upon it. It means constructing systems of transformations that can be carried out on or with this object. Knowing reality means constructing systems of transformations that correspond, more or less adequately, to reality. Knowledge, then, is a system of transformations that become progressively adequate."[94]

The phrase "more or less" adequate here is disappointing, but we must recognize the difficulty of the problem. Piaget will not go so far as to accept a naive "picture theory" even from a sophisticated philosophy like that of Wittgenstein. What is important for our purposes in this essay is Piaget's sense of an active engagement with reality by the knowing subject.

The idea of "adequation" also is troublesome, requiring some sense of final goal or norm as a measure of "more-or-lessness." The norm, of course, is cultural, the many systematic logics, cultural *langue*, that tend to force adequation into ego adaptation. But since these subsystems or logics do not project an all-inclusive logic that determines the individual systems, the individual is free to restructure even the most recalcitrant logic of adequation. What we are given is not a universal grammar or innate structure but the potential for assertive transformations, the too rich signification of *langage*. Piaget is interested only in that cognitive phase that has begun to move beyond Cassirer's primitive consciousness of "momentary gods." On this level he makes use of the mathematical principle of transformation to describe a truly active principle of cognition.

> The nativist or apriorist maintains that the forms of knowledge are predetermined inside the subject and thus again, strictly speaking, there can be no novelty. By contrast, for the genetic epistemologist [Piaget himself] knowledge results from continuous construction, since in each act of understanding, some degree of invention is involved; in development, the passage from one stage to the next is always characterized by the formation of new structures which did not exist before, either in the external world or in the subject's mind.[95]

"Some degree of invention" is crucial to Piaget's developmentalism. Observable on the ontogenetic level, it also, by extension, characterizes the phylogenetic level and gives a historical dimension to man's structuring capacities. We may, therefore, extend Piaget to argue that man is not bound by his "uniform nature," and in the process of his cognitive development he continues to restructure the meaningful systems of his world. Lucien Goldmann, drawing sociological implications from similar psychological insights, expresses this interchange between self and world most clearly; "*tout* comportement humain est un essai de donner une *réponse significative* à une situation particulière et tend par cela méme à créer un équilibre entre le sujet de l'action et l'objet sur lequel elle porte, le monde ambiant."[96] So it is also in the realm of language, and here we must once more align language with cognition although without speculating on the origins of either. In the development of language capabilities a complex process emerges whereby the given system of adequation is tested by the individual's articulation to experience. Thus all cultural systems are subject to Piaget's "continuous construction" (to the freeplay of *langage*), to the resistance that articulation itself expresses toward too repressive logics of adequation.

There can be no reconciliation between Cassirer and Piaget on the question, "Which comes first, logic or language?" But we must recognize that each man directs his attention to a very different dimension of cognition and language usage: Cassirer to poetry or noncasual utterances, Piaget to prose or casual utterances, and we may, I think, justifiably question whether the two theories are exclusive on all levels. Cassirer defines a version of creative language use based on a prelogical emergence of self-consciousness: the vital separation of self and other that activates the contradictory drives to maintain and dissolve that separation. At this unlocatable moment, which is the origin of human history and yet itself not historical, man's self-awareness is contingent; the inner and outer worlds are flickering mirror images of one another. It is the moment of metaphor in Cassirer's philosophy, a probable impossibility, the unity of difference. This moment is dissolved into difference itself or deferred fulfillment by Derrida; it is a repeated and repeatable moment that Derrida wants to see as the enduring and ahistorical condition of man, and for which he coins the term "*differance*."[97]

But this condition, as I have argued, can only "show" itself, and that best in the tenuousness of Cassirer's metaphor, as presence and absence. Thus metaphor can be seen either as creating its own presuppositions or as self-destructing into those presuppositions. Moreover, Piaget's first stage of logical development, simple abstraction, necessitates its own presupposition in something like the violent individuation of Cassirer's metaphor (or, for that matter, Derrida's *differance*). One cannot act upon objects without individuation, without affirming its violence and reaching out to close the gap. Nor can this act be repeated—each repetition being different and, perhaps in one sense, psychologically more adequate (as proof of mastry or belonging to culture)—without affirming Derrida's vision of deferral (*differance*). As this rudimentary stage gives way to "reflective abstraction," man transforms himself into the user (consumer) of his world. But here too abstract systems fail to reach complete adequacy; by their very nature they cannot, for they are the developments of the more rudimentary forms of consciousness, showing themselves in individual actions, subject to constant revision as a result of man's fundamental drive toward a deferred fulfillment.

If we may speak at all of the "history" of man, we cannot oversimplify it (as, for example, readers of Cassirer tend to do) into a linear evolution from primitive to sophisticated thought, from metaphoric poetry to metonymic prose, or from a state of nature to a condition of culture. The developmental process, Piaget argues, is repeated in every generation, ontogenetically in every individual. The rudimentary metaphoric expressiveness, Cassirer shows, remains within all men at all times. The systematic possibilities of prose ("writing") and logical thought, Derrida teaches, are not strictly developments from, but also are the "given" conditions of, all individuation, poetry, and knowledge. Perhaps the most adequate explanation of this complex system is to be found in Cassirer's theory of the human condition that everywhere and always ranges between "ineffables" of different orders, between rudimentary (self)consciousness and abstract collective systematicity. History, therefore, is a human projection (is man-made); it is no more and no less than the record of man's struggle for adequation and is itself (as historiography) a struggle for such adequation. Observable in the acts of the individual, history marks the interpenetration of the outer on the inner, but does not evidence the collapse of the one into the other else history would be silent; *langage* would not show itself.

Modern, perhaps better designated "post-modern," literary theory has been obsessed with the idea of "silence," but from two very different perspectives. I give only extreme examples. In the radical theory of Ihab Hassan, based on the neo-Freudian utopianism of Norman O. Brown, a militant antiformalism leads to an overemphasis of the experiential, the sensual, the corporeal, or immediate at the expense of defending inarticulateness. Language as a formal and limiting system is associated with society, with repression and sublimation so that it is

> no wonder that language, which is traditionally man's largest repository of private as well as public meaning, should be held in discount. . . . By minimizing the role of sublimation in the future

> [the prophets of our time] also minimize the role of language. . . . The modern revolt against verbal discourse may be thus seen, at bottom, as a revolt against authority and abstraction: the civilization that Apollo sponsored has become totalitarian, and the tools he gave man to live by have become machines fueled on abstractions. Because all meaning is ultimately rooted in the flesh—assertions may be regarded as affirmations of the body—meaninglessness is a correlative of abstraction.[98]

Hassan, in the sixties one of the many voices of intellectual revolt in the United States, now seems himself to have been silenced, but not by his own strategies. Rather he is the victim of a social/political revolution that moved diametrically away from his idea of the sensuous inarticulate to what we might term the structural inarticulate. This is the realm of Derrida's "deferred meaningfulness" and Lévi-Strauss's "surplus of signifier." This philosophical shift moves away from the existential by means of a remarkable extension of Saussure's idea of the "arbitrary" relationship between signifier and signified, between the diacritical system of potential meaningfulness and the realm of individual experience.[99] This, as Fredric Jameson points out, is what Lévi-Strauss has in mind when he argues, with Kantian overtones, for being aware of the "discontinuity" between "experience and reality"; "to reach reality one has first to reject experience, and then subsequently to reintegrate it into an objective synthesis devoid of any sentimentality."[100] Derrida, of course, finds Lévi-Strauss not antiempirical enough to support his theory of signification as "freeplay," as the "disruption of presence."[101] For Derrida, and even appropriately for Michel Foucault, the result of this thrust away from the existential is a tendency toward antisubjectivism, antihumanism, and anti-historicism. With an emphasis on deferral and anonymity, on a meaningfulness that is not articulated but that dwells in the gaps of articulation, comes another version of the writing of silence. It is not necessary, however, to opt for either of these extremes.

Hassan and Derrida, through their very different fascinations with silence, have both hypostatized the arbitrary "bar" that Saussure rather innocently drew between signifier and signified, $\frac{\text{signified}}{\text{signifier}}$ or $\frac{\text{thought (concept)}}{\text{accoustical image}}$. But perhaps no one has treated Saussure's formula with more suggestive violence than Jacques

Lacan. For Lacan the relation between signifier and signified (S/s) does not so much describe a discrete state of affairs (the arbitrary association of one set of sounds with a thought, like the Saussurean example where the sounds of the word "tree" embody the concept of "treeness") as it signifies a "function." That is, the formula (S/s) does not itself transcend language to describe it; it rather functions as a sign of the condition of language use. Saussure's formula, literally inverted by Lacan, signifies the problematics of the relationship: $\frac{\text{Conscious and Preconscious}}{\text{Unconscious}}$ where the "bar" is "arbitrary" only in the sense that its existence as Freudian "censor" or "repression" is real enough but unlocatable.[102] The reason for this problematics is that for Lacan the "unconscious is structured like a language,"[103] and like a language is apparently neither wholly inner nor outer, neither wholly conscious nor unconscious, neither wholly individual nor communal. The unconscious for Lacan is remarkably within and outside the individual as "the discourse of the Other,"[104] and this, I suggest, "necessitates" the Saussurean bar as a sign of the struggle, both inner and outer, between the individual and collectivity. The "continual" formation of the ego (which process comprehends the echo-relationship of ontogenesis and phylogenesis in Piaget's theory, the struggle for equilibrium) is an expression of "need" both as individual desire for fulfillment and as collective (linguistic) deferral of fulfillment.

The necessity of the bar for Lacan is not unlike the necessity of some conception of the emergence of man from Nature into Culture in Lévi-Strauss's philosophy, the positing of an originary moment that nevertheless, as Lévi-Strauss realizes and Derrida emphasizes, must also be scandalously violated. The bar is a bar between Nature and Culture, between conscious and unconscious, between individual experience and collective signifying structures only because we "need" it as a presupposition for its own denial. The bar for Lacan is seen as repression in two interdependent ways. The first is "metonymic," a form of Freudian displacement, in which the movement from signifier to signifier "hides" the location of the unconscious desire and thereby situates the bar of repression. The metonymic movement that will not allow the emergence of the repressed desire into the consciousness nevertheless expresses that desire through the movement from signifier to signifier as a form of voracious consumption, a repression of a fundamental psychic need seeking fulfillment, which in turn is both promised and deferred by the diacritical nature of the signifying system itself. It is this "linear" flow that characterizes what I described in part 1 as the metonymic drive of narrative, the seeking for an ending that is perpetually deferred. It is, of course, echoed in Faulkner's hero Ike McCaslin, whose desire to end the flow of his family history conflicts directly with his desire to father his own son, to begin the family once again in innocence. Ike's seeking to pay off the family's debts returns on him in that devastating repetition where his dreams of a world of plenitude, of homogeneity (the union of white and black) are shattered by his own shouts of deferral: "*Maybe in a thousand or two thousand years in America*, he thought. *But not now! Not now!* He cried, not loud, in a voice of amazement, pity, and outrage: 'You're a nigger!'" (*Go Down, Moses*, p. 361). Such "debts" are never paid; desire and need turn, through repetition, into exploitation.

Ike's cry, furthermore, brings us to the other function of the bar of repression in Lacan's theory: metaphor. It is metaphor that expresses the very emergence of the process of signification from the unconscious into the conscious. Metaphor, as Jakobson argued, calls attention to itself as metaphor. It is, for Jakobson, the function of the selective activity of language usage that emphasizes both difference and similarity and is, for Lacan, both conscious and unconscious. Ike's cry "in a voice of amazement, pity, and outrage" marks the violence of such a "crossing of the bar" in Lacan's theory,[105] but rather than the simple expression of repressed racial hatred, Ike's cry, "'You're a nigger,'" is metaphoric, signaling the repression of an unvoiced signifer even as the voiced signifier, "'nigger,'" forces us to see that repressed signifier as a signified, as, very simplistically stated, "personal." What is repressed, a most typical Faulknerian theme, is the entire history of the McCaslin family so tangled in the scandal of incest and here manifest again for Ike in the child of the white Roth Edmonds and the unnamed yet "related" black woman. Ike's cry is at once a condensation of this history into the metaphor of racial "otherness" and a division that shatters his dream of fulfillment; it is a metaphor that allows us to see the metonymic flow of eternal deferral, a metaphor the "presence" of which reveals the "absence" that makes its showing forth possible. In this, metaphor serves a profound function, perhaps an essential one. It at once affirms the necessity of the bar in order that it be violated; it speaks in the momentariness of its articulation to experience that mutuality of presuppositions that makes every metaphor both the force that shows the structure of the signifying system and an assertion of itself over against that system.

To some extent, my view of the bar as necessary explains Derrida's distrust of the idea of "arbitrariness"; Lacan's shift away from Saussure is justifiable in terms of Derrida's argument against those dualisms between Nature and Culture, experience and signifying structure, speech and writing that almost always eventuate in the metaphysical elevation of the former over the latter, the treating of Culture, structure, writing as "fallen" or "deadening degenerations" of Nature, experience, speech. But Derrida's powerful argument in his *Of Grammatology*, taken within its own terms, must not be seen as simply inverting this traditional metaphysics; Derrida does not simply privilege writing over speech. In his analysis of Rousseau he arrives at a position of mutual presuppositions. The bar is necessary as that which "shows" itself, in its transgressions, as repression, as that primal Faulknerian repression/transgression of the taboo of "incest."[106]

> Even that which we say, name, describe as the prohibition of incest does not escape play. There is a point in the system where the signifier can no longer be replaced by its signified, so that in consequence no signifier can be so replaced, purely and simply. For the point of nonreplacement is also the point of orientation for the entire system of signification, the point where the fundamental signified is promised as the terminal-point of all references and conceals itself as that which would destroy at one blow the entire system of signs. It is at once spoken and forbidden by all signs. Language is neither prohibition nor transgression, it couples the two endlessly. That point does not exist, it is always elusive or, what comes to the same thing, always already inscribed in what it ought to escape or ought to have escaped, according to our indestructible and mortal desire.[107]

For Ike McCaslin the promised but unarticulated signified which must be repressed only to violently erupt is that tangled experiential realm of incest and miscegenation, but this opening is culturally and personally destructive.

We must not, of course, privilege any sign, even one so profoundly descriptive as "incest," for the signifier incest, as we have seen in the discussion of *Go Down, Moses*, is merely metaphoric, an expression of the activity of language engaged with experience. It is a term that may well have only the function of a "rhetorical" strategy, divided from the world of things even as it reaches toward that world and teaches us the use of things. Thus even as metaphor (desiring) presupposes metonymy (consumption) it disrupts it (it does not replace it) in order to show it. Émile Benveniste, describing the function of the sentence as a fundamental unit of language usage, puts emphasis on the active force of "showing." "C'est dans le discours, actualisé en phrases, que la langue se forme et se configure."[108] Perhaps this same idea has been more expressively and inclusively put by Kenneth Burke. Literature, like proverbs, Burke suggests, might well be seen as "*strategies* for dealing with *situations*. Insofar as situations are typical and recurrent in a given social structure, people develop names for them and strategies for handling them. Another name for strategies might be *attitudes*. One tries to change the rules of the game until they fit his own necessities."[109] Changing the rules of the game, as I have argued, is what *langage* as inclusive system, as deferred fulfillment, and as the potentiality of all games makes possible. It is the function of the game to "fit" necessities, to "show" itself in strategies or in "attitudes" toward experience and specific occasions. These rule changes describe the limits of history.

Just as there is no one logic, for Piaget, that is adequate to all experience, so too there is no one system (game) that remains adequate for all men at all times. We have, therefore, a history comprised not of neat homogeneous evolution, of universal sameness, but a series of emergences that form the cultural, cognitive, and linguistic contexts for those individual members who in their everyday activities continue to ratify their operational, explanatory powers. On its abstract level history is not unlike that "series of series" described by Foucault, the emergence of cognitive systems at certain places and times that draw an ordered set of propositions into the limits of

Knowledge.[110] But a countering extension of Piaget's theory allows us to remain mindful of the ever-present individual within the collectivity. Beyond the level of "simple abstraction" is an admittedly more mysterious form of prelogical cognition that tends to fragment experience into Cassirer's "momentary gods." Herein we confront the essence of what Derrida calls "freeplay," for it is this movement counter to mere stereotypical collectivity, yet, in acculturated man, always within collectivity, that threatens to recenter any static, culturally ratified system. Derrida's claim that there are no universal a priori centers is correct; man's history is a constant series of overlapping systems each holding to its elusive hegemony for its space and time.[111] But this is not far removed from Piaget's idea of man's constant struggle toward equilibrium, a basic human condition that resists on the one hand a lapse into primitive apocalypticism (the sin of Ike McCaslin) and on the other hand the loss of individual being through absorption into the tyrannous collectivity of stereotype (the fate of Roth Edmonds).

The relation of language and thought that gives us our world makes language itself a model of human culture. The very structure of language contains within it the limits of a temporal, collective, and static system (though not a universal system as "sameness") and the possibility of an individualistic and dynamic freedom. The tension between the two makes possible a revitalized concept of history. This extensive characteristic is manifest in the concept of "style" (which will occupy us in the next part) through the metonymic and metaphoric functions of language. Thus we might argue that language is composed of both poetry and prose, although apparently there is no absolute separation between them. The old New Critical radical organicism, itself a metaphor, fails to fully acknowledge this relationship and, as a result, fails to define the full power of language as both system and individual utterance. To some extent, the old form/content dichotomy also must be refocused, for the relation of language and thought forces us to see the relation of form to content in terms of a broader spectrum of possibilities. Again, at the extremes (where distinctions are clearer but not absolute) metonymy must be seen as a process of structuring content in terms of linear, logical sequences;

metaphor structures content in terms of immediate, spatial, symbolic identities. The content of each is functionally different because of the cognitive formalizations called into activity; that is, the content of each impinges upon our minds *as content* only because it is structured as it is. There is, effectively, no way to separate the two.

Faulkner's *Go Down, Moses* once more serves us as an instructive example. If history as "collectivity" shows itself only through individual acts of consciousness, "intentions"; if, as I have argued through Derrida, the inner and outer worlds interpenetrate and mirror one another; then each individual is at once the totality and the possibility of history. Ike McCaslin's fate is the result of an internalization of the more romantic ideal of inner/outer confrontation; this internalization is, I believe, what Lionel Trilling meant by the "opposing self."[112] Ike's fear of the ledgers (what Derrida would call his "phonocentric" fear of writing) drives him to defy his own history by constantly seeking immediate experience, by reaching for an ever-receding Nature. Faulkner's story is a powerful and devastating vision of modern life, particularly of the American dream. The death of the frontier, the exploitative violence that European man wrought on the new world, the collapse of the hope for rebirth into innocence, all are themes of *Go Down, Moses*. The narrative of Isaac McCaslin tells the "real" story of the death of Natty Bumpo, the end of the dream of natural plenitude; only Faulkner will not allow Ike to die. He lives as the constant echo of our American heritage, giving the lie to the dream of innocence. The American myth is vitiated by language because the innocence of experience is corrupted by the "commonness" of utterance; the delusion of bountifulness is exploded by the twin images of scarcity and desire.

It is "Pantaloon in Black" that draws into focus the complexity of Faulkner's novel and the philosophy of language that the novel shows. We have seen to what extent the story pits its hero Rider against the nameless sheriff, and how in this confrontation are juxtaposed the idea of "individuality" and the idea of "stereotype." Rider's continual seeking for some relief from his personal sense of loss drives him into stereotype. His questioning violates his individuality; his self-doubt, fear, and hallucinations inevitably force the outer world, the "others," to encroach upon the sanctity of his inner being. We are confronted again by Freud's paradox of the interplay of life and death instincts, for Rider is never so alive as in his headlong plunge toward death. More significantly, Rider is never more individual, never more the "named" person, than when he confronts the white world, forcing the sheriff to un-name him as an-other, as "Boy" or "nigger" (to echo Ike McCaslin's epithet from a different but related context). The sheriff's instinctive retreat into stereotype shows the inadequacy of that stereotype to deal with experience. "Pantaloon in Black" plays itself out on a stage of very complicated interactions, revealing the unlocatable point of intersection between *parole* and *langage*; between individual experience and the myth of the human condition. But these relationships are askew, turning back upon themselves as each mirrors or reflects the others, spiraling inside/outside and outside/inside like the twisting of DNA chains. I offer the following diagram as a poor two-dimensional representation.

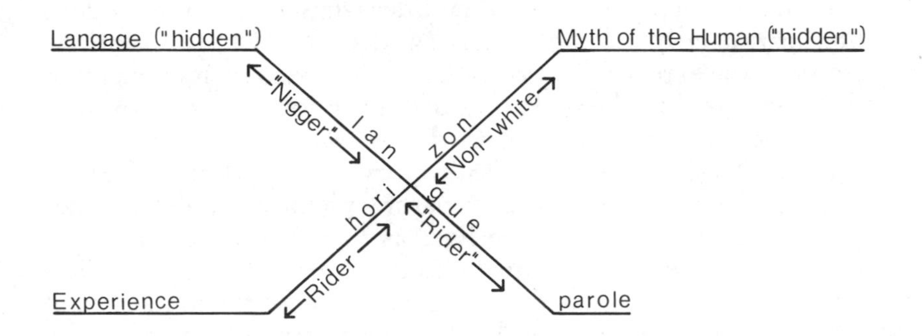

One must see this diagram as an illusion of perspective, for the figure is "actually" twisting on itself so that *parole* and *langage* are in some way on the same level as will then be also myth and experience. There are, therefore, no levels, and the pivotal point of crossing is an imaginative point where inner becomes outer. What matters is the idea of a point where *langue* and horizon appear to intersect. It is here that the critic situates himself, observing that "nigger," as the displaced fragment of a differential system, as the mere possibility of distinction, as "otherness," flows through the cultural horizon of the sheriff where it signifies "nonwhite" to force its way into the particularity, individuality, of the realm of *parole* and do battle with the proper name "Rider." But this flow is, as the arrows indicate, reversible, just as is the flow along the horizon axis. Moreover, each axis apparently deflects into the other, for Rider's personal experience as "named" individual mirrors the impersonal myth of the human as primordial lack, as desire for the always deferred fulfillment of the Word made flesh. There are, therefore, no clear limits to a cultural horizon and the *langue* that expresses that horizon—and no points of contact except those of cultural ratification; they are merely revealed, as *langage* and myth show themselves in *parole* and experience.

The cultural functioning of *langue*, as opposed to the hidden logic of *langage*, is always on the edge of appearing as fixed and delimited. But *langue* fluctuates between the limits of national character and local color, and, therefore, is a ghostly cultural system, not unlike a cultural code. If *langage* tends toward the wholly arbitrary, *langue* tends toward the highly motivated—at its most stultifying, toward the stereotypical. *Langage* is capable of many *langue*, sometimes overlapping or in conflict. We might borrow from information theory a definition of this idea of *langage* as a "situation of maximum information," as the ideal of perfect freedom of choice poised to generate specific messages.[113] The problem is, of course, that this maximum or ideal state is essentially nonfunctional. Umberto Eco argues that we produce meaningful communication in part by delimiting choices, by designing (culturally) subsystems within the maximum state of perfect freedom. "A message selected from a very large number of symbols (among which an astronomical number of combinations may be possible) would consequently be very informative, but would be impossible to transmit because it would require too many binary choices."[114] Represented by the formula $I = N \log_2 h$, where I is information, N is the number of possible choices, and h is the number of symbols available, Eco states that "in order to make it possible to form and transmit messages, one must reduce the values of N and h."[115]

Such a reduction is essentially a limit placed on the expressive power of the system, and for all practical purposes it is a limit placed on the experiential field to be encoded (a limit imposed by the design of the subsystem). The experiential field is not part of the semiotic subsystem, but limits placed on the semiotic subsystem tend to censor or repress the field of experience by limiting the range of what may be truthfully articulated. Thus the experiential field remains *in fact* unlimited, and as such is always an anarchical threat to any delimited system (*langue*). Referentiality, as Eco describes it, is a necessary condition for the design of any semiotic system because the semiotic system is constructed to control the flow of information from the experiential field, and this is so even if referentiality is not a part of the system's "semiotic functioning."[116] We have, then, here come full circle to repeat the Platonic and Wittgensteinian paradox that language can produce meaningful statements about states of affairs in the world regardless of the empirical truth or falsity of those statements. It is always possible to subdivide, to specify an experience below the range of a semiotic system's permissible functioning; to do so is to redesign the system; to do so reveals the desire to break through the culturally sanctioned limits of meaningfulness by allowing the infinite potentiality of *langage* to intrude upon the cultural historical functioning of *langue*. This desire, a response to the discovery of absence, the discovery of something missing in all subsystems, also can be designated as "invention" (the intention to produce change, creativity as revitalization). Invention is largely a matter of mapping from experiential stimuli to perception to expression; radical invention is a new way of seeing the world, a revolutionary articulation to experience that is prelude to "new semiotic conventions."[117]

The literary critic must be ever-mindful of these complex distinctions and interrelations as he engages in the interpretation of an individual literary work. But before I move on toward more specific discussions of literary hermeneutics, it will be helpful to revise once more the ten preliminary observations about language made earlier in this part.

1. *Langage*, as *logische Raum* or myth, comprehends the systematic interpenetration of *langue* and *parole* (cultural horizon and personal experience). *Langage* gives us our world, the "how" it is.

2. *Langage* shows itself as *langue* only through intentional acts, through *parole*, through "articulation to experience." *Langage* (myth) comprehends richness of meaning as both a surplus of empty signifying power and a surplus of immediate experience.
3. These are surpluses of different orders: (1) that of a signifier showing itself in metonymy as arrangements of states of affairs, as deferral of completeness, as narrative flow; (2) that of immediate experience showing itself in metaphor as intuition of the particularity of things, as the inexpressible desire for (hence, absence of) completeness, as momentary and lyrical arrest. Neither metonymy nor metaphor exhausts the other. We can say either: (1) "metonymy cannot *replace* one metaphor with another metaphor without loss" or (2) "metaphor cannot *identify* one metonym with another metonym with out loss."
4. *Langage* functions as a dynamic medium of expression, as *energia* not *ergon*, but in poetry and prose there is a functional distinction between the metaphoric and metonymic uses.
5. As *energia*, *langage* gives meaning to our experiences. *Energia* is the gift of *langage* to all humankind. It may be corrupted into repressive *langue*, but it may never be wholly appropriated to the ends of personal authority. In literature the metaphor/metonym tensions reproduce the drive toward the equilibration of defamiliarization and demystification. Metaphor disrupts the metonymic flow of prose by raising out of the flux of familiar experience the strange or typical. This is the form of narrative history as a discontinuous series of emergences. Prose is metonymic, the logical or causal arrangement of perceived reality into patterns, the subsuming of the part under a general category of the whole (Knowledge). This is the mode of systematic philosophy.
6. As *energia*, *langage* acts on the attention of the listener or reader, involving him in an "act of interpretation," and through its own dynamic structure as text it structures his perceptions. This is not a passive activity, for the particular

instance always opens out onto historical systems; the immediate experience opens outward to the encroachment of the mythical.

7. Language, consequently, is a way of knowing; the study of *langage* belongs to the discipline of epistemology.
8. Below the logical structure of metonymic language, into the realm of metaphor, metonymic language itself cannot easily venture. This is the basis for the traditional struggle between literary criticism and poetry, philosophy and art. This struggle is, however, necessary; it shows the energy of man's human condition.
9. There are, therefore, limits beyond which metonymic prose and metaphoric poetry cannot go, but that need not be seen as a severe restriction on the creative freeplay of *langage* as individual articulation or dynamic system.
10. *Langage* as system can neither describe its own origins nor its hidden structure. These, however, show themselves through usage, through the intentionality of articulation to experience (*parole*) and through the repressive, delimiting possibilities of culturally ratified subsystems (*langue*). It is necessary to say that *langage* does not exist; it is itself necessary.

Part Three

Stylistics

Although there is a vast body of material professing to be stylistic analysis, there is, as yet, no general agreement about the aims and scope of this paradiscipline. In recent years, perhaps reinforced by the New Critical dichotomy of poetry and prose, stylistics seems to have fallen into two divisions: (1) the analysis of *literary style*, which has its peculiar aesthetic or poetic values, and (2) the analysis of a general or *linguistic style*, which has its rhetorical or prosaic values.[1] This bifurcation reinforces the division (real or imagined) between literary criticism and linguistics. In this part my interest is in whether one may legitimately define a "literary style," and this involves a close look at what Leo Spitzer called stylistics: the measuring of minute surface details of a literary text against our intuitive grasp of the text as a whole, and beyond that against the historical milieu of author and work.[2] Yet the focus on surface qualities does not relegate style to mere "decoration" as many classical rhetorical theories would have it. Style is more substantive than "figures of speech" that simply embellish the presentation of an argument to make it more pleasing and, hence, convincing. Style is a matter of technique, but it is not only technique.

Clearly, I have raised again the dilemma of the form-content dichotomy. The trend in linguistically oriented approaches to stylistics is either to ignore or openly to affirm the dichotomy. Michael Riffaterre says, "*style* is understood as an emphasis (expressive, affective, or aesthetic) added to the information conveyed by the linguistic structure, without alteration of meaning."[3] Richard Ohmann is somewhat more perceptive than Riffaterre, although finally of the same opinion.

> What *is* content and what *is* form, or style? The attack on a dichotomy of form and content has been persistent in modern criticism; to change so much as a word, the argument runs, is to change the meaning as well. This austere doctrine has a certain theoretical appeal, given the supposed impossibility of finding exact synonyms, and the ontological queerness of disembodied content . . . divorced from any verbal expression. Yet at the same time this doctrine leads to the altogether counterintuitive conclusion that there can be no such thing as style, or that style is simply a part of content.[4]

Louis T. Milic borrows an analogy from information theory to demonstrate the function of style in sending a message. In a simple code consisting of only two symbols, *A* and *B*, and rules that restrict expression to two messages encoded as *AAA* and *BBB* (the redundancy a safeguard against transmission errors), stylistic variations can be seen as messages written *AAB* or *BBA*. The message *AAB* is recognized immediately as carrying the same cognitive content as the message *AAA*; the variation may be a mistake, insignificant because it does not distort the message, or it may be a stylistic choice of the author, also insignificant because it does not alter the information content.[5] At best, it can function to add "emphasis" or "local color."[6]

Ohmann, Riffaterre, and Milic represent an extreme view of the separability of style (form) and content, a view that eventuates, whatever the efforts to avoid it, in a version of the "decoration" theory. They see style, correctly, as manifesting itself in a surface quality, but, ironically, they rob it of any real value by reducing its influence over content. Ohmann, Riffaterre, and Milic reflect their debt to what Gerald Bruns has defined as the "rhetorical" tradition of stylistic theory.[7] The message, or informational content of a text, they argue, is fixed; it is unchanged by stylistic variations, but this too leads to an "altogether counterintuitive conclusion": because style is an isolable element of any text, it is finally insignificant or trivial.

Conversely, under the pressure of New Critical aesthetics, literary style is seen to be *fused* (to reuse the Coleridgean term) with content. It has an undeniable surface quality that can be grasped immediately by any sensitive reader; but the surface, as Spitzer argued, is wedded to content, and the organic wholeness of the text is, finally, irreducible. Here style is raised to its most concrete level; the embodiment of the creative act of mind gives the text its privileged functionality, or what John Crowe Ransom called "texture."[8] It is not, therefore, in the theory of fused content and form that style disappears; rather it is in Ohmann's, Riffaterre's, and Milic's decoration theory that style almost evaporates in its triviality. Style is *never* so transparent.

All language use is marked by style, and therefore, the terms *literary* and *linguistic* are misleading. We would, perhaps, be better served by Karl Uitti's distinction between "individual" and "interpersonal" style.[9] Interpersonal style belongs to the realm of communication theory, where style must be as nearly separable from content as possible in order to avoid distortion of the message. The function of style here is for emphasis or clarification, but at its extreme it has little aesthetic value. Interpersonal style adheres to conventional formulae, to communal and historically relevant devices or "figures"; but it is not superfluous, even if it *tends* toward the trivial, for without it the disembodied content would never find its way to the intended reader or listener. The ideal would be a kind of "white writing," or what Roland Barthes has described as "degree zero." On the other extreme, individual style pushes toward the level of pure poetry, where the symbolic function of language takes on the mysterious existence that Cassirer characterized as a transcendental relationship between perceiver and perceived. Here our attention is shifted away from primary concern with the "what" of the message to the "how" of the expression. The symbol is not merely a name for a thing, but is, in the poetic function of language use, at one with the thing it names. The separation of form and content, therefore, is more problematical. At an ideal (or idealistic) level of poetic consciousness, style is wholly individual, the opposite of "degree zero." This is pure metaphor, the romantic dream of immediacy or presence, "that is, equivalence of the author's literary intention and carnal structure. . . . So that style is always secret; but the occult aspect of its implications does not arise from the mobile and ever-provisional nature of language; its secret is recollection locked within the body of the writer."[10] At this extreme, Barthes claims, it is improper to speak of *a* style, for there are many styles, each of which raises the "writer above History as the freshness of Innocence."[11] Purely individual, purely metaphoric, and completely personal style would mark a free moment in duration, the expression of the writer's identity as incorporeal "voice."

Two major concerns, then, define my interest in style as I move toward the construction of a literary hermeneutics. First, style manifests itself in its surface qualities, what might better be called the physical or sensual characteristics of language. Consequently, it is the most available (though sometimes the least observed) characteristic of any literary text; as Spitzer suggested, it is the starting point for interpretation. Second, style fluctuates between the discrete and the conventional. Behind style, in the realm of human cognitive processes, are affective meanings characterized by their position along a line leading from metaphor to metonymy; but on the sensually apprehendable surface, stylistic techniques are characterized by positions along a line leading from the individual to the interpersonal.

Since no text, wherever it might lie along these continuous lines between extremes, ever becomes wholly individual (to be so would be to be totally obscure) or wholly conventional (a negation of the author's or speaker's identity), there is always a combination of individual and interpersonal qualities in its style. This is the essence of the text's communicative powers; there must be a context of the conventional as well as an individual expression. A study of style, then, encompasses the traditional divisions of interest in all literary criticism: the author, the work, and the reader. From this basis, returning to the preliminary observations with which I began my discussion of language in part 2, I can describe the following triad of issues to be discussed in part 3.

1. Style is the individual existential projection of an author's perception of his world. This perception is ordered (structured) in the cognitive-expressive transaction that takes place between the author and the cultural-historical and linguistic conventions of his day involving his conscious or unconscious "collective individuality."

2. Style is the *dynamic* meaning-structure of the work itself, its surface or aesthetic qualities *as work*.

3. Style is the affective structure of meaning that sets up *controlled* responses in the reader. This phase of the communicative transaction enables the reader to enter the world of the work and finally to step through time and across space to enter the author's world *as* he saw it.

STYLE AS EXISTENTIAL PROJECTION: THE AUTHOR

Interest in the relationship between the individuality of an act of language usage and the general, cultural system of language has led to what many linguists call the "deviation theory." Simply stated, this theory explains the individual aspects of any linguistic utterance as deviations from the general linguistic norm. The relationship is vaguely parallel to Saussure's distinction between *parole* and *langue*; in communication theory it is like the relationship between message and code. For the literary theorist, however, there is an unavoidable trap in deviation theory because it is impossible to differentiate poetic deviations from all other deviations. Of course, the trap operates only if one wishes to articulate a theory of special (aesthetic) language usage, a poetics.

The term *poetics* in itself is troublesome. Merely to use it is to raise the specter of the entire tradition of aesthetic theory, which originated with Aristotle and has as yet found no culmination. Does the term imply a theory of language usage (creativity) radically deviant from normal communication? Is the difference one of kind or degree, the former, of course, too radical to be designated "deviation"? Coming at these issues from a linguist's point of view, Jonathan Culler has bravely undertaken to sort out the primary questions and to offer tentative conclusions to some of these ancient problems. He is not altogether successful, but his struggle is instructive.

In defining what he calls "structuralist poetics" Culler engages in a broadly sweeping critique of structuralism (with its linguistic or Saussurean biases), and he also promotes his own theory of literary reading, which he sees in terms of what he calls "naturalization." Naturalization is a mode of making a text intelligible; it assumes a motivation toward meaningfulness, the desire to make sense. Naturalization, moreover, can be aestheticized by viewing it within the limits of a general, literary intertextuality; literary intelligibility is a function of cross-referencing between texts and general categories of texts. Culler borrows from Todorov the term *vraisemblance*, which implies both our ability to perceive connections, resemblances, and a kind of statistical sense of probability (i.e., that a text we are reading is likely to echo other texts of a particular tradition). I will quote at length from Culler to illustrate the scope of his sense of intertextuality.

> One might distinguish five levels of *vraisemblance*, five ways in which a text may be brought into contact with and defined in relation to another text which helps to make it intelligible. First there is the socially given text, that which is taken as the "real world." Second, but in some cases difficult to distinguish from the first, is a general cultural text: shared knowledge which would be recognized by participants as part of culture and hence subject to correction or modification but which none the less serves as a kind of "nature." Third, there are the texts or conventions of a genre, a specifically literary and artificial *vraisemblance*. Fourth, comes what might be called the natural attitude to the artificial, where the text explicitly cites and exposes *vraisemblance* of the third kind so as to reinforce its own authority. And finally, there is the complex *vraisemblance* of specific intertextualities, where one work takes another as its basis or point of departure and must be assimilated in relation to it. At each level there are ways in which the artifice of forms is motivated or justified by being given a meaning.[12]

What Culler argues here and elsewhere is that intelligibility depends on recognition, on conventional knowledge of a special kind. Motivation (as borrowed from Saussure) implies cultural stipulation; the intelligibility of any text arises from its bound relationship to a somewhat vaguely conceived literary *langue*. Motivation and intelligibility are the production and recognition of certain conventional strategies for making sense, strategies of cultural referentiality, formal integrity, generic type, and self-conscious literariness (artificiality), all of which express society's aesthetic value system. Such conventions are empty and superficial, finally; they are, I would claim, matters of surface style, and Culler's poetics is itself little more than a conventional theory of stylistic conventions, consciously cut off from anything resembling a true interpretive procedure.

Leaning heavily on the recent theory of Roland Barthes, Culler follows the trend of structuralism in collapsing all content into form ("stylistic surface"). "To read is to participate in the play of the text, to locate zones of resistance and transparency, to isolate forms and determine their content and then to treat content in turn as a form with its own content, to follow, in short, the interplay of surface and envelope."[13] Use of the term "play" here, however, is specifically differentiated from Derrida's concept of "freeplay" (which Culler sees as a kind of logical trick),[14] and this raises several problems. One cannot play Culler's reading game without knowing the rules, and such knowledge implies a kind of literary competence that has a limiting function like the cultural function of Saussure's *langue*. Literary competence is cultural and artificial (unlike the implications of an innate linguistic competence in Chomsky's universal grammar, for example, or the innate reasoning capacities in Lévi-Strauss's binary theory). Culler's literary *langue* is a holding action against the anarchic freeplay of *langage*; and, aware of the ideological implications of this theory, he attempts to defend it simply by anticipating the attacks of ideological opponents.[15] But the issue here is not whether Culler's concept of competency or *langue* implies political and psychological repression; it does imply that. The issue is to what degree is Culler's theory useful for understanding literary texts?

Thus several implications of Culler's approach are of particular importance to our investigation here of the concept of style. The *langue* of competence for Culler functions in much the same way as Frye's literary myth, as a closed system of possible conventions available to any intelligent (competent) reader in his struggles to understand a particular text. But whereas Frye attempts to give his closed system both historical and psychological justification, thereby breeching the system to locate a meaningfulness that is both cultural/historical and a reflection of individual desire, Culler carefully wards off any such extra-systematic projection. As a result, "meaning" is trivialized; one is bound within a system merely to recognize the possible givens of that system. The repressive nature of Culler's competency is (1) historically insensitive, unlike Saussure's *langue*, which is in a state of continual readjustment, and (2) hopelessly superficial because meaning is not in any sense content or experience, but merely empty form, a set of algebraic counters organized into patterns (like the linguist's grammar rules). The suggestion of cultural referentiality is severely limited by the idea of artificiality. For Culler, style and content are not merely separate; contentless form is all the meaning we have.

Culler's theory emphasizes in part his reading of the narrative theory of Frank Kermode onto the "readerly-text" theory of Barthes. The key is closure on all levels. Competency is a closed set of possible intelligible forms; *langue* is a closed system of conventions (conventionalizing even the functions of social/historical referentiality), and the individual text is marked by its own drive toward closure, its "sense of an ending."[16] Without this interrelated set of closures, intelligibility is at hazard. The style of literature, its essential "literariness," is to resolve (naturalize) all openness according to conventional wisdom. *Meaning* is a term we should drop, as Culler does, in favor of the information theory jargon, *intelligibility*. Culler's structuralist poetics, therefore, results in the most radical of all decoration theories, for literariness can only be seen as manifest on the stylistic surface of a text and as readily available to any competent reader whether or not that reader can detect meaning in the text.

It seems that we must, with regard to style as well as to general language functioning as discussed in part 2, break through the limits of closed literary systems if interpretation and understanding of literary texts can ever eventuate in meaning. To this purpose I have broadened the functioning of motivation by introducing into it the concepts of "intentionality" and "articulation to experience"; that is, by introducing the idea of the author. As a consequence, it is impossible to speak of any determining system or *langue*, or of the process of naturalization as Culler defines it, without confronting a profound ambiguity. Any individual text (*parole*) both is situated in a cultural system (*langue*) and also creates or situates that system. A single *parole*, moreover, may situate (and be situated in) many systems at once. Competency, as Culler defines it, is too limiting (if comforting) a concept; as the "system" that "makes literary effects possible,"[17] it trivializes the function of the author in making both conscious and unconscious choices. Like many linguistically oriented structuralists, Culler's expressed interest in the idea of authorial control is illusory, perhaps contradictory. Limiting conventions provide a context for the author to write against, Culler claims, and the author may even "attempt to subvert" those conventions. But, alas, the context is ultimately "the context within which [even the author's subversive?] activity takes place."[18] Subversion is a hollow word, and the limiting literary context precedes and determines *all* literary expressiveness.

Borrowing from both the structuralists and, perhaps less willingly, from the Anglo-American New Critics, Culler extends his theory of naturalization to the lyric, and in so doing he expresses a very traditional attitude toward the authorial function in literary composition. A naturalized lyric reveals unambiguously its reflection of conventional surface qualities like popular verse forms and rhyme patterns, general patterns of metrical and phonic organization. "We naturalize such patterns in a very formal and abstract way by showing how various features contribute to patterns which help to assert the monumentality and impersonality of poetry. . . ." The only "value" of this assertion, Culler says, borrowing from the aesthetic humanism of Wallace Stevens (hence, also from the lingering romanticism of Kermode), is that it convinces us "that the making of fictions is a worthy activity."[19] The radical "impersonality" of the theory (which belongs to both the New Criticism and structuralism in their different ways) removes poetry (all literature) from the realm of the real and locates it irrevocably in the realm of the artificial. However one may struggle to relate fiction to life and human experience, the former always seems to contain its own justification for being.

There is an unfortunate and undeniable aestheticism in such a fiction theory; the removal of the authorial function, and consequently the denial of nonconventional or empirical referentiality, leaves us only with the surface of stylistic play. The impersonality theory takes two different forms under the different influences of structuralism and New Critical contextualism, but the effects on literary hermeneutics are similar just as the superficial operations of their interpretive procedures often appear to be alike. In Culler's structuralist poetics, for example, the first person implications of the lyric poem are conventionalized; the pronoun *I* functions as a "shifter" (like "here" and "there"), as an empty orientation term. When the "I" calls attention to itself as so functioning, literary naturalization has occurred, and we are aware that we are reading poetry. Given Culler's emphasis on fictionality and textual closure (the poem's "monumentality," he calls it), this particular antireferentiality in his theory can be as New Critical as it is structuralist. Given his borrowing from linguistics the idea of literary competency, his antiempirical bias, and emphasis on cultural conventionality, Culler's theory seems more comfortably in the structuralist camp. In either case, impersonality virtually contradicts the issue of style. For the structuralist critic, impersonality emphasizes the play of language reflecting its general diacritical nature *as opposed to* language's expressive capacities. It emphasizes language's medium-as-message function *as opposed to* its content-carrying function. It emphasizes its systematic and nonempirical powers to generate endless meanings *as opposed to* its subservience to human experience. From the New Critical point of view, impersonality emphasizes the immediate, experiential (aesthetic) nature of the act of reading *as opposed to* mediated communication. It emphasizes the ineffable mystery of the human spirit (man's "fictionalizing" capacities) *as opposed to* man's conventional and articulate wisdom. It emphasizes the density of language, its self-justifying, self-referential opaqueness *as opposed to* language's transparent referentiality. In both traditions style is radically dehumanized, dispersed into the systematic freeplay of *langage* tempered by the conventional, interpersonal limits of *langue* on the one hand, or apotheosized into the eternal, inexpressible, and sacred on the other hand.

Culler's efforts are not consciously directed toward a union of these two traditions, but his desire to define a truly special sense of literariness (surely a legacy of Anglo-American aesthetics) within the boundaries of a structuralist philosophy makes his discussion usefully revelatory of the problems that modern literary theory faces in discussing literary style. Culler's positing of a conventional system of literary competency may, in fact, be the only solution to the dilemma, but it must not be seen as a trivial sort of deviation theory: the playfulness of fiction *as opposed to* the play of meaningful signification. Moreover, Culler's approach founders on internal contradictions, yet it is nonetheless considerably more convincing than traditional deviationist ideas. Samuel R. Levin is representative of a statistically oriented version of deviation theory; he argues that "a given linguistic element produces a stylistic effect because its occurrence has zero or near zero probability of occurring where it does."[20] A high degree of probability defines the norm, the basis, of course, for improbable deviations. There are several obvious problems in this theory, particularly when it is applied to literary texts. Primary among them is how to determine the norm (as it is a problem for Culler in defining conventional literary competency). Any norm is abstract; no individual utterance embodies a norm, nor is the norm simply a sum of all individual utterances. For the most part, a major thrust of modern linguistics has been toward the formulation of a general linguistic norm. This is, fundamentally, a descriptive effort, championed by men like Leonard Bloomfield and Chomsky, as opposed to prescriptive stylistics like that of Strunk and White's handbook, *The Elements of Style*. But the focus here is on language in general, and there is no room for even a special literary competency like that promoted by Culler.

The dilemma faced by Levin, therefore, is that either literary style is a special form of all stylistic deviations or literary style must be considered outside the realm of the normalizing system altogether. Levin argues bafflingly that "all deviations, poetic or otherwise, are ungrammatical, and ungrammatical sequences are deviant. But not all ungrammatical sequences are poetically *deviant*."[21] This distinction is of no help at all; it merely removes the question to another level requiring that a distinction be made between poetic and nonpoetic ungrammaticalness (which has an even more absurd implication in the distinction between meaningful and nonmeaningful deviations). Levin "solves" the problem on this level rather weakly by positing what he calls a distinction in the "degrees of ungrammaticalness" between poetic and nonpoetic deviation.[22]

It is perhaps better, although still not wholly satisfactory, to distinguish between deviations that are ungrammatical (or "agrammatical"), and therefore outside the system, and deviations that are, to borrow Roman Jakobson's term, "antigrammatical."[23] Agrammatical deviations can be cast off as meaningless, but antigrammatical deviations exist both within and outside the general system. The result of this terminological shift is to emphasize both the individual act of language use (*parole*) and the normalizing structures of *langue*. In this way we might better understand what Barthes means by the argument that beyond the level of style there is implied "a vision which is eventually moral . . ." or "sociological."[24] The literary artist in some way finds his identity as artist in the struggle between his personal style and the normal style of his language system; he also finds himself embroiled in the tension between his private moral responsibilities and commitments and the system of morality imposed upon him by his society. The two levels are intimately related if we take seriously Wittgenstein's claim that "the limits of our language mean the limits of our world." To challenge the fixities and definites of language is to challenge the moral norms and restrictions of society. To be always *somewhat* in contention with society is, perhaps, the human condition, but I italicize *somewhat* because this is always a matter of degree.[25]

Such a schematic sense of oppositions, of course, is too easy; even in the realm of art it is too reductive. But the complexity of being a "good" member of a society, which involves neither the surrender to a programmatic political determinism nor the assertion of inviolable personal freedom, is surely intensified for the inviolable personal freedom, is surely intensified for the literary artist. If language gives us our world, the use of language involves agonizing moral commitments; and it is this moral content, reflecting the artist's identifying voice, that underlies all serious literary productions. In his fine article, "Literature as Act," Richard Ohmann makes this point by expanding the terminology of "speech act theory" to define the expressive action of the literary artist as a peculiar kind of illocutionary performance. "Illocutionary action is action on a social plane. It relies for success on those things that make up a society: for instance, definitions of role and relation, stable distribution of power, conventions of intimacy and distance, manners."[26] The artist, alone in his study, cut off from the daily humdrum activities of familiar experience, can hardly avoid the tension between himself and his society as he engages the interpersonal norms of cultural language use with his own personal style. The degree to which he challenges the norms can only be known after the fact; that he will confront them is assured by the human condition, for no individual is so in touch with the abstract structure (the surplus of explanatory power) of the general system of *langage* that he can write in the wholly impersonal anonymity of Derrida's "freeplay." To write "situates" *langue*, cultural values, and meanings, as it activates the infinite potentials of *langage*. The writer's moral commitment may issue as more or less positive or negative, for himself or for the reader, but his commitment will be made, and the necessity of this commitment, a fall from innocence and purity, reflects an essential historicism on both the cultural and stylistic levels.

This historical dimension of literary style is not, as Karl Uitti claims, a new phenomenon in language theory. Through men like Condillac and Humboldt, he sees it eventuating in the very influential work of Edward Sapir. "His analysis of poetic creation as the creative deployment of resources involving two layers of an inner form versus the outer restrictions of the specific linguistic system . . . remains faithful to the most profitable dualisms modern thought has produced."[27] That dualism has its source in Cartesian "mentalism" and the dichotomy of mind and body. It has pervaded my discussion from the beginning, surfacing in the form/content dichotomy and the poetry/prose or individual style/interpersonal style distinctions, as well as in the philosophical argument of part 2 describing the mutuality of inner and outer worlds. Transformed into the historical perspective of the interplay of individual moment and continuous pattern it is, indeed, a profitable dualism, and clearly it works profitably for Sapir.

> Language is itself the collective art of expression, a summary of thousands upon thousands of individual intuitions. The individual goes lost in the collective creation, but his personal expression has left some trace in a certain give and flexibility that are inherent in all collective works of the human spirit. The language is ready, or can be quickly made ready, to define the artist's individuality. If no literary artist appears, it is not essentially because the language is too weak an instrument; it is because the culture of the people is not favorable to the growth of such personality as seeks a truly individual verbal expression.[28]

The give and take between individual expression and social restrictions quickly becomes historical for Sapir, defining what he called linguistic "drift."[29]

This idealistic position is remarkably similar to that of the Prague Linguistic Circle. From a more positivistic point of view, with its emphasis on the study of the synchronic system, the Prague theorists do not reduce the importance of the individual creative act.

> Le langage poétique [the poetic use of language] tend à mettre en relief la valeur autonome du signe . . . tous les plans d'un système linguistique, qui n'ont dans le langage de communication qu'un rôle de service, prennent, dans le langage poétique, des valeurs autonomes plus ou moins considérables.

In the matter of the dialectic of poetry and general language, the Prague theorists are again at pains to define the importance of both terms.

> Le langage poétique a, du point de vue synchronique, la forme de la parole, c'est-à-dire d'un acte créateur individuel, qui prend sa valeur d'une part sur la fond de la tradition poétique actuelle (langue poétique) et d'autre part sur le fond de la langue communicative contemporaine.[30]

The Prague theorists are less concerned than Sapir with the individualism of language usage, but they are also well aware that a literary *langue* (*langue poetique*) cannot operate wholly apart from the general pattern of social communication (as Culler proposes) and, therefore, no conventional system can wholly trivialize the role of the author in the communicative transaction.

I would argue that the personality of the artist is never unimportant, not because we can read from his biography directly into his individual works, or vice versa, but because on the level of his own cognitive awareness we find the structuring principle of those works. This is why literary criticism has turned more and more to the philosophy and psychology of human consciousness for its principles of interpretation. It is crucial to remember, however, that consciousness and linguistic capacities are structurally related, and that to map from the structuring power of the mind to the structure of the work, a modified version of Coleridge's identification of poetry and the poet in the poetic imagination, is less than an exact, one-to-one transfer. The innate grammar of the human mind posited by Chomsky has, theoretically, the explanatory power to justify his effort to isolate and describe it, but because there are dimensions to language beyond the local systems of communal utterances, much of the descriptive effort is speculative projection. In this sense these innate structures, and this is particularly true of Lévi-Strauss's theory, do not explain anything. They are no more than logically perceived "potentials" for cognition; they are rules that become meaningful only when they enter into the communicative transaction between subject and object, only when articulated to local or individual experience. Lévi-Strauss's theory of binary oppositions is simply a principle of juxtaposition; meaning arises when the mind juxtaposes two or more perceived objects—an act that is at once a "situating" of the objects (as in Wittgenstein's states of affairs) and the implication of a desire or motivation or attitude toward that situation.

There are, of course, many forms of this activity. The existential-phenomenologist philosopher Maurice Merleau-Ponty has made us aware of an act of juxtaposition that takes the form of bringing certain objects in the perceptual field into primary focus—or foreground—while relegating the rest to an undifferentiated background. This is, perhaps, the most fundamental version of cognitive attention, a separation and identification of the world of things analogous to the literary act of "defamiliarization."[31] There is also a temporal juxtaposition of items, a relationship established across time and thereby involving memory, and there is a more complex exclusive/inclusive juxtaposition, the sorting out of items into groups or categories. No doubt there are more, reflecting Kant's theory of the fundamental categories of the understanding as well as supporting Piaget's thesis that there are many logics.

Below this system of logics we find the rudimentary consciousness that is the focus of Cassirer's philosophy, his projection of a first "violent act of individuation." Here is the most fundamental assertion of the ego, the awareness of the self as distinct from the other. Yet we need not overemphasize either the egoistic or the hierarchic/developmentalist aspects of Cassirer's theory. As Heidegger claims: "The origin of language is in essence mysterious. And this means that language can only have arisen from the overpowering, the strange and terrible, through man's departure into being. In this departure language was being, embodied in the word: poetry. Language is the primordial poetry in which a people speaks being."[32] It is not merely a primitive activity; it is an enduring condition. The emergence of the ego is also a situating of the collective context, and therein language and consciousness gain the power to manage and participate in the undifferentiated otherness. The end of this projection of order is what Piaget called "reflective abstraction" and the programmatic and communal function of language as thought. Moreover, this communal level is that which is most available to Chomsky's linguistic study—and to Chomskyan stylistic analysis. Here language, at its most "instrumental," disguises much of its creative or poetic power; "originally an act of violence that discloses being, the word sinks from this height to become a mere sign. . . ."[33] But again the instrumentalist eclipse of poetry is never total. The world of literary art, we remember, divides two extremes. To borrow from Heidegger once more, this is "the great poetry by which a people enters into history" and that "initiates the molding of language."[34]

The poet's impulse is to open *langue* by an appeal to the freeplay of *langage* in order to activate what we will have to call language's "poetic function," and this may explain why society, conservative of its operational systems, treats its artists as children, resists the poet's challenges that would seemingly repeat the socially repressed trauma of the violent birth of consciousness or being. One of the forms of this repression is to declare the poet a nonbeing by means of a theory of literary impersonality. The poet is always a radical when he challenges the conventional in language and general culture.[35] Yet his is an essential function and, as I have presented it, a broadly conceived form of deviation that never allows language and society to become static, that asserts our historical being by situating both *langue* and *parole*. His articulation to experience, his language, gives us his identifying style as well as society's conventions and cultural style.[36] There is, of course, nothing of the mystically visionary or prophetic in this function. The poet's relation to his culture's norms is an extremely complex arrangement; his challenge to those norms must not be seen simply as ideological or as always a conscious activity. The literary artist may reveal himself to be the most revolutionary at the very moment he feels himself to be most in tune with his culture. The poet's act of articulation to experience is an act of critical interpretation; he reveals the limits of culture's norms, often exposing the contradictions that reside deep within, at the base of, cultural ideology. As always, the poet's identity, his style, is as much given to him as it is created by him.

STYLE AS DYNAMIC MEANING STRUCTURE: THE TEXT

In general, there are two significant questions that must be answered in the development of a viable literary hermeneutics: (1) how do we interpret a text and (2) how do we evaluate it? But the latter is an extremely complicated activity involving both interpretation and the individual and cultural value systems that can be brought to bear on the text. Value judgments are intimately and unavoidably a part of literary interpretation, yet they are less objective (partly because they are subject to historical variations) and less easily methodized. My focus so far in this essay has been more or less on interpretive methodology, and I have, I hope, allowed the evaluative dimension of literary criticism to emerge as it will. Now, however, it is no longer possible to ignore it.

In discussing the stylistic structure of the individual text, I will start, once more, with the relatively value-free methodology spawned by Noam Chomsky's transformational-generative grammar. Samuel R. Levin has attempted to differentiate between poetic style and "casual" language use by extending Chomsky's transformational models. He also borrows from Roman Jakobson the idea that "the poetic function [of language] projects the principle of equivalence from the axis of selection into the axis of combination."[37] This very important observation by Jakobson will occupy us in more detail below, but for the moment it can be simplistically stated that Levin takes the "principle of equivalence" as it is applied to the structure or arrangement of structures within an individual text as the basis for his own stylistic principle of "coupling."[38] Coupling describes how, in syntagmatic units of an individual text, the positional arrangement of one syntagm parallels the positional arrangement of another (or others) thereby *structurally* establishing equivalence between the two. More simply, the poetic arrangement of words, what in the past we have euphemistically called "poetic license," tends to force the reader to see certain groups of words as equivalent—sometimes in contradiction to their conventional semantic import.

Richard Ohmann, also defending the use of transformational grammar in stylistic analysis, lists three major "characteristics of transformational rules" that are valuable to the literary critic.

> 1. "A large number of transformations are optional" and will allow the critic to identify typical patterns used by individual writers.
> 2. "A transformation works changes on structure, but normally leaves *part* of the structure unchanged." Hence "sets of sentences which are transformational alternatives seem to be different renderings of the same proposition." Again this aids in the intuitive recognition of the stylistic variation which is simply a surface quality added to the informational content.
> 3. "A third value of a transformational grammar . . . is its power to explain how complex sentences are generated. . . . Writers differ noticeably in the amounts and kinds of syntactic complexity they habitually allow themselves. . . ."[39]

The approaches of both Levin and Ohmann are interesting and valuable, but they are also limited by the nature of the transformational principle itself. Levin admits that his idea of "coupling" ignores "features like meaning, metaphor, imagery, etc.,"[40] a rather casual dismissal of what has traditionally been regarded as the very essence of poetry. His problem, basically, is in his rendering of Jakobson's "principle of equivalence." Two groups of words arranged in parallel are not necessarily equivalent in poetic discourse—at least they are not mathematically (or logically) equivalent as Levin suggests. The syntactic parallelism results in a semantic modification of meaning; neither element *means* quite what it meant in isolation. It is not easy to ignore meaning.

How to read a poetic text must be analogous to how to write one. Levin wants to explain poetic "unity," that "contextual" unity which extends beyond the limits of the individual sentence (or the limits of a syntagm). But this unity is achieved in the writing by a process of continual readjustments between the parts, not by establishing a simple series of parallel structures. The poet begins by arranging a group of words in a meaningful order, perhaps several lines, a single line, or even part of a line. As he writes, adding to and developing the intuitive thought that set him at his composition, he must go back to rewrite what he first set down. Throughout the process of selection, arrangement, and limitation there is a forward and backward movement, the old being rearranged to accommodate the new, while the limits of the new are refined by what has already been written. Is there not always a lingering trace of this process inscribed in all texts? Does this not indicate a very fundamental openness at the heart of even the most tightly constructed text? Levin's concept of equivalence, however, seems to describe a mere string of parallel structures. Rather than a tensional relationship between closure and openness, Levin's approach reduces organization to the idea of unrestricted addition. His method is purely statistical and value free. There is little or no way to distinguish between parallel structures or groups of such structures; they simply follow one another in linear fashion; their only measure is quantitative.

As a result, style has come to mean nothing more than an intuitively recognizable pattern of optional transformations. The stylistician's job is to catalogue the choices made by an individual writer. Ohmann's list of the advantages of a transformational stylistics emphasizes this rather mechanical type of analysis, and it does not satisfy the analyst of style who intuitively distinguishes between highly individual and conventionally interpersonal styles. The catalogue of choices must also reflect the frequency with which the options are *normally* exercised. This would give us a statistical accounting for the difference between individual and interpersonal styles. But it also forces us to admit that certain transforms are "more normal" than others, and this results in the same problems we encountered above in establishing a statistical norm that will be sufficiently stable to explain why certain transforms are unusual.

Michael Riffaterre, trying to avoid the tyranny of the general norm, sees style as a deliberate breaking of established and predictable syntactic patterns in the individual text. The reader, having been led to expect a certain pattern, is "surprised" by a "stylistic device" that alters that pattern. This requires a sense, not simply of a string of equivalent structures, but rather of some contextual interplay between small segments of the text and the text as a whole. The notion is vaguely New Critical in its emphasis on contextual unity at the expense of the norms of general language, but there are crucial differences. First, there is no way to distinguish between radical and mild breaks in the textual pattern; all stylistic devices are the same. Second, the text is fragmented into the predictable pattern and the individual stylistic devices that break that pattern; there is, then, no real textual unity in the New Critical sense. Finally, without the norm of general language use there is only one way to identify stylistic devices: by charting the response of native speakers, graphically marking in the text their "surprise" points. This affective analysis will occupy our attention more completely below; for the moment I will claim only that this too gives us no way to distinguish between stylistic devices. The measure is again wholly quantitative, for apparently the more surprises a text contains, the more individualistic is its style.

Riffaterre also effectively cancels out the realm of conventional stylistics, and surely this is counterintuitive. Conventional stylistic devices, those special uses of language that have an assigned stylistic value, certainly exist. They change, even disappear, as society changes, but they are important to any culture for interpersonal communication. They range from the conventional, and significant, stylistic opening of a fairy tale, "Once upon a time," to "bankrupt expressions" like "in the last analysis," which Strunk and White have rather unsuccessfully (and, in the last analysis, unnecessarily) attempted to excise from the English langauge.[41] There is nothing in either of these stylistic devices that would cause surprise in the native speaker. As conventional devices, they are easily recognizable, essentially transparent phrases used either as an identifying marker ("Once upon a time" characterizes what is to follow as a particular kind of literature: a fairy tale) or simply for emphasis ("In the last analysis man is doomed to suffer ecological disaster!").

On the level of such conventionality poetry cannot exist, yet the poet will, and it is a favorite device of modern poets, use conventional stylistic devices in a context that "deconventionalizes" them. At this point the quantitative aspect of such devices is transformed into a qualitative value. T. S. Eliot takes the most common and familiar elements of linguistic use, conventional greetings, and works them to his larger and "defamiliarized" purpose in *The Waste Land*:

You ought to be ashamed, I said, to look so antique.
(And her only thirty-one.)
I can't help it, she said, pulling a long face,
It's them pills I took, to bring it off, she said.
(She's had five already, and nearly died of young George.)
The chemist said it would be all right, but I've never
been the same.
You *are* a proper fool, I said!
Well, if Albert won't leave you alone, there it is, I said,
What you get married for if you don't want children?
Hurry up please its time
Well, that Sunday Albert was home, they had a hot gammon,
And they asked me in to dinner, to get the beauty of it hot—
Hurry up please its time
Hurry up please its time
Goonight Bill. Goonight Lou. Goonight May. Goonight.
Ta ta. Goonight. Goonight.
Good night, ladies, good night, sweet ladies, good
night, good night.

Once again I am led to conclude that, even on the stylistic surface, poetry struggles against prosaic linearity. The metaphor/metonym paradigm I used to describe the distinction between poetry and prose applies to my analogous distinction between individual and interpersonal style. The metaphoric nature of poetic language asserts semantic overlap, not mere logical equivalence, between the structural elements of the text. This is the deeper implication of Jakobson's theory, one that is beyond the explanatory power of transformational grammar. Instead of linearity, in poetry we have circularity, a somewhat metaphorical notion supported by a long tradition of poetic theory from Lessing's *Laocoön* to Joseph Frank's "Spatial Form in Modern Literature" and Murray Krieger's "The Ekphrastic Principle and the Still Movement of Poetry."[42]

The organic, self-sufficient poem promoted by New Critical aesthetics is also, however, a very limited concept of poetry. It has traditionally been most adequate as a description of those short lyric poems that are structured around the elaboration of a single metaphor. It fails, particularly in longer works like novels and narrative poems, to explain the crucial relationship between poetic language and ordinary discourse. On the other hand, the transformational approach to stylistics cannot effectively describe the short, metaphorically centered, lyric. The norm-deviation theory is reductive in its consideration of the truly qualitative use of language in poetry. Consequently the two extremes may be brought together only through the paradigmatic relationship of metaphor and metonymy. This forces us to focus our interpretive attentions on the text, wherein the structuring principles are manifest on the level of style, but also insists that we not cut our interpretations free from the important dimensions of author and audience in the aesthetic experience of literature.

STYLE AS THE "AFFECTIVE" STRUCTURE OF MEANING: THE READER

In turning to the third of the triad of issues that I defined as the central interests of stylistics, we will become more aware than ever of the indissoluble relationship among all three. The affective level of style, which in terms of literary criticism involves the reader's act of interpretation, is perhaps the key to a general literary hermeneutics, but our discussion will take us back to the level of expressive language, to the author's projection of an encoded message and the form of the message itself. The affective dimension of style is the most often ignored, a victim in literary theory of New Critical fallacy hunting (the "affective fallacy") and in linguistics of antibehaviorism.[43] Admittedly, the affective approach is dangerous, running the risk of turning literary interpretation, to say nothing of evaluation, into pure impressionism. On the other hand, it seems unavoidable, and it does not necessarily lead to such pitfalls.

Riffaterre, among the linguists, has moved most boldly into this area. Reviewing many of the problems in traditional stylistic investigation that we have encountered in our discussion above, problems of establishing norms, of identifying and analyzing devices that are truly stylistic and not simply aberrant usage, Riffaterre claims that only by studying the responses of a large number of native language users (or by defining an "average reader") can the analyst know what style is. "If linguistic analysis cannot discriminate these [stylistic] elements from irrelevant ones, it is because their potential is not realized in the physical body of the message, but in the receiver. . . ."[44] This theory is not mere impressionism, however, for Riffaterre sees it as part of the transaction between author and reader that is mediated by a structured text. "The author's consciousness is his preoccupation with *the way he wants his message to be decoded*, so that not only its meaning but his attitude towards it is conveyed to the reader, and the reader is forced to understand, naturally, but also to share the author's view of what is or is not important in his message."[45] The concept of "shared" attitudes emphasizes the dynamic relationship that exists between author and reader; it is a relationship wherein the author, through his style, is able to compel the reader's attention—to "force" the reader to participate in the original mental activity that molded the text. Here Riffaterre seems to be echoing that very intense communication between author and reader described by Poulet as the reader's mind occupied by the thoughts of another.

Traditional norm-deviation theories of style are inadequate to explain this transaction. In something like a New Critical narrowing of focus, Riffaterre proposes that the stylistician "substitute" the text of the message (or the poem) for the linguistic norm.[46] A stylistic device is identified as "the insertion of an unexpected element." Style is a textual pattern suddenly "broken by an element which was unpredictable," unanticipated. One must presume that such a "breaking" is purposeful and that all breaks in the pattern are not the same; they can be distinguished by what Riffaterre calls their "degree of unpredictability."[47] The more unanticipated the break, the more impressive is the stylistic device.

Riffaterre, therefore, is not proposing a New Critical explication de texte. True to his affective approach, he identifies textual deviations, or stylistic devices, by studying the reader's responses. His aim is to avoid what he calls Spitzer's impressionism, the analytic approach of the "philological circle," which begins with the isolation of a single important or outstanding detail of the stylistic surface of the text but then constructs a general hypothesis of the meaning of the text based on this detail and the critic's general intuitive sense of the work as a whole. Finally, the critic, according to Spitzer, refines his general hypothesis in a series of "to and fro" movements that test it against all of the other details of the text. He knows he has reached the right interpretation, Spitzer claims, by intuition—an "inner click."[48] For Riffaterre, there are no value judgments involved in the selection of outstanding stylistic details, and there is no intuitive perception of the text as a whole. Only the fact of *noticing* a detail is important. The stylistician has only to chart the "responses" (noting *where* they occur most frequently) of native speakers as they read the text. As a result he achieves a statistical portrait of the "average reader."

In this effort to avoid value judgments, however, Riffaterre seriously restricts his theory. He resorts to a rather empty behaviorism, a stimulus-response theory not far removed from Bloomfield. Moreover, both Riffaterre and Bloomfield were anticipated by the behaviorist criticism of I. A. Richards. Richards, too, would ignore content; he argues that what a poet thought or believed is unimportant to the experience of readers. What really counts is the organization of his text and the intensity of response elicited by it. The greatest works for Richards are those which hold in balance the greatest number of potentials for action, or impulses, in the reader. Richards also posits an average, or "right," reader statistically created from the various responses of all actual readers, but he goes beyond Riffaterre, finally, by tying the "right" reader's response to a "standard" that is more or less equivalent to the author's response to his own work.[49]

The average reader and standard response of Richards and Riffaterre, however, seem to offer little improvement over the norm-deviation theory; the problem of distinguishing between stylistic devices remains. Still trying to keep their methodologies value free, Richards and Riffaterre claim that some responses are more intense than others, but is intensity alone a significant distinction? Is intensity a matter of textual structure, or is it simply an impressionistic measurement of the kind Riffaterre sought to avoid?

In addition, is it possible to claim that reader response is wholly free from semantic influence—and more importantly, from value judgments? Is a "surprising" stylistic shift surprisingly good, or bad? If good it would enhance the content; if bad it would confuse or contradict it. At the base of this problem is Riffaterre's form-content separation. "Style is understood as an emphasis . . . added to the information conveyed . . . without alteration of meaning." Yet style as mere emphasis, it would seem, depends heavily upon the information conveyed for its *surprise* value.

Riffaterre's rejection of the norm-deviation theory, even though his arguments against such a theory have merit, leads him farther away from the epistemological and aesthetic interests of the literary critic. The pseudoscientific objectivity of his analytic approach also robs his theory of any high-level interpretive power, and he has ignored the poetic context/prosaic code relationship that is central to the study of literature. The entire distinction between individual and interpersonal style has been transformed, by the stimulus-response theory, into a distinction between unpredictable and predictable structures or surprising and commonplace language usage.

Roman Jakobson suggests a slightly revised version of the poetry/prose distinction that will return us to this most basic question. Furthermore, Jakobson's approach emphasizes the broader aspects of stylistic analysis involving the author-work-reader triad. "The principle of similarity underlies poetry; the metrical parallelism of lines, or the phonic equivalence of rhyming words prompts the question of semantic similarity and contrast. . . . Prose, on the contrary, is forwarded essentially by contiguity. Thus, for poetry, metaphor, and for prose, metonymy is the line of least resistance."[50] There is nothing in this distinction that recalls the absolute separation of poetry and prose demanded by New Critical organicism. Poetry, what Jakobson would call the "poetic function" of language, can occur in contexts that are, by common agreement, not poems. These might be called little poems in the midst of prose, but because poetry differs from prose only on the level of function, there is no absolute distinction. The difference between poetry and prose is a matter of structure, although this involves, necessarily, the semantic dimension as well.

The distinction between metaphor and metonymy, to which I have frequently referred, was developed by Jakobson from his analysis of clinical studies of certain speech disorders known as aphasia. Concentrating on aphasia in the "encoder" (the speaker who formulates the message to be transmitted to a listener or "decoder"), he classifies disorders into two categories, paralleling each of the two phases of the encoding process. The first phase is "selection," where the encoder, using the principle of "similarity," chooses from categories of more or less equivalent verbal elements those elements that will be combined into the speech chain or statement he wishes to transmit. The second phase is "combination," where the selected elements are arranged by "contiguity" into the statement. (For the decoder the process is reversed. He receives the message fully arranged and must break it down into its elements.) The first phase is metaphoric, based on the principle of "equivalence" (in the broad sense that includes the poles of synonym and antonym), and the second is metonymic, based on sequential arrangement that emphasizes progression through a series of its parts (or associational parts). Unlike metaphor, which emphasizes the immediate and atemporal identity of elements, metonymy derives from a chain of logical extensions moving from the categorical to the particular.

These phases of communication are ordered temporally and logically; aphasic disorders of the second phase may leave the operations of the first phase relatively unimpaired. The encoder is still able to make selections, but his speech is reduced to single units or childlike fragments. An aphasic disorder of the first phase, if extreme (*aphasia universalis*), can wholly block the encoder's linguistic operations. If the disorder is only partial, the speech may be reduced to single words or morphemes that seem to function metaphorically. These words have meaning only in the immediate presence of the perceived object; the word is so closely identified with what it represents that it ceases to exist if the object is removed. This two-step operation can also be observed in the speech development of children. The selection stage appears earliest and consists of small metaphoric units. The combination stage follows (under the guidance of developing logical capacities as well as training) moving the child into the area of metonymy.

Jakobson's insights have exciting implications for literary theory when viewed in the broader perspective of the philosophy of language and the prose-poetry distinction I have been attempting to develop. The metaphorical function of language, with the principle of equivalence as its basic structure, echoes to some extent Cassirer's conjecture on the primitive genesis of language. The "violent act of individuation" that is accompanied by the first efforts at language use is, for Cassirer, a poetic expression that opens the way to multiple linguistic functions. First, it is language as a personal projection from the individual toward the newly recognized other, perhaps nothing more than sound—but meaningful sound, like the child's cry for its mother. This is a fundamentally individuating action even if the communication involved is rudimentary. As Jakobson says, it is the "first verbal function acquired by infants; they are prone to communicate before being able to send or receive informative communications."[51] When this prelinguistic form of assertion enters the realm of language usage it bifurcates into two very distinct but interrelated functions. These are represented by the poles of metaphor and metonym and reflect the interdependence of two linguistic and cognitive functions that Piaget, we should remember, characterized as logical as well as developmental in his "genetic epistemology."

The realm of what we traditionally call lyric poetry, above the rudimentary assertion of self yet below the logical and systematic structure of prose, seems always driving toward the violent individuation that forms the heart of romantic aesthetics; it is accompanied by an all-absorbing engagement with the particularities of nature, a fascination with the primitive and the untutored, and a rejection of the conventional and static. The romantic emphasis is on the immediacy of lived experience (its individuality), which in part defines the idealist's stance as opposed to the positivist's philosophy of language. The former, represented in part 2 by Cassirer, keeps an eye on the miraculous fusion of diversity into unity and situates metaphor at the basis of the lyrical experience and at the origin of language in general. This philosophy, however, articulates not the achievement of the ideal of the individual as much as the enduring desire for such an ideal. The positivist viewpoint, as in the theories of Wittgenstein and to some extent Chomsky, fastens the philosophy of language to metonymic functions, to the structure of arrangements of states of affairs. Here romantic desire is transformed into functional management, into group identity, games and rules, into the positivistic ideal of "belonging" to the world. It is not impossible, as I have argued from the beginning, to see these two very different approaches as mutually corrective, one of the other, rather than as mutually exclusive. The temporal and logical relationship that exists between metaphor and metonymy here reflects the Lacanian theory of metaphor as the violent eruption of language as signifying system, an eruption that situates the "bar" of repression (cultural, linguistic, psychological) depicting the inevitable degeneration of metaphor into metonymy and, paradoxically, the necessary presupposition of metonymy for the emergence of metaphor. This functioning is particularly obvious on the level of stylistic analysis, where the interplay of metaphor and metonym is seen to deny either a position of privilege.

Many unanswered questions still remain, and in confronting these Jakobson further develops his insights into the nature of metaphor. "The set (*Einstellung*) toward the *message* as such, the focus on the message for its own sake, is the *poetic* function of language."[52] This is another, more descriptive, way of saying what has often been claimed, that metaphor (and, a fortiori, poetry) is always about itself. Because metaphor embodies the fundamental cognitive operations of the mind (in itself and in its tension with metonymy), it preserves in its articulate and articulated structure these operations in potentia. As the essence of poetry, we may recall, it is *energia* not *ergon*. Poetry *about* poetry no longer need be seen simplistically as autobiography or the poem that recounts the ardor and joy of its own composition. To be sure, poetry (metaphor) calls our attention not simply to poems but to the full range and capacities of language itself. In this sense, poetic communication is at once more direct, more intense, and more rare than that of prose. George Henrick von Wright, quoting Peter Winch, describes this basic and profound communication as "empathic understanding," which is "not a 'feeling'; it is an ability to participate in a 'form of life.'"[53] I would extend this claim even further, for such a communicative transaction may be participatory life itself, the communal and self-conscious act of critical awareness that exposes the power of language (*langage*) to situate man in the midst of "meaning."

To conceive of metaphor as a form of cognitive organization solves one of the principal dilemmas of modern aesthetics. The New Critics, we should remember, were forced by their doctrine of organicism to consider the short lyric poem, structured around an extended metaphor, as the purest form of poetry. Yet according to Jakobson, poetry exists only in the broader context of prose. "[Metaphoric] selection is produced on the basis of equivalence, similarity and dissimilarity, synonymity and antonymity, while [metonymic] combination, the build-up of the sequence, is based on contiguity. *The poetic function projects the principle of equivalence from the axis of selection into the axis of combination*. Equivalence is promoted to the constitutive device of sequence."[54] Poetry, with its basis in the "principle of equivalence," arises only through the "principle of projection," through the violence of metaphoric intrusion into the realm of metonymic prose. Poetry, however, is not simply metaphoric; a poem is not simply a metaphor, extended or otherwise. Pure metaphor, like the New Critics' "pure poetry," is an ideal projection; for a romantic philosophy like Cassirer's it is the expression of a nostalgic desire in the sense that Schiller called "sentimental." Remarkably, such longing presumes a nonmetaphoric (metonymic, prosaic?) context as a ground for idealistic projection. We are returned once more to Derrida's paradox: one must project the priority of prose ("writing," the metonymic function) in order to define the originating force of poetry as located in prose. Therefore, there is no need to speculate about origins, certainly not on the level of style, and this explains why Jakobson sees a continual "competition" between metaphor and metonymy.[55] "Similarity superimposed on contiguity imparts to poetry its thoroughgoing symbolic, mutiplex, polysemantic essence. . . . In poetry where similarity is superinduced upon contiguity, any metonymy is slightly metaphorical and any metaphor has a metonymical tint."[56] The importance of this "principle of impurity" cannot be understated, for because of it Jakobson's "projection theory" of poetry never results in the radical disparity between poetry and prose, "literariness" and nonliterariness, that so restricts the New Criticism. Nor does Jakobson privilege any specific genre, as the romantic theorists privileged the lyric.

Nevertheless, Jakobson's approach is not without troublesome ambituities. When the "projection theory" is read in combination with his general communication chart, there is implied, as Mary Louise Pratt astutely notes, some sort of special "poeticalness" about the poetic function; if nothing else it is the dependence of poetry on surface, stylistic devices such as "versification."

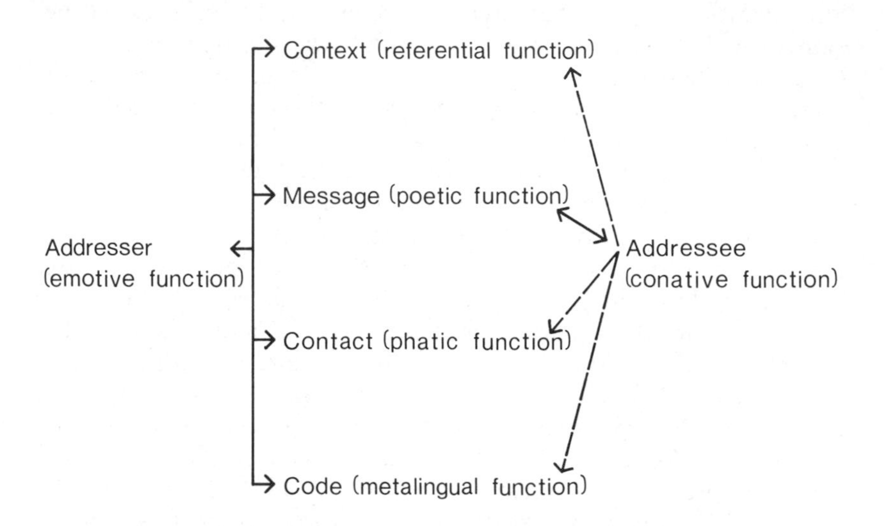

> The referential, emotive, and metalingual functions seem to be distinguished from each other in terms of subject matter. Utterances with these functions carry information about the "context," the addresser's inner state, or the code, respectively. The phatic function, on the other hand, is defined contextually by the speaker's intention to "establish, prolong or discontinue communication." To define conative utterances Jakobson proposes a logical criterion, that imperatives lack truth value, in addition to the criteria of grammatical surface structure and referent.[57]

As Pratt argues, the poetic function is of a wholly different nature, "a focus on the message for its own sake." The dominance of this function makes any utterance poetic, but does the dominance of this function "exclude" the others, which are not marked by focus on themselves for their own sake? The radical nature of this self-reflexiveness would seem to close out the other functions, but can this be so if poetry expresses a desire to communicate that surely involves phatic and emotive functions and perhaps others?

Pratt's narrow reading of Jakobson emphasizes the radical isolation of the poetic function rather than what I have called Jakobson's "principle of impurity," but our differences here are finally minimal. Seeing Jakobson caught in the traditional (romantic, New Critical) trap of dividing literary and non-literary style, Pratt suggests that the poetic function fails to distinguish between truly poetic functions and cheap imitations like advertising jingles; both, she rightly notes, are prone to the self-conscious use of stylistic devices such as versification. She further suggests that the projection theory, so narrowly drawn, would profit from an extension that would include cultural/historical context, as well as considerations of intention and affective response. Through my emphasis on the principle of impurity in Jakobson's theory, I am merely suggesting that Jakobson himself anticipated the inevitability of such an extension.

The essential fact is that literary style cannot be seen as radically removed from the general system of communication. It is not at all clear that we can even define a special literary style other than through a concept like that proposed by Culler as "poetic competency." Such competency is nothing more than a subclass of values within the general cultural *langue* and is barely distinguishable as a subsystem. Literary style is at the service of the collective will, on the most functional level operating as a system of models for "good writing" (interpersonal style) and at the other extreme as "touchstones" of sublime expressiveness (personal style). We might borrow here a term from eighteenth-century literary criticism and define literary style in this sense as a reflection of cultural "taste," but we should not be fooled by simplistic arguments that literary taste is nothing more than the result of a self-serving elitism of an academic fraternity. The line of demarcation between "highbrow" and "lowbrow" is anything but clear; moreover, the elitist academy is itself an indulgence of society, a projection of socioeconomic wishes and even the expression of society's high ideals. That the academy rarely fully satisfies these wishes and never lives up to these ideals is a problem that, although it is vitally significant, is too complex to consider here. What is significant is that with regard to literary taste the academy performs (or attempts to perform) the very tasks that society charges it to accomplish: it engages in the codification of the aesthetic values that best seem to serve the interests and needs of the culture.

In the revolutionary zeal of literary theory in the 1970s, the romantic ideal of literariness as "high seriousness," as marked by an "innately" and "mystically" human experience, has been overthrown. Perhaps we have been too hasty here, failing to cull from that which had grown too rigid in its ascendency and needed rethinking the more interesting and still significant concepts of basic human wishes and desires. Ironically, what replaces the romantic ideal is a concept of literariness defined by its special adherence to cultural expectations. Taste is, therefore, acquired and not innate, but the difference is ultimately a slight one since both continue to reflect some more basic human need to project or intuit a humanistic capacity to create and respond to art. The acquired taste theory is more complex than the innate taste theory, the former actually subsuming the latter. The determination of literariness in the former projects an elaborate storehouse of linguistic devices stipulated as literary, ranging from lists of stylistic techniques to broader cultural signs that allow us to make preliminary judgments of value on the basis of such factors as jacket designs or even where books are sold (outdoor stalls, bus terminals, or college bookstores, for example). The elaborateness of this acquired system not only argues against the relative simplicity of romantic aesthetic taste but also disallows even the possibility of an ideal or "right" reader whose "competency" is complete, without blind spots.

Jakobson's projection theory, expanded beyond the idea of mere self-reflexive literary texts, reveals the ever-receding boundaries of literary style and, more than that, exposes literariness as a characteristic of mind and cultural context. The projection theory must not be allowed to narrow to the purity of Kantian aesthetic contemplation. Involved in the surprise of metaphor's disruptive stylistic surface is the "projection" of a desire to communicate, what I have above termed motivation. There is a sense in which the disruptive poetic function is in itself a special sort of phatic device—a signal that "poetry" is being articulated! Two aspects of this motivation are seen in relation to the idea of "literariness" and the concept of literary style as an identifying mark. The first involves what many theorists in various terms have defined as the intention to produce art. Eliot sees it as a struggle to enter the Tradition, Bloom as the "anxiety of influence," Said as a "beginning intention." In all, it is a seeking of a confirmation of an identity *as* artist, what on one level is "to be known by one's style." This confirmation is an extraordinary process involving extraordinary personal risk, and that calls attention to the second aspect of what I have called motivation: cultural ratification. Pratt discusses a similar twofold interrelatedness in terms of the interplay of "illocutionary" and "perlocutionary" activities. The intention to produce art necessitates an audience's willingness to read the work *as* art. Such willingness exposes the power invested in the audience to grant or not to grant the artist an identity *as* artist. Artistic confirmation, therefore, is a special, cultural activity that hints at something like the indistinct range of literary competency or the fluctuating boundaries of a literariness within cultural *langue*.

The risk involved is in part the one that has obsessed Bloom as a form of anxiety. To be granted identity as artist ambiguously involves entry into the Tradition and yet resistance to all the models contained in the Tradition. The movement is partly mimetic (to write in the literary style of others) and partly revolutionary (to articulate one's own style). The risk is personal and cultural. The artist challenges the cultural subsystem of literariness by disrupting cultural expectations, but on either side of success lies "anonymity." To submit too much to the dictates of the system makes one a mere imitator; to unleash too much freeplay into the bound play of the system may result in a total failure to communicate. Therefore, it is not so much the assertion of an inventive new style that marks one's entry into the system (this is the point of view of the artist); rather, one is assured of a place among the artists only when one has been imitated (this is the point of view of the critic). Bloom's anxiety theory perhaps puts too much emphasis on the former whereas it is the function of the latter, as critical confirmation, that is most important. Umberto Eco speaks directly to this point. "When only one person in the world is able to falsify a *mode of invention* (i.e., not to copy a given painting, but to paint according to the same type of inventive procedure) the code proposed by that painting has not yet been accepted by a culture; when it becomes possible to paint *à la manière de*, then the invention (as a code-making proposal) has succeeded semiotically; a new convention exists."[58] Somewhat contrary to the tradition of "inimitable" style as the mark of genius, here it is the very *effort* to imitate (successfully or unsuccessfully is of no matter), the recognition of the possibility of imitation, that establishes a convention, a "new" convention, by the way, that typically would bear the artist's name, as in "Faulknerian style." This process of confirmation is also profoundly historical. Pratt's use of speech act theory leads her to liken it to the contractual relationship between audience and storyteller,[59] what I spoke of in part 1 as the "occasion" for myth singing. We might note that because of the problems of distribution, written forms of literature and plastic art forms often must wait for cultural ratification resulting in a lag in the communication arc; but the procedures are the same: the identifying confirmation situates the artist at a time and place, within a shifting tradition of artistic values and general cultural expectations.

Ironically, this identifying confirmation carries with it a negative implication. To be designated as an artist with a style worthy of imitation is tantamount to being put to death. Such identity conferring is fixating, stereotyping, a condition eagerly sought but almost always vigorously resisted when achieved. To be named an artist, to be interred in one's identifying style (Faulknerian) is to be deprived of life. If my language here seems excessive, take it as a counterreaction that urges that we be careful not to overinterpret the fact of "poetic projection" even as we see it revealing the very dramatic desire for identity. The naming of the artist *as* artist is itself nothing more than a metaphor—a metaphor for "authentic" historical being, and the achievement of named identity, as a deadening act of confirmation, disguises at its heart (below the stylistic surface) a profound struggle that defies naming. That struggle, never named or only falsely named, is an essential absence that makes metaphor possible, only now we must not see it as a simple stylistic device (like the interplay of proper names, stereotypes, and metaphoric tensions in "Pantaloon in Black" or the metaphoric functioning of Lucas Beauchamp's family icon discussed in part 1). Stylistic "deviations," as revolutionary or even anarchistic, are foremost the expressions of the *need for* metaphor, the *desire for* identity that is endlessly repeatable and defiant of stereotyping; the opening of the space for emergence into identity can only show its authenticity through deadening metaphorical superficialities.

Who, then, is the author we "name" so easily and dismiss with such cavalier impersonality? Gerald Bruns notes that Barthes's answer to this question contains its own essential mystery. Barthes focuses on what he calls the "diathetical analysis of the modern verb *to write*," which reveals a grammatical functioning in that verb not unlike that found in the sentence, "It is raining." The "subject" here "is neither active nor passive but is rather the purely grammatical agent of a self-motivating activity"; the sentence, as all literary sentences metaphorized by the self-conscious use of the verb *to write*, "possesses a phantom or mythical subject." Bruns interprets: "we no longer think of the speaker in a poem or the narrator in the novel as the author who exists outside the work as a transcendent originator of meanings; we think of him instead as a nameless and departed god, an irrelevance, and in his stead we attend to the figure whose identity is found precisely in the activity by which the poem or novel unfolds."[60] Actually, the issue is even more complicated, for we make a series of designations with regard to authors that are complexly interrelated. In part this series is characterized by the now famous critical distinction between "*énonciation*" and "*énoncé*,"[61] between the act of articulation and the fact of the articulation that contains a vestigial or repressive "I" as a mere grammatical marker. There is, therefore, an "I who writes" and an "I who (apparently) speaks" in the text. But there is more, for our ability to distinguish between a grammatical "I" (which functions like a first person narrator/character in a story or as a "shifter" on the level of style) and an "implied" author (on whom we confer the deadening identity of the name of the artist) reveals to us the emptiness at the heart of all articulation, the unnamed and unnameable "authentic" self of an "I who lives," and who is more than the artist as stylist. Here we see the openness at the heart of intentionality both on the level of style (as the intention to produce art) and on the ontological level (as the intention to speak being, to enter the world of language, culture, the symbolic order). The whole concept of literary style and the identity of the artist reveals, reflects, and opens for us the more profound (and vital) question of emerging being discussed in part 2 as forming the basis of the philosophy of language in general. It is our only contact with "authentic being," not as a determinate subjectivity nor as a "biographical individual" but as the lack or need for being that is both the primordial motivation for the generative movement of language and the gift of language to man.

The importance of our awareness of this tertiary level of authenticity is that it introduces into the theory of literary interpretation an idea of authorship, a humanistic dimension that is, finally, not distorted by solipsism or egoism. The authentic self is, paradoxically, an absence at the heart of expression, but the negativity of such an idea is only a matter of logical procedure. One can arrive at a sense of such being only by inverting the logic of noncontradiction, the very method Derrida gleefully, playfully took from Heidegger. What results is a vision of being not as ego-isolate but as active, emerging-into, as *ekstatic*. Many would call this "ego-loss,"[62] but it is more significant to see it as a motivating assertion of the human, which situates the nonhuman. There is a danger in this, the danger that we will come to believe our metaphors and claim dominion over all that we survey, but the corrective for this may well be the essence of literature's cultural functionality (its "fictionality"). It is in literary activity that attention is called to the limits of metaphor, to metaphor's disruptive, stylistic, identity-conferring function that reveals a vital emptiness, a desire below the surface. This is the "force" of metaphor, which also "proves" the historical extensiveness (as opposed to intensiveness) of humanism. I am reminded of Jorge Luis Borges's wonderful story, "The Library of Babel," wherein the universe (all the universe man knows) is allegorized as an infinite library containing all possible expressions of human knowledge in the form of innumerable texts that exhaust the logical possibilities of linguistic utterances. Borges's library functions in a way similar to the functioning of what I have called *langage*, as a potential for meaningfulness vastly more powerful than man himself. But despite the paranoiac worries of the story's narrator, the library does not wholly dispense with the human. "Perhaps my old age and fearfulness deceive me, but I suspect that the human species—the unique species—is about to be extinguished, but the Library will endure: illuminated, solitary, infinite, perfectly motionless, equipped with precious volumes, useless, incorruptible, secret."[63] Man always fears his extinction, the possibility that he will, for a variety of reasons, disappear from the universe. The verbal universe of Borges's story, however, makes such extinction inexpressible, for a "perfectly motionless" and "useless" verbal universe is essentially flawed, dumb, inarticulate. It would in no way exist or endure without motion and use, without man to assert his own authentic being and at the same time situate the Library as powerful, signifying system. It is man's activity driven by his need to achieve being, that creates (corrupts) the perfectly still universe in which he lives. That universe, of course, is not the physical world, which does very well without man, but the "intelligible" universe, which is, logically, the only context within which man can be defined. Man cannot, even so clever a man as Borges, articulate his own nonbeing; he cannot "speak" his own "silence." He can articulate his own emergence as historical being, for his metaphors disclose the vitality of his motivating (and motivated) force. Less than the "unique" being that his romantic dreams promised, man, nevertheless, is a necessary power within the powerful structure of any system of articulation.[64]

We have here gone far beyond the efforts of Samuel Levin to employ Jokobson's insights in the explanation of poetic unity. Levin saw the projection theory only as a series of parallel structures coupled in linear fashion. But Jakobson's "principle of equivalance projected into the axis of contiguity" suggests much more. To move beyond the unifying structure of a single metaphor inevitably risks the influx of some metonymic qualities; the extension of metaphors over a long sequence defines temporality. There is, therefore, no reason to insist on the ideal of a pure poem (a single metaphor) promoted by the imagists and adopted by the New Critics as the measure of creativity and the identifying function of artistic naming. We can, however, understand the New Critical emphasis on the poet's drive toward purity, on the struggle to activate language's poetic functionality. The ideal will never be achieved, but the poetic use of language makes this failure the key to both the cultural and personal dimensions of "creative" writing. I am describing here an extended version of what Murray Krieger calls poetry's "ekphrastic principle." Krieger redefines the traditional prosodic term *ekphrasis* to mean not simply a poem that imitates plastic art but one that achieves a sort of "archetypal" status by denying the linear nature of language in a metaphoric drive toward unity.[65] In my extension "ekphrasis" becomes the metaphor that "belies" its own "ek-stasis," which in its failure to fix, name, and "presence" opens for us the being-there of the author as an "I who lives."

Michael Riffaterre's observations on style are also useful on this point. The breaking of patterns established in the text serves the vital function of calling attention to the text as (literary) text. The "anticipations" of the reader are linear; the pattern once established promises to continue, but to shatter this pattern forces the reader out of his linear mental set and back to a reassessment of the recalcitrance of the particular, discrete moment that defies and demystifies the whole. Stylistic devices, therefore, are not mere decoration; and Riffaterre's theory pales beside the implications that poetic style has a profound meaning all its own, that poetry connects us with the author's and our own essential being-there. By jarring our cultural mental set, by threatening our logical (metonymic) structures of language (inverting the principle of noncontradiction), it makes us aware of our existential condition as men. Therefore, the stylistic breaks themselves must be more than merely disruptive; they assert a deeper meaningfulness in the metaphoric/metonymic tensions of the text.

On the cultural level, a poem that merely jars us for the demonic pleasure of disrupting our sensibilities would be viciously anarchistic. There are such poems, but this is the dialectics of poet and society carried to its extreme. In fact this violates the very nature of metaphor, the essence of which is unity, albeit a "new" unity. On the level of linguistics, the anarchistic poem would be simply agrammatical, totally divorced from the cultural system of language that defines the communal world. It runs the risk of being "meaningless"; at its worst it is wholly personal and psychotic. Metaphor, as we know it in our literature, revitalizes language; it does not destroy it. It challenges culture; it may even replace it, but it does not negate it. This is the force that moves diachronically across the synchronic structure of culture, the force of the individual moment that resists the dehumanization of fixities and definites and gives them *new* life. My analysis, therefore, has worked its way outward again to the original question of poetry's relationship to general language use. Here we confront the puzzling problem of history, but without the historical dimension literary interpretation remains incomplete.

HISTORY AS EXISTENTIAL

Literary criticism necessarily involves a historial perspective. It is something more than the formalist absolutism of the New Critics, which relates the individual work to history by mere analogy, and less than reductive sociological historicism, which explodes the boundaries of the literary context into the blur and flux of the work's temporal milieu. Traditional literary history has struggled between these extremes for centuries, but with little success. The varieties of historical perspective seem to be stymied by a dilemma, repeated by Barthes: we are permitted to have *either* literary criticism *or* literary history but not both.[66] Yet no one can deny the absurdity of such a theoretical separation. Literature, like man himself, is bound off in time; the creation of literature is temporal, for (1) it is itself a process that ultimately activates a corresponding process of thought in the reader, and (2) it is, in its epistemological dimension, existential, an individual moment of articulation within a general context.

The historical perspective that underlies my arguments in this text has its origins in Hegel and is refined under the influence of Heidegger; it is born of dialectical thinking only to necessarily transcend that logic. The recalcitrant individual moment never evaporates into the universality of Time. Nor is it ever fully free from it. Historiography is essentially a metonymic intellectual actvity; it demands that the individual moment be given a context—one that "makes sense."[67] But the life of the mind refuses the easy lure of metonymy, and it is this realization that enabled Croce, Dewey, and many others to claim that history must always be rewritten. The historian, if he is sensitive to the uniqueness of moments of consciousness, stands at what Eliot calls the limitations of human understanding. Only the "saint" can easily occupy this most essential of paradoxical junctures.[68] The historian, bound by his temporal, logical, and metonymic language, must force his historical point of view to admit the timeless. His only option is to rewrite continually, and his narrative must never deny the discrete moment in its rush to make systematic and self-regulating the general structure or pattern.

The historian and the critic, therefore, are partners in a joint enterprise, for the critic brings to the historian's metonymic abstractions the constant reminder that the unique moment "corrupts" the universal. Both retreat from the rebellious questioning of the artist, and neither should be confused with the artist, yet neither must fall into the logician's or philosopher's abstractionist methodology. The dilemma of the historian and critic, or that ideal hybrid creature, the historical critic, is that he must dwell between poetry and prose, metaphor and metonym, between the structure of individual human consciousness and the structure of cultural systems. Perhaps he does so at the risk of resigning the glory of either.

In this context Geoffrey Hartman's claim that modern formalists have simply failed to be formalist enough is very instructive. The New Critics were apparently content to confine their interests to the structures of individual works. The possibility that behind these works were deeper structures that derived from the interplay of individual consciousness and social systems was largely ignored. Such a backward movement was condemned as radically idealist, leading to Crocean historiography and the diminution of the work's importance. Yet it need not go so far in this direction; Crocean historicism runs the risk of becoming ahistorical. Again, history demands the balance between the individual and the universal.

The poetic drive toward metaphor gives us the necessary dialectic for historical movement, for metaphor dissolves into its own genesis, even to the suggestion of its rudimentary sources in the primitive act of individuation. It is, in this very movement, the essence of history, being-there, with all its spatiotemporal implications of the place and moment where being shows itself. For the true primitive (ancient or modern), whose awakening self-consciousness drives him to seek unity with the outer world, metaphor functions as existential projection, not as a transcendent ego but as an escape from the ego. As egoist, man is doomed; the diversity of experience demands a never-ending series of unrelated momentary projections, each asserting a self and an other and eventuating in a discontinuous series of apocalyptic moments much like those of Faulkner's romantic egoist, Ike McCaslin. For the egoist this is a devastating pattern of repetition (fate) and fragmentation. Yet from another point of view, it is the uniqueness of the individual moment metaphorized on the stylistic surface of the literary text that enables us to say with the New Critics that the poem is whole and self-sufficient. This can no longer be interpreted as cutting the text free from time; rather it emphasizes the text's temporal existence: the humanistic struggle for self-consciousness within the pattern of all human consciousness. The moment of consciousness can happen only as it does, when and where it does.

Herein lies the value of poetic communication. It is not simply that author and reader share a common linguistic code that enables the one to understand the message of the other. That there is such a shared code is self-evident. True communication lies beneath the code; what is shared is the existential condition of man, the "concern" for the human. On the level of this existential awareness is founded a communication between author and reader that invites the latter to enter the world of the former, to live through the details of the author's world, which becomes a simulacrum of the reader's own human condition. The reader's and author's worlds are different, separated by time and space, but *in the work* the two worlds meet in a communion of souls. The metaphoric text draws its life from the critical, self-conscious interpenetration of author and culture, but once full born it breathes on its own, surviving the fading consciousness, the "authentic" being, that bore it. This metaphoric status tends to disguise the text's origins-as-emergence because the text seems to speak out of its time to readers in other lands and in other cultures. It thrusts itself into the future of readers yet to come. It defies our metonymic reductions and continually asserts its own being as text, yet it also inexorably draws its readers back to its own time and place, to the emptiness beneath its shining surface, to the force of articulation to experience that marks the limits and the possibilities of being-there for all humankind.

Part Four

Toward a Literary Hermeneutics

Briefly stated, there are two basic, and traditional, concerns in hermeneutic philosophy; they have tended to divide the history of hermeneutic theory itself, but they are not fundamentally contradictory. Rather, they seem to reflect different layers of interest. Perhaps the oldest tradition is associated with Biblical exegesis, where the concern is with the interpretation of individual texts and their transmission (that is, with the history of the interpretation of a text). This is the narrower of the basic concerns and has parallels with the New Criticism, although it never ignores historical meaningfulness altogether. It merely tends to restrict its historical perspective by isolating texts in particular historical moments. This tradition is still very much alive; Paul Ricoeur said as recently as 1965 that "we mean by hermeneutics the theory of rules that govern an exegesis, that is to say, an interpretation of a particular text or collection of signs susceptible of being considered as a text."[1] The approach is doggedly scholastic and generally antiromantic; it promotes objectivity in interpretation, a positivistic attitude, and emphasizes the importance of methodology as a series of logically defined interpretive steps that will, *of necessity*, lead the interpreter to the *true* meaning of the text. It is well represented by philosophers like Emilio Betti and literary critics like E. D. Hirsch, Jr. Behind these men are the works of Schleiermacher, and to some extent Dilthey and Husserl. Its similarity to the positivistic and methodology-centered linguistics of Chomsky is apparent, even if the stated goals are quite different.

The second basic concern, much younger in its full development (although like all philosophical movements prone to trace its origins to antiquity), reflects much broader interests. Under the influence of Heidegger, and to a lesser extent of Merleau-Ponty, this hermeneutic tradition seeks through the point of view of the phenomenologists to focus on the fundamental activity of "understanding," in both its epistemological and ontological dimensions. It is epistemological because "understanding" has its base in the self-conscious act of knowing the world; it is ontological because this act of knowing originates in a Heideggerian assertion of being. This tradition often appears to be broadly metaphysical, psychologistic, and idealistic, although such designations must be wary of the Heideggerian "deconstruction" that challenges them. The tendency is to disregard the centrality of logical methodology and the emphasis of the older tradition on apodictic knowledge. Some of its leading exponents are Hans-Georg Gadamer, Rudolph Bultmann, and, more recently, Richard Palmer.

HISTORY AND INTERPRETATION: FIRST VIEW

The exegetical tradition of hermeneutics, the first of the two positions outlined above, defines its primary goal as the establishing of "norms" for determining "right" and "wrong" interpretations. The end is apodictic knowledge, and the methodology, what Emilio Betti calls "historical objectivity,"[2] is designed to escape the damnation of subjective (romantic) judgments. As a result, the methodology becomes mired in a relativistic historicism. Betti's historical objectivity is essentially a development of the hermeneutic theory of Wilhelm Dilthey. The interpreter, for Dilthey, must be able to transcend his own personality in order to enter into the consciousness of another being (the author) from another time and place. Only by doing this can one discover the true—and determinate—meaning of the text. "Meaning" must not be allowed to suffer interpolation at the hands of the critic, and in this sense the text is said to be "autonomous," having a meaning locked in time. This version of textual autonomy, obviously, is not New Critical.

The approach can best be grasped by outlining what Dilthey established as the three main areas of interest for hermeneutic theory.

1. *Erlebnis*: simply "life" but in the broader sense of "existential consciousness" or what Richard Palmer translates as "experience."

2. *Ausdruck*: "expression" or perhaps more literally an existential projection. For Dilthey, expression was the realization of *Erlebnis*, its objective manifestation in one of man's "gestures": art, politics, philosophy, and many others.
3. *Verstehen*: "understanding." The crucial element of Dilthey's hermeneutic theory is understanding; it is this capacity of mind that allows us to grasp sympathetically the actual thought process of another mind.[3]

Dilthey says of this third area of interest: "Understanding is the rediscovery of the I in the Thou; the mind rediscovers itself at ever higher levels of connectedness; this sameness of the mind in the I and the Thou and in every subject of a community, in every system of culture and, finally, in the totality of mind and universal history, makes the working together of the different processes in the human studies possible."[4] For the purposes of hermeneutic theory, we must understand that this I-Thou relationship (the end of all interpretation) is achieved only by passing through the concrete "expression"—the text itself. "Above all . . . the grasping of the structure of the inner life is based on the interpretation of *works*, works in which the texture of inner life comes fully to expression."[5] The "autonomy" of the text in the exegetical tradition becomes primary, whereas the concept of "understanding" is no more than a basic assumption; the text is an objectified, formed, or structured expression of lived experience, the existential projection of a particular man living at a particular time and place.

Such autonomy is defended, however, at the expense of the interpreter's involvement; the text is free from interpretive superimpositions, but it is lost in the historical moment of its creation. This historical relativism is admittedly the aim of the hermeneutic theory of E. D. Hirsch, Jr. He uses the term *autonomy* in the sense of Husserl's object of "intentionality." Hirsch quotes Husserl to the effect that "the same intentional object may be the focus of many intentional acts."[6] That is to say, the literary text remains essentially unchanged although it is subjected to a variety of different interpretations. More importantly, the text is the product of the author's creative act, of, in an expanded sense, his "intention." It is on this basis that Hirsch defines the "meaning" of a literary work as the product of the author's determining will (including all the conscious and unconscious factors of his environment that affect his will). Meaning, then, is historical, determined by the spatiotemporal locale of the author. There is also a secondary meaning for Hirsch, which he labels "significance." It is a "present" meaning arising from the critic's *subjective* judgment. Despite its basis in the idealistic assumptions of a possible "inter-subjectivity" voiced by Dilthey, proponents of hermeneutics, like Hirsch, insist that the methodology of the interpreter must be objective, scientific, and value free in contradistinction to the critic's subjectivity. Clearly, Hirsch divided interpretation and evaluation in order to focus on the former without the befuddling problems of the latter, but he fails to explain fully what we must all intuitively confirm, that such a theoretical bifurcation of interests has little of the same purity in practice. Can an interpreter really avoid some degree of subjectivity?

The affirmative response to such a question is made by Hirsch as a result of his primary emphasis on methodology. If an exact logical interpretive process can be established, there is little room for subjective wanderings. The methodology makes the interpretation for us if we follow the rules. Meaning becomes, in this positivistic notion, almost identical with the interpretive procedure itself, and the result is an extremely narrow kind of historical determinism. Admitting that his concept of intention is fraught with vagueries, that we cannot *know* what was in the author's mind as he wrote, Hirsch argues that we must, on the basis of *textual evidence*, deduce what was most probably his intention. Thus the methodology avoids the charge of "psychologism." Hirsch sees the text as an object in experience, but a determinate object that can be interpreted without conjectures on the psychological condition of the author. The methodology is statistical. Given several variant readings of a text, or a portion of a text, the interpreter's role is to establish "evidence" (including all the known factors of the author's life, his works, his social-historical milieu) that can be used to determine the relative rightness or wrongness of the variant readings. This evidence forms a closed context of possible meanings, and the correct meaning of an individual work is determined by that context. The interpreter can then decide which of the variant readings is most nearly correct by deciding which of all possible interpretations satisfies the greatest number of determining possibilities.

The methodology is value free because it is wholly quantitative, a result of Hirsch's importation of Husserl's empiricism. It lacks the exactness that the ideal of apodictic knowledge might seem to demand; it delivers only a "high probability of truth," but Hirsch is a practical man in such matters. He would not claim that even this statistical approach is free from the vagueries of evidence gathering. More importantly, the methodology is wholly relativistic, and in the end this denies any true autonomy to the text, that more radical New Critical autonomy. The work must be seen as a product of its times, and art's contribution to the structuring of history is severely undercut. We are confronted here with the picture of an artist spoken *by* his historical context. Everything is reduced to simple pastness; the context of the work is static and closed, and the continuity of past and present is ignored or even denied.

HISTORY AND INTERPRETATION: SECOND VIEW

Hirsch's understanding of autonomy contradicts my goal in this essay of establishing a historically sensitive hermeneutics. We can quickly agree that any work must be seen as in some sense free from the reader's (interpreter's) determining influence, but it is also free from the illusion of the *determining* influence of its own historical milieu. Paradoxically, the work is related to both past and present, for only in this relationship can it be said to be truly autonomous (irreducible to either the reader's or author's point of view) and at the same time a *part* of the continuous flow of such objects in experience that make up the dynamic flow of history. Perhaps, then, it is better to drop the term *autonomous* altogether, for it is distorting in either its New Critical or relativistic usages. This forces us to a much broader sense of hermeneutics and perhaps a more complicated methodology. The interpreter's approach, I would argue, is inevitably less logical and statistical than Hirsch admits, and flirts with the dreaded "psychologism." We might describe the literary text more accurately as "finite"; it is not "autonomous" because its very nature opens it to a vast world of experience and discourse.

To accomplish such a theory we must return to Dilthey's triadic relationship of *Erlebnis*, *Ausdruck*, and *Verstehen*. In so doing I reject Dilthey's limitation of the latter, "understanding," to the mere process of entering into the consciousness of the author, his lived experience or *Erlebnis*. Hence, from the beginning I admit that the separation of interpreter's and author's consciousnesses is problematical, but the blending of the two consciousnesses leads us to a broader sense of communication than Hirsch provides through his dichotomy of meaning and significance.

The virtue of Hirsch's methodology is that it is simple and logical (much like Chomsky's analysis of linguistic structures). But it generates problems for itself as a methodology. This is most clear in Hirsch's development of a genre theory, his answer to the problem of how we "share" a meaning that is so narrowly circumscribed by the closed context of possible meanings—a context that may well be very remote from our present sense of significance. Hirsch's difficulty here is similar to Chomsky's in explaining communication in language systems, and their solutions are remarkably alike. Both fall back on a general category of shared experiences or capacities. For Chomsky this is rigidly determinative as it takes the form of "innate reason." For Hirsch it is milder, a matter of mere "convention" or "heuristic" devices that take the form of genre types. Both appeals are to the rationalist's argument from "necessity" in order to posit an explanatory general law that will "cover" all the individual variations known as specific expressions.[7]

Hirsch assumes that an author works within a finite category of experience (including the formal and thematic aspects of that category), which he calls an "extrinsic genre." This category can be known by the interpreter whose approach involves the elimination (by statistical probabilities) of all of the implications of the extrinsic genre that are "false" when applied to the specific text. By a process of gradually narrowing the focus, the interpreter arrives, finally, at the "intrinsic genre," which is apparently no more than the text itself as product of the author's determinate intention.

Hirsch has here committed himself to the traditional implications of the hermeneutical or philological circle. Leo Spitzer, however, suggests that the philological circle necessarily involves both a "psychological" and a "grammatical" dimension.[8] The first risks the damning label of "intuition" or even "mysticism" as it seeks the necessary inner structure of the author's mind *via* his works; the second restricts itself to the stylistic surface of the text. The psychological dimension pushes toward the irrational but, in combination with the grammatical, has its ground firmly in the finite text of the work. "To understand a sentence, a work of art, or the inward form of an artistic mind involves, to an increasing degree, irrational moves—which must, also to an increasing degree, be controlled by reason."[9] The intuitive aspect of the philological circle springs from the necessary "anticipation of the whole," which enables the interpreter to measure specific details against his intuitive assumptions about the text's unity. Schleiermacher, Spitzer claims, considered this in theological terms as a leap of faith; Hirsch, more secularly, calls it a "guess."[10]

Hirsch's "extrinsic genre" is a broader context than the textual wholes Spitzer is here speaking of; but Spitzer also expands the vibrations between parts and wholes into the realm of social history, and at this point he develops an idea of literary "context" very similar to what I have called "occasion" in part 1. Hirsch is well aware of the basic structure of this methodology, but the influx of the irrational (necessitated by the methodology itself) does not conform to his positivistic and statistical approach. On the deeper level, where a hermeneutic methodology must be developed, we find that an analysis that measures details against the whole, cannot proceed without the intuition of the whole, that deep-seated sense of unity and identity that is essentially metaphoric and thrusts toward the prelogical and irrational. The fate of Hirsch's hermeneutics, like that of Chomsky's linguistic analysis, is that its very methodology leads it, in part, away from objectivity.

This being the case, we might wonder why it is advantageous to restrict our interpretive approach to a narrow sense of "meaning" like that proposed by Hirsch. Can we not profitably expand hermeneutic procedure to include the problematical relationship between the reader's subjectivity, the text's finite existence, and the author's historical milieu? Dilthey's triad of *Erlebnis*, *Ausdruck*, and *Verstehen* can then be seen in the author-work-reader relationship I have so laboriously developed above. The result of such an expanded sense of literary hermeneutics supports Gadamer's assertion that interpretation "is an encounter with Being through language."[11] Nevertheless, the eloquence of this claim should not open it to the charge of mere psychologism or mysticism, for the interpretive methodology remains grounded in the part/whole relationship of finite text and cultural context, work and occasion, and has its concrete basis on the level of grammar. The focus necessarily remains on the text, for it is the finiteness of that text, its movement between past and present, that provides the key to the interpretive act as vehicle for communication between reader and author. There is a sense in which the act of interpretation defines the text, situates it in its cultural context, and thereby defines or situates the text's culture. Murray Krieger calls this an *as if* critical commitment;[12] but giving credit where it is due, the text can as easily be said to present itself, as one among many texts, to make itself available for interpretation.

Textual interpretation is, then, a profound kind of "translation"—from authorial past meaning into present significance—endowing the text itself with a more comprehensive meaning that encompasses the potentials for both. Translation is not an inappropriate word. Rewriting a text of one language system in another, separate system has long been the interest of hermeneutics. But even this narrow kind of translation must not be seen as the simple transfer of a message from one set of linguistic signs to another, semantically equivalent, set of signs, or as a game of transforming one set of codes into another. Such a semantic transfer is probably impossible; at best it results in so-called literal translations, which are always unsatisfactory. As Heidegger demonstrates in all of his philosophical writings, translation is never an "innocent process."[13] Translation calls into question the very limits of interpretation, for not only must it operate on the informational level encoding and decoding, on the level of signifiers generated within the culturally motivated system of *langue*, it must also concern itself with the general semiotic functioning that treats of the relationships between signifiers and signifieds, more broadly, between articulation and experience, or word and world.[14] Georges Mounin confines the field of interpretation to the latter operations, to a concern with the function of language as "index,"[15] but I hope that approach will seem too narrow a characterization following my discussion of the problematical interplay of *parole* and *langue*, language and experience.

The translator, by means of striking at the very heart of language's capabilities, the play of signifiers as well as the phenomenological activity of signifying as "intentionality," crosses from his world to that of the author; he establishes communication on the deepest level, penetrating to the very core of the author's existence and making it compatible with his own. Surely this is nothing less than Gadamer's "encounter with Being through language," and it involves an intuition of the potentials of all human consciousness as they are located in the author's horizon of consciousness. The translator must then be able to bring that consciousness to existence through his own consciousness. This is understanding at its fullest dimension and at its most problematical, for it involves not only the gap between language systems but also the historical and cultural differences between the author's world and that of the translator.[16]

THE HERMENEUTICS OF *VERSTEHEN*: CONSCIOUSNESS

Through the methodological paradigm of translation we confront the tradition of hermeneutic theory that necessarily involves historical consciousness. Moreover, in so doing we do not find it necessary to abandon interest in the text, or language in general, for the intimate relation between consciousness and language itself—its metaphor/metonym tensions, which reveal the author's encounter with his particular world of temporal flow and discrete moments—becomes a tool for the interpreter as he strives to penetrate to the deep structure of meaning. The interpreter, nonetheless, begins with his own consciousness as he confronts the text, and he is never free of it. As Richard Palmer says of Heidegger: "Understanding is the power to grasp one's own possibilities for being, within the context of the lifeworld in which one exists. It is not a special capacity or gift for feeling into the situation of another person, nor is it [simply] the power to grasp the meaning of some 'expression of life on a deeper level.'"[17] Understanding begins and ends in the interpreter's own existential awareness, but always within the context of history.

There is a crucial sense of will (or "intention") in Heidegger's phenomenology, in the act of consciousness that places the self in history (on another level, in tradition), thereby making the being of self and relationships with *other* beings possible. "Only as a questioning, historical being does man come to himself; only as such is he a self. Man's selfhood means this: he must transform the being that discloses itself to him into history and bring himself to stand in it. Selfhood does not mean that he is primarily an 'ego' and an individual. This he is no more than he is a we, a community."[18] Man is both, an individual whose very individuality comes to be in a community—in history. Without the context of history he cannot be an individual and without the multiplicity of individuals there can be no historical context.

Art, therefore, can be described in terms of "disclosure," for the foundation of every individual work (act of consciousness) is what Heidegger calls "Earth," and it is on the ground of Earth that man builds his World, makes, through an act of historical consciousness, his works. This creative act makes a place in time for the works of man, just as it makes a place in history for man himself. The work of art captures *formally* the tension of consciousness as it struggles to bring forth World on the vivid but opaque foundations of Earth. The work is, then, part of its World and is composed of and on Earth, but it is also at the same time a situating of World and Earth. It has its freedom as well as its belonging. Heidegger can, therefore, describe the individual work (being) as a strange, violent, disruptive emergence that nevertheless opens up the space/time continuum for the situating of a World that becomes the familiar dwelling place of the individual, a dwelling place that will subordinate the individual, even repress it as it also exploits the Earth for the World's purposes.[19] Heidegger, of course, discusses these complex movements and countermovements as characteristics of language. His sense of the mysterious originality of poetry and its later codification into a poetic tradition is not far from that of Cassirer, even to the use of very romantic terminology to describe the relationship between the primordial nature of emergent being and the cultural/historical context of that original poetry. "The origin of language is in essence mysterious. And this means that language can only have arisen from the overpowering, the strange and the terrible, through man's departure into being, embodied in the word: poetry. Language is the primordial poetry in which a people speaks being. Conversely, the great poetry by which a people enters into history initiates the molding of its language."[20]

We must remember here that Heidegger's use of the term *origin* is special, indicating an abiding power that is always available in language. Language contains the forces of both gathering together and dispersing in conflict, the tension of metaphor and metonymy that makes possible the emergence of the individual at a time as well as the absorption of the individual into the flow of temporality. Poetry, therefore, is not merely a metaphor; it is the force of gathering, violent estrangement, that creates a space for a metaphor, an opening in the fabric of being (context or text) that only a "pure" metaphor in its dynamic enduring could fill, if only such metaphors were ever at hand. In a very real way, as I have argued from the beginning, it is the failure of metaphors, their "impurity," that signifies intention, will, and emergence; on the stylistic surface it is the weakness of the metaphoric unity, its always-openness to metonymy, that best reveals its power. How far, for example, should we extend the unifying claims of "My love is like a red, red rose"; as far as blood and thorns, root rot and aphids? The dissolve is the other side of emergence, and literature most forcefully calls our attention to this powerful interplay. Without it we would have no sense of the timeliness of time, nor of the true dimensions of history.

A FURTHER NOTE ON LANGUAGE

Heidegger's student Hans-Georg Gadamer placed even more emphasis on the linguistic orientation of hermeneutics than did his master. Gadamer extensively developed the distinction between the poetic use of language and the instrumentalism of scientific discourse. Rejecting the latter as a vitiation of the true power of language he says, "everywhere [the] word is seen in its mere sign function, the primordial relationship of speaking and thinking is turned into an instrumental relationship."[21] We are returned once more to the New Critical distinction between poetry and prose, but it is no longer seen as absolute. The denial of that New Critical separatism is justified by a move away from textual formalism toward the structuralism of human consciousness. This is the expansive sense of formalism advocated by Geoffrey Hartman. Gadamer eschews the formalist analysis, which never sees beyond the autonomous text, never penetrates to the deep structure of consciousness. The essence of language, he claims, is experience (Dilthey's *Erlebnis*); the poetic or primal use of language springs from the Heideggerian disclosure of space and time.

But we do not here abolish all distinctions between what we have for many years called poetic and philosophic languages. These are, Heidegger expresses it, always in the same "neighborhood"; they are "held apart by a delicate yet luminous difference, each held in its own darkness." They are "parallels" that "intersect in the infinite."[22] The difference between the two is chimerical, now this—now that, a kind of optical illusion not unlike the metaphoric use I made of the "principle of indeterminacy" from quantum theory in part 2. It is a question as to whether we look at poetry as emergence or as object. The former is a poetic way of determining, the latter is a logical or philosophical way of determining. Again Heidegger poses the dilemma:

> No thing is where the word is lacking. A thing is not until, and is only where, the word is not lacking but *is* there. But if the word is, then it must itself also be a thing, because "thing" here means whatever *is* in some way. . . . Or could it be that when the word speaks, *qua* word, it is not a thing—in no way like what is? Is the word a nothing?
> . . . If our thinking does justice to the matter, then we may never say of the word that it is, but rather that it gives. . . . What does it give? To go by the poetic experience . . . , the word gives Being.
> . . . [This is] the intuited secret of the word, which in denying itself brings near to us its withheld nature.[23]

There is no question that we sometimes (as stylisticians, as literary critics?) see the poetic word as a thing, as a presence that conceals its power to disclose the historical emergence of being. But we must not allow that perspective to solidify; we must perceive poetically, allow the poetic word to deny itself and reveal its powers of "giving," its original function as primordial naming.

In this sense, as Murray Krieger has claimed, poetry contains its own interpretation and remains to some extent always beyond the grasp of philosophical criticism, on the other side of "wonder," which is disclosed by the actual (perceptible) decomposition of what we have too literalistically designated as the substantiality of metaphor.[24] Heidegger proposes a remarkably expressive formula for this paradoxical interplay between poetry as emergent being, strange, uncanny, and language as the logical or familiar expressing "thingly" permanence. "The being of language : the language of being."[25] Such a phrase, with all of its rhetorical/poetical suggestiveness, cannot help but remind us of similar poetic devices so popular among the practitioners of eighteenth-century "heroic" verse. It is filled with the witty twisting of logic made possible by grammatical inversion, and what emerges is something far beyond a dialectical struggle between the opposed half-lines that face one another across the inarticulateness of the colon. The same words on either side of the caesura do not have the same meanings, but each side necessitates the other to situate its meaningfulness, even as it dissolves that meaningfulness into the "neutral" zone that opens between them. The distance between the word as thing (the being of language) and the word as giving (the language of being) makes possible the Heideggerian idea of poetry as speaking being. In the light of my earlier discussions, we can translate this poetic line into another expression, fully aware of the dangers of translation as well as its intimacy with the methods of interpretation. "The belonging of language : the language of belonging." This translation is not without loss; its distance from the original, however, is precisely the issue. The "belonging of language" is its fallen status as cultural systematicity, as *langue*, or even further as "literary value." These are the fixities and definites of interpretation, the scholastic rules that form the basis of literary handbooks. They are not without use; they are to be used. The "language of belonging," conversely, is that which defines our world, the familiar, delimiting, even repressive "world of our fathers." It is in part the realm of the function of the giving of identity; for the literary artist, it is the possibility of receiving the deadening "name of artist." Yet even if this version of Heidegger's paradox is sadly degenerate, its very inadequacy as a definition of the interpretive procedure opens up once more the path to "original poetry." In the inarticulate space marked by the colon the "text for analysis" emerges as neither a composite of culture's rules nor an expression of the personal (stylistic) struggles of the author. Nor is it possible to conceive of the appearance of this text as a simple dialectic of the two forces, for where is the place of transition, the fading of one into the other? The text is both and neither; it is the locus of the interpenetration of forces that dissolves into questions concerning the power of language to solidify into the thingly words of cultural rules on the one hand and the "given" power of self-assertion (will) that articulates itself as "seeking identity" on the other hand. Concealed within such a text is "being-there," the force of emergence into and the situation of history.

This is the essential historicity of literary hermeneutics, a historical perspective that must be preserved in its full ambiguity. The text, in its tensional revelation of the battle between the author's drive toward primal consciousness (being-there) and, in opposition, the systematicity of society, reveals the *possibility* of history and provides the *foundation* for communication. The text stands mediately between the author's world and the reader's world and draws author and reader together in its own unique structure while it asserts its own and man's being in time. "The claim of the text must be allowed to show itself as what it is. In the interaction and fusion of horizons the interpreter comes to hear the question which called the text itself into being."[26] As an event of consciousness the text "claims" a finite "presence" that defies any reduction of it to either wholly private or wholly public status. It is both; it shows itself not as a thing that is but as an opening, a space for being-there. The articulate text preserves the creative act that gave it being and invites the reader to disclose that creative power within it, but that disclosure opens thereupon a broader context, the occasion or World (the enabling horizon of man's always original emergence as being).

THE "TEXT" AS INTERPRETATION: IN DEFENSE OF ROMANTICISM

In *The Order of Things*, Michel Foucault characterizes romanticism as the "discovery of man"; he does so in order to attack all the other familiar "isms" that we associate with the romantic period, in particular: subjectivism, humanism, historicism, symbolism, and transcendentalism. Foucault is the defender of the rationalistic "systematicities" of the classical period (the seventeenth and eighteenth centuries) against the irrationality of romantic self-indulgence. There is, despite his denials, a polemical purposiveness—something of a missionary zeal—in his writing. For Foucault the "discovery of man" was not a triumph but a disastrous (and temporary) fall into the decadence of a sinful egoism. It resulted in the cult of the "self," in the claim that the thinking, feeling, speaking "subject" (man) was the measure of all things.[27] Viewed broadly, there is some justification for Foucault's observations on the excesses of romantic theory, but he is, finally, too anxious to make his point and fails to acknowledge the philosophical complexity of romanticism's "discovery." To cite only one example, Foucault seizes upon the concept of organicism and uses it to characterize the romantic way of thinking. This is traditional, but unless one is careful, it is distorting.

Organicism proclaims, as we have seen with the New Critics, the principle of the "folding inward" upon the self, the emergence of all particular phenomena, including man, from hidden, mysterious origins that are the nuclei for each individual organic whole. Thus man can be explained only by a search for origins, by retracing the interminably regressive steps back toward his birth into consciousness. Organicism, however, cuts two ways, a fact that Foucault glosses over. On the one hand, it promotes the worship of unique particularity and originality; in the arts it encourages the cult of "original genius," and it supports an exaggerated respect for the new, the avant-garde, the revolutionary, and even the strange and the grotesque. On the other hand, as it focuses on the particular it also proclaims the universal sameness of all phenomena, since the organic principle operates everywhere and at all times according to the same laws. It is possible, by embracing the paradox, to jump from awe in the face of the particular to sublimity when confronted by the universal, from the immediacy of experientiality to the abstractness of transcendentalism, from the perspctive of individual being to the perspective of cultural-historical becoming, from radical existential discontinuity to historicist continuity. It is true that man thus becomes the symbol of all order and the reference point for all interpretation, but the essential nature of his being is clouded by the mystery of time itself.

Foucault would carve out for himself a place between the extremes; neither the individualist nor the transcendentalist, he eschews the subjective, the particular, and the humanistic as well as the universal, continuous, and divine. To do so, however, is not to reject romanticism but to come to dwell within its limits, to "bracket" the really tough questions in order to focus on the narrow ones that deal with the myriad systematicities that claim neither concrete existential viability nor universal justification. It seems a sterile occupation that forces him to walk a very thin line at the risk of being continually off balance. If one returns from Foucault's polemical treatment of romanticism to specific romantic texts, one is both enlightened and disappointed, for the strange and frequently ironic revision of eighteenth-century rationalism in Foucault's modern dress points up the true complexity of the romantic "vision."

In his post-romantic masterpiece, *Sartor Resartus*, Thomas Carlyle embraced all of the romantic "isms" that so offend Foucault—and much more. The extraordinary hero of this work, Diogenes Teufelsdröckh, is obsessed with the "discovery of man" and repeatedly asks the ancient question, "Who am I?" giving it a full romantic flavor.

> Who am I; what is this me? A Voice, a Motion, an Appearance;—some embodied, visualized Idea in the Eternal Mind?
>
> . . . this so solid-seeming World, after all, were but an air-image, our Me the only reality; and Nature, with its thousandfold production and destruction, but the reflex of our inward Force, the "phantasy of our Dream. . . ."
>
> Stands he [man] not thereby in the centre of Immensities? [Pp. 160, 169][28]

The influence of German romantic philosophy is clear, and if more evidence is called for we need only refer to the "egoism" of the Everlasting No and Everlasting Yea chapters, the sentimentality of the *bildungsroman* form borrowed from Goethe, and the notorious chapter on symbols where Carlyle's transcendentalism comes to full flower. "In the Symbol proper, what we call a Symbol, there is ever, more or less distinctly and directly, some embodiment and revelation of the Infinite; the Infinite is made to blend itself with the Finite, to stand visible, and as it were, attainable there!" (p. 276).

The book is an encyclopedia of romanticisms, but to read no further is to misrepresent both the complexity of *Sartor* and the romantic period. After all, what does it mean, exactly, to stand in the "centre of Immensities"? If this is a phenomenological question then Teufelsdröckh can be read in terms of Georges Poulet's description of man in his *Metamorphoses of the Circle*. Man stands alone, in silence, confronted by the multiplicity of the experiential world, which he must mold into an order around himself as center, which he must articulate into meaningful patterns of language.[29] If we take Carlyle's "work philosophy" a step further we approach the phenomenological theory of Maurice Merleau-Ponty in the idea that "doing" is the measure of man; man thus discovers himself through his "creative," bodily motions into the world.[30] To slide into Heideggerian language, "work" can be seen as coming into "presence," man's achievement of "being-there" in time or history. If we emphasize Carlyle's transcendentalism we gain another, though not contradictory, perspective, for man as the symbol of God in the world becomes the new Adam, the namer and orderer of life's plenitude under the auspices of divine law.

These interpretations, among others, are all possible—that is, defensible; they are forms of critical or philosophical discourse that express very much the same romantic idea. Man is "centered" in these theories either as the force or order in a universe that he creates wholly for himself or as a mediator between heaven and earth, but it takes only a moment's reflection to realize that this "discovery" of man's centrality has very little stability. Early in *Sartor* Carlyle sets up the course of his discussions in such a way as to call all explanatory systems, all definitions of man, into doubt. Chapter 5, "The World in Clothes," purports to defend the famous "clothes philosophy," yet as the sometimes skeptical, sometimes adoring "editor" of Teufelsdröckh's manuscript plays one system off against another we learn, in fact, that the vaunted clothes philosophy itself is derived from a more general definition of man as the "tool-using Animal." What we are actually given in this chapter is a half-serious, half-satirical glimpse of man's confused world of systematicities, of the plurality of discourses through which we articulate humanism. Between the absurdly simplistic idea that man is the laughing animal and the more complex but still inadequate idea that man is the tool user, there exists a seemingly endless field of explanatory systems. If man is the center of all of these theories, he gains from it an elusive presence at best.

Furthermore, in this brief catalogue of theories, to which list we could add endlessly, we find a startling anticipation of the recent systematics of the French anthropologist, Claude Lévi-Strauss. Carlyle's "editor" argues "Still less do we make of that other French Definition of the Cooking Animal: which, indeed, for rigorous scientific purposes, is as good as useless. Can a Tartar be said to cook, when he only readies his steak by riding on it?" (p. 152). Carlyle, of course, had no way of knowing the complexity of Lévi-Strauss's crucial definition of the "raw and the cooked," or the definition of man that emerges from his binary oppositions of nature and culture. But if this dismissal of a proto-Lévi-Straussian theory carries no real force, Carlyle's inclusion of it absorbs even Lévi-Strauss into the mainstream of the romantic obsession with discovering and defining man, and it leads us to wonder whether or not the task has even yet been accomplished.

I am here, admittedly, playing with Carlyle's use of irony, but irony may be the most important characteristic of the romantic and post-romantic eras. While a plurality of defining systems seems inescapable given the cataclysmic nature of the romantic "fall," the adequacy of any one system is always in doubt—is, crucially, always subject to the accidental nature of lived experience, to the additional detail or particularity that will not fit into the system or to the appearance of a rival system. The romantic willingness to dwell between the extremes of particularity and universality, to embrace discontinuity and continuity, insures this vacillating movement and makes history possible. The ironic tone expressed by Carlyle's "editor" toward the definition of man as the "Cooking Animal" turns back upon the "clothes philosophy" itself. It also explains the necessary vacillation of the "editor," who at once shows admiration and skepticism for the philosophical system he is presenting.

The "immensities" that Carlyle speaks of do not define man so much as call attention to his orders, to his uses of language, sign systems, and symbols. Ranging between the extremes of particular, chaotic experience and universal orderliness, man is capable of defining his "me" only in more or less adequate systems that establish his relation to a world that slips and flows from his grasp. These systems, or "discourses," form what Foucault calls "an immense density of systematicities, a tight group of multiple relations."[31] *Sartor*, because it is a discourse about discourses, reflects on the inadequacy of any individual system and ironically on itself insofar as it presents itself as a system, but it thereby establishes the firm ground upon which man emerges into being; through his articulation of "self" into a world. Attendant upon this hesitating definition of man, moreover, is the ironic self-criticism of the text, which clearly anticipates the skepticism of a more modern philosopher like Jacques Derrida, who both proclaims the necessity of seeing man as a language-using animal, the necessity of hypostatizing the verbal sign, and also doubts language's power to confer being on man or the world in which he seems to dwell.[32]

Sartor is not merely a treatise on symbolism, transcendentalism, or historicism, although it embodies all of these discourses by distancing them from the text, by removing them to the status of an-"other" text that is the object of the text that we read. I submit, then, that the "me" of which Carlyle speaks in *Sartor* is not easily defined in terms like Foucault's discovery of man. What Carlyle tells us is that romanticism never discovered man, but it did initiate a profound humanism in its ironic awareness of man's historicity as a language-user. Romanticism is not a movement but the assertion of the possibility of movements; it is not the discovery of man but of the positive and negative limits of subjectivity; it is not the worship of continuity but the honest confrontation of discontinuity; it is not a simplistic reduction of language to thought or individual cognition but the awareness of language as both a genuine "tool" and an almost mythical context—each extreme necessary for the emergence of the "me" into the world, however tentative and subject to decay this emergence may be.

Carlyle's concept of the "me" is a complex proposition. It is the "self" or "individual," alien, alone as the "only reality." It is Teufelsdröckh, the shy, withdrawn scholar, whose origins are mysterious and whose future is unknown. Carlyle's "me" is also a borrowing of Coleridge's echo of divine consciousness, and this typical romantic vacillation between particular and universal parallels precisely the extreme limits of the clothes philosophy. Clothes (as linguistic signs), on the one hand, carve up the undifferentiated chaos of the experiential world into Kantian space-time categories, yet clothes (as symbols) must be pierced through so that we may experience the divine "One." Is this far from "the being of language: the language of being?" Who, then, is Teufelsdröckh? He is, most obviously, the hero of a work that Carlyle called a "kind of Didactic Novel."[33] As the dilettantish professor of "Things in General" he clearly satirizes the tradition of German idealistic philosophers who were universal system builders; as a consequence, the systematic nature of his own philosophy is subject to ironic doubt. There is, of course, no real distinction between Teufelsdröckh and his clothes philosophy; to speak of one is to speak of the other. He, like his philosophy, is a "mighty maze"; his being never becomes distinct because "a noble complexity, almost like that of Nature, reigns in his philosophy" (p. 148). He is boundless in the way that his philosophy is boundless; a professor of things in general, he is all things in general. He is at best a metaphor, a "name," which has a peculiar kind of presence in the text but no "thingness" nor "centrality." "Teufelsdröckh has . . . contrived to take-in a well-nigh boundless extent of field; at least, the boundaries too often lie quite beyond our horizon" (p. 148).

If Teufelsdröckh provides no heroic center for *Sartor*, he has a more profound function, within the text and beyond it. Carlyle tells us that this book "contains more" of his "opinions on Art, Politics, Religion, Heaven, Earth, and Air than all the things"[34] he had written to that time. Such a pastiche cries out for form because it has neither the neat Aristotelian plotting of a novel nor the rigid logical development of a didactic tract. What is needed, of course, is a clothes philosophy. Thus Teufelsdröckh's all-encompassing philosophy suggests a total orderliness or finite structure of "surplus" explanatory power that would be adequate to all occasions; it is the illusion of order surrounding the multiplicity of "things." The clothes philosophy, even as it is ironically distanced, casts, through the ghostly presence of Teufelsdröckh, a semblance of universal orderliness over *Sartor*; and Carlyle's text, like the clothes philosophy, asserts itself as a "Library of General, Entertaining, Useful or even Useless

Knowledge" (p. 149). It is no doubt the prototype for that very similar library that Borges named "Babel." Borges negatively and Carlyle directly situate "man" in that library, the former out of the necessity for motion, emergence that also situates (opens the space for) the library, the latter out of the historian's need to recognize that man "is" only because he "belongs." "The being of language: the language of being" : : the belonging of language: the language of belonging. Teufelsdröckh, without origins or ends, who dwells nowhere and everywhere, surveys a boundless world of men and books, of men in books. "The joyful and the sorrowful are there; men are dying there, men are being born; men are praying,—on the other side of a brick partition, men are cursing; and around them all is the vast, void Night" (p. 138).

Like all characters in literary works Teufelsdröckh comes to be a character by virtue of the text itself, but there is obviously a significant difference in the way Carlyle uses this device in *Sartor*. Because Carlyle's hero must in some way exceed the boundaries of his text while he also remains within it, Teufelsdröckh is both the namer and the named, the author and the character; through Carlyle's series of frames within frames (Teufelsdröckh's philosophy, Hofrath Heuschrecke's letters and tracts, the editor's manuscript, and Carlyle's text), through the overlapping and intersecting of discourses, it becomes impossible to determine which frame contains all of the others, which text is the encompassing one. Each ironically comments upon the other, and where inadequacies are revealed in one discourse another seems to fill the gap. Moreover, and this is crucial, there is room for even more, for even greater experiential particularity (which supports the illusion of *Sartor* as completely adequate discourse), and for other discourses (perhaps the reader's, or Lévi-Strauss's, or Foucault's). This is the structural basis for *Sartor's* rhetorical appeal and the force behind its quintessential hermeneutical assertiveness; Murray Krieger, borrowing from Rosalie Colie, has, after all, defined the "art of interpretation as the filling of gaps."[35] The reader, like the editor, is confronted with a demanding task, the measuring, one against the other, of two orders of "immensities": one of experiential plenitude and the other of discursive systems each projecting beyond itself a universal adequacy.

The purpose of such a centerless text is not to define man;

Carlyle has postponed indefinitely the wonderous "discovery" that Foucault speaks of. Even though the text has no center, all "subjectivity" has not necessarily been abolished. The irony of such a centerless system is that it seems to demand subjectivity. The textual "black hole" is not a void but a vortex; it is the possibility—even necessity—of a "virtual" center, of a voice that speaks being. It is not merely space, openness, dispersion, emptiness but the gathering into greatest density, solidity, being within openness. The text seeks to draw us into man's most human activity, the author's act of articulation, and if successful it reveals to us therein the textual limits of the author's subjectivity. *Sartor* is autobiographical (as well as biographical) insofar as it shows the presence of Carlyle engaged with his world, and, through the text, engages the reader in the author's vision. Without the presence of his voice, the activity of his articulation, we would have no text, but, equally, without the reader's engagement, which completes the communicative transaction, the author's voice would remain silent. The reader's attention, therefore, is drawn not to Teufelsdröckh nor to Carlyle, but to the text as act, as system bounded by and encircling the density of life, which opens outward into the terrifying onrush of pure temporality yet closes against this chaos by asserting its real presence as text. Unlike Foucault's "anonymous" discourses, Carlyle's *Sartor* breathes with the life of Carlyle's world. It is truly *work*. Carlyle argues, "Hence, too, the folly of that impossible Precept, *Know Thyself*; till it be translated into this partially possible one, *Know what thou canst work at*" (p. 238).

As "work" it also demands much from its reader; the act of interpretation is, like the dynamic nature of the text, a continuing process with no guarantees of total understanding. The text of Teufelsdröckh's philosophy comes to us, we should remember, not as an ordered treatise but in six paper bags containing scraps of paper and labeled with six zodiacal signs, and, once again, Carlyle uses this device to reflect his own text. There is, perhaps merely fortuitously, a parallel between Teufelsdröckh's six bags and the serial publication of *Sartor*. The hint of universality in the zodiacal signs is undercut by the fact that there are only six used, just as the hint of completeness in *Sartor* is undercut by its fragmentary appearance in print. More significantly, however,

Carlyle has here anticipated Ludwig Wittgenstein's "zettelistic" method of constructing the text of his *Tractatus*. The reader of such a text, like Carlyle's editor, is called upon to actively participate in the forming of it. The myriad explanatory and interpretive schemes of the text speak for the possibility of all interpretation, and the order of it stands for the possibility of any order. The range of Carlyle's text is deliberately broader than that of Wittgenstein; Carlyle is not willing to bracket the realm of symbolism or transcendentalism, but both men have a clear sense of the presence of the subjective and the call for interpretation.

Carlyle's text whirls precipitously from the ridiculous to the sublime, from political and social commentary to pure philosophical speculation, from detail to system so that the reader, dizzied by the range of thought and feeling, is caught up in the spectacle of life's fullness. What emerges is not Knowledge in the sense of conventionalized structures of order but the very activity of knowing, and this plunges the reader into the profoundest kind of communication. Quoting Novalis, Carlyle says that "it is certain my Belief gains quite *infinitely* the moment I can convince another mind thereof" (p. 272), but the term *convince* need not be taken to mean "domination." We need to be convinced only of the richness of the Belief, of the dynamic and searching nature of its activity; that is, the great writer convinces us not so much by the content, the *what*, of his discourse but by the process, the *how*, of its saying. We are not bound to believe *what* he believed but *as* he believed, to be awakened to the extraordinary force of his engagement as man, his commitment as writer, whereby he projects himself into (and, because of his originality, out of), his own historical point in time.

The romanticism that promotes such a theory is itself a daring philosophical commitment. It has been both fondly and derisively characterized as a fall from grace, and, in a way, so it is. For the romantic like Carlyle, through the irony of his discourse, there is an implicit admission that the Word of God has fallen to the level of man's language. It is, then, man who creates man and his world through his acts of articulation. But this creation is thereby subject to time itself, which necessitates a continual reproduction of the "me," a continual recreation of man's world. As Teufelsdröckh bemoans, a man must always "thatch anew" the very being he gives himself. This is the punishment man suffers for his fall into language, and it is, unfortunately, almost always accompanied by the sin of pride as man discovers that he is the only measure of his achievements and failures.

Modern man has, I fear, been unable to rid himself of the guilt accompanying his fall. Forced to rediscover himself at every moment, he finds himself with a most difficult role to play, and one cannot blame him for his recent efforts to deny his subjectivity, to remove his guilt-ridden "me" into the collective anonymity of laws and systems. This so-called ego loss, as a breaking down of the psychosocial structures of repression that define the ego, has sometimes set for itself a too easy enemy, for the romantic egoist never really confronted the outrageousness of repression that his self-assertiveness concealed. The romantic concept of being did become rigidly dialectical, rigidly commited to the universality of the psychosocial paradigm of master and slave;[36] and this the modern theorist of ego loss could well disassemble into its more complex and meaningful suggestiveness, but ego loss in any more confining sense comes at great sacrifice, comes only with the loss of man's articulating powers, his voice—only with the loss of true being to a world of accidental, anonymous systematicities. If man has already killed God, he is now in the process of destroying himself, of dehumanizing his very being in a desperate effort to shake off his guilt.

But is this not a greater sin than any dreamed of in romanticism? Rather than an acceptance of the accidental it is a removal of the terrifying threat of time to a meaningless, atemporal set of laws, structures, or systems of propositions that give us "orders" without "things." Romanticism, on the other hand, transforms accident into necessity, and, therefore, accident is never *only* a matter of chance but is also a principle of systematicity itself, very much in the sense that the term is used in musicology. "Accident" is the insertion of a foreign element into a natural (naturalizing?) context, a willful alteration of the key signature that breaks the pattern without resulting in chaos. It adds complexity, depth, richness, and "meaningfulness" to the passage. The foreign element is not naturalized by the dominant system of which it has become a functioning part; it is part of the totality of the piece yet is outside it; it is, then, a willful accidentalism that expresses the very possibility of change, of the unexpected and strange made compatible but not merely familiar.

Such accidentalism is the very essence of the literary artist's creativity, and indeed his being. It opens all systems to his challenge and gives space for the emergence of his voice in his text. For the literary artist there are no movements, only the possibility of movement, and, therefore, his act of articulation is not historical but expresses the very possibility of history. Joseph Conrad, addressing this problematic sense of literary creativity argued: "Fiction is history, human history, or it is nothing. But it is also more than that; it stands on firmer ground, being based on the reality of forms and the observation of social phenomena . . . .[37] There is nothing easy about this creativity, for it defies systematic reductions, critical impositions, and scholarly stagnation. Nor can it easily resolve itself into a self-satisfied egoism. In the full irony of Heidegger's paradoxical/poetical formula, one gains one's *individual* being-there only *dependently*. Interpretation of man's literary efforts to express this multiform being, moreover, demands a risky participation from the reader, the wagering of his own subjectivity against its rediscovery; but given this, the reader penetrates beyond interpretation into understanding, into a true historical communication. Furthermore, by opening outward to both life's fullness of particularity and the endless range of man's systematicities, the artist, and the texts through which he expresses himself, cannot be confined within narrow limits. The greatest literature strives to achieve a modestly privileged position in culture at large so that it is an acculturating object. Literature above all of man's endeavors expresses not so much the irreducibly human but rather the motion of humanism.

TEXT AND CONTEXT IN INTERPRETATION

The crucial issue in Foucault's rejection of romanticism is finally not the triumph or failure of the "discovery of man" but the means available for any definition of man. We find in his polemics the limits of this defining activity; man can be characterized either historically, as only a moment in time, or abstractly, as only a collectivized, dehumanized "we." To put this same dilemma in other terms, man can be defined either existentially, as a fragment of the manifold of experientiality subject to the destructive force of temporality, or rationally, as a fragment of an orderly structure arranged spatially across the flow of time. The former tends toward history and the latter toward myth, but in fact, these two perspectives are not as distinct as the infamous debate between Jean-Paul Sartre and Claude Lévi-Strauss seems to indicate.[38] Both men are prisoners of their own terminology, for in the effort to carve out a stable position each falls victim to man's fundamental inability to separate the concepts of space and time. It is, moreover, the refusal to make such a separation that marks Carlyle's *Sartor Resartus*, that informs his two orders of immensities and makes his text an exemplary literary act.

The portion of the structuralist movement that has evidenced a militant antihumanism and antiexistentialism handicaps itself in its polemical pose.The general concept of system, derived in part from Saussure's insight into the diacritical nature of the system of verbal signs, plunges man into a world of structural relationships without beginning or end, into what Foucault has called the "already begun."[34] For Derrida such a system can have no privileged center that gurantees man a world of meaningfulness and value; hence, man's human condition is a revamped version of the old existentialist conundrum of condemned freedom, only what remains is not Sartrian "nausea" but Nietzschean "freeplay."[40] As with Foucault's "relativistic systematicities," there is no room for the subject and no place for existential meaningfulness. There is no Hegelian, transcendental telos, no Freudian privileged unconscious nor Jungian archetypal guarantees, no Cassirerian origins, no Marxian idealism or materialism; all the ideological demigods of our modern world nave been pulled down, and man is left with the significance (if meaninglessness) of the system, or its manifestation in liguistic codes. Hugh M. Davidson, however, quite accurately characterizes Roland Barthes's structuralist universe of linguistic codes in a way that also reveals the significant flaw that emerges within the extreme structuralist position. The systematic nature of language codes, like the concept of system itself, "sounds and is . . . quite mechanistic, but Barthes has found a way to animate the machine. His main concern has shifted from structure to structuration, seen as an autonomous activity with a life of its own, almost independent of men, for, as he has said, man is no longer the center of structures."[41] That this "machine" is an idealized projection and its "animation" is too often merely illusory, I hope I have been able to demonstrate in my discussion of Chomsky's activity of transformation in part 2. Yet the possibility of motion within the system/machine speaks of the necessity for an animating force that the system/machine generates within itself. It is the Heideggerian opening for being or the humanistic flaw that breaks the silence of Borges's great "useless" library. Failing to give attention to this opening, structuralist writing frequently evidences a serious ennui, a placid acceptance of the world that structuralists have defined for themselves, and a frightening, almost neurotic, antipathy to the personal. As a result, structuralist critics struggle desperately to write themselves out of existence.

I hasten to add here that Foucault represents an extreme position in this movement. In many respects his protest is not unlike that of the Anglo-American classicist writers of the early twentieth century. T. E. Hulme, T. S. Eliot, Ezra Pound, and W. H. Auden, also attacked romanticism for its fragmenting individualism and its egotistical hubris. They emphasized the importance of belonging to the tradition, of comparative literary studies (as opposed to nationalistic historicism), and, as we have seen in part 3, they developed a poetic style and theory that is not unlike the structuralist theory of the impersonal writer.[42] But these classicists were finally no more than anticipators of the newer classicism that defines Foucault's approaches to culture. For Eliot the tradition was always infused with the "individual talent," and the general emphasis on comparative study was narrow if not eccentric. The impersonal stance of the writer, moreover, was never fully antiexperiential. The ideal of existential commitment, moral responsibility, and historical development pervades Eliot's poetry. It is still the artist, holding to a man-centered, post-Kantian universe, who must strive for the vision of the saint. If Eliot finally embraces a system of universal significance, it is an orthodox, Christian scheme dominated by a god devoted to man and not to the expansive cosmos.

Foucault's concept of the "already begun" and Derrida's

parallel idea of the freeplay of language codes (both men's militant antihumanism and antisubjectivism) clearly reflect the influence of Lévi-Strauss on the human sciences, but Lévi-Strauss is far less radical (as Derrida laboriously points out), far less narrow in his perspective. Rather than a sweeping dismissal of romanticism, his polemical focus has been directed primarily against a specific development of romanticism: against the subjectivist vision of French existentialism. This has been a favorite target for Foucault as well; his concept of the already begun inverts the infamous idea, articulated by Sartre, that "existence precedes essence."[43] The effect of Foucault's argument is to rob existentialism of the crucial emphasis Sartre wants to place on the necessity of individual commitment and responsibility, of the very possibility of willed progress or revolution, but it is Lévi-Strauss who most instructively engages Sartre in debate. For Lévi-Strauss, the idea of the already begun is more pervasive than the somewhat restrictive cultural concept advanced by Foucault; it springs from his early discussions of the idea of "mana" and is developed into his general theory of the "zero-signifier" or the idea of a "surplus of signification" that I discussed in part 1. Man's existence, or perhaps better stated, man's self-consciousness, is preceded by a kind of "essence," Lévi-Strauss argues, in the form of a structured cosmology. It is not clear whether this precedence is merely a matter of a preset in the mind (an innate structuring capacity) or a system much vaster than man into which he is born but over which he has little command. In either case, the structuring potential for meaningfulness engulfs man with a systematicity far more powerful than his finite consciousness.

It is perhaps easier (and surely appropriate) to describe Lévi-Strauss's concept by contrasting it with Cassirer's more romantic idea of "mana." Cassirer defines "mana" as a "supernatural power." "In this light, the whole existence of things and the activity of mankind seem to be embedded, so to speak, in a mythical 'field of force,' an atmosphere of potency which permeates everything, and which may appear in concentrated form in certain extraordinary objects, removed from the realm of everyday affairs, or in specially endowed persons, such as distinguished warriors, priests, or magicians."[44] This field of force Cassirer sees as anonymous and pervasive, present in many societies no matter how remote from one another in time and space. It is the "background against which definite daemonic or divine images can take shape."[45] On this level, Cassirer is not far afield from Lévi-Strauss who sees mana as a floating signifier, an indeterminate *potential* meaningfulness that makes possible our lower level concentration of its power into particular, nameable concepts. Both men agree that this power is beyond mere words; it is a mystical realm of silence.

But at this point the two diverge sharply. Cassirer thinks of mana in mythico-religious terms. It is the ground of consciousness that emerges along with man's first traumatic awareness of the self as separate from the all-embracing and anonymous other. Mana-consciousness has both a positive and negative aspect; it is expressive of the desire for oneness, for a return to the comforting womb of Nature on the one hand, and of repulsion, separation, and taboo on the other. It is a virtually irrational sense of loss and gain, which for Cassirer is a condition of consciousness that can be transcended only at the other extreme of man's full development by his powers of rational projection. Language, we should remember, operates between these extremes, between the poetic level of pure metaphor and the prosaic level of logical metonymy. For Lévi-Strauss mana is not a condition of consciousness but the prior context for consciousness. The floating signifier (mana as a field of force) is discovered by man, as infinitely functional, when he comes to consciousness (an ever-present awakening, not a historical event). As a result it remains an anonymous context that confers on man no privileged position in the cosmos. Rather than focusing attention on man as the language user who struggles to transcend himself (and his language through language), Lévi-Strauss reduces man to a mere part of the grand schema that precedes and survives him. This leads him specifically to reject all those subjectivist philosophies of reflexive self-consciousness that attribute to man the responsibility for creating his world (Cassirer) or the responsibility for projecting a better world (Sartre).

On the crucial issue of man's active role in the universe, therefore, Lévi-Strauss and Sartre find themselves grasping diametrically opposed points on a spinning wheel, but one cannot help noting that these points are positions without particular privilege on the same circle. Despite their differences, both espouse very similar propositions with regard to man's present condition as man. Lévi-Strauss's cosmological vision posits that man was born into an a priori systematicity; only man's self-delusion has caused him to fall into egoism and selfishness, and has bolstered him with the false hope of progress. Man is enslaved by his institutions, not the least of which are those evolved from the structure of language; he is trapped by his culture, which is no more than a corruption of his egalitarian, economical, and ecological myths.[46] Sartre finds man in the middle stages of his development from savagery. Contrary to Lévi-Strauss's lingering Rousseauism, Sartre sees man's natural state in a Hobbesian perspective, as warring and exploitative. Man's freedom from a priori values and meanings (like Ivan Karamozov's claim that without God all is legitimate) allows him selfishly to exploit others in order to satisfy his own need, to fill his preternatural lack. Culture has become, then, a systematic enslavement of the many by the few. For both Sartre and Lévi-Strauss man is enslaved, and for both, some remedy must be found in an ideal world.

If there is a real difference between these views it arises from their prophetic implications. Lévi-Strauss seeks for man a freedom not inferior to that posited by Sartre; only, for Lévi-Strauss, that freedom is freedom from Sartre's historicism and dread of responsible choice. Sartre argues that man is uniquely man "because he is able to be historical" (wherein history is no prior condition for man); man is uniquely man because he can project for himself a future that is better than his present.[47] Sartre's fear of Lévi-Strauss's anthropology is one with his fear of all gnosticism. He challenges man to free himself from the enslavement of his institutions, to transcend himself and ultimately his bound historicity. If he is somewhat pessimistic about man's chances, it seems more to reflect a distrust of easy solutions and totalizing, fatalistic systems, than the "mythizing of history" charged to him by Lévi-Strauss. For both men history carries a burden of suffering.

Yet I am tempted to argue that, despite their many differences, the terms of the existentialist-structuralist debate have actually drawn the two men closer together. Sartre argues persuasively that the true role of his existence philosophy is to act as a dialectical challenge to Lévi-Strauss's anthropology.

> Anthropology will deserve its name only if it replaces the study of human objects by the study of the various processes of becoming-an-object. Its role is to found its *knowledge* on rational and comprehensive non-knowledge; that is, the historical totalization will be possible only if anthropology understands itself instead of ignoring itself. To understand itself, to understand the other, to exist, to act, are one and the same movement which founds direct, conceptual knowledge upon indirect, comprehensive knowledge but without ever leaving the concrete—that is, history or, more precisely, the one who *comprehends what he knows*. This perpetual dissolution of intellection in comprehension and, conversely, the perpetual redescent which introduces comprehension into intellection as a dimension of *rational knowledge* at the heart of knowledge is the very ambiguity of a discipline in which the questioner, the question, and the questioned are one.[48]

Lévi-Strauss, unlike some of his followers, has never wholly left the ambiguity of his discipline. In *Tristes tropiques*, perhaps his greatest book, he seeks to write himself out of existence in a positive action, by an intense self-consciousness that allows him to dissolve his self in comprehension without denying the countermovement that introduces comprehension into his very subjective experience. The structuralist methodology of Lévi-Strauss does not deny existence any more than Sartre's existence philosophy ignores the comprehensive abstract *knowledge* of anthropology. The following passage from the *Scope of Anthropology* reveals the extent to which Lévi-Strauss's definition of a "pure anthropology" finds its articulation in personal, particularized experience.

> Of all the sciences [anthropology] is without a doubt unique in making the most intimate subjectivity into a means of objective demonstration. We really can verify that the same mind which has abandoned itself to the experience and allowed itself to be moulded by it becomes the theatre of mental operations which, without suppressing the experience, nevertheless transforms it into a model which releases further mental operations. In the last analysis, the logical coherence of these mental operations is based on the sincerity and honesty of the person who can say, like the explorer bird of the

> fable, "I was there; such-and-such happened to men; you will believe you were there yourself," and who in fact succeeds in communicating that conviction.[49]

Those who attack the philosophers of existence by claiming that experience is an illusion are themselves deeply deluded by their vision of orderliness. There is no such blindness in the philosophy of Lévi-Strauss.

I return now once more to my claim that literature is a privileged form of discourse. This is not to say that literature has any direct line to Truth nor that the literary work encompasses more of life more accurately than other human endeavors. My claim is essentially a modest, if important, one: that literature is a peculiar kind of human endeavor that can be defined only in terms of its own experiential value. It is a part of the totality of human history and Knowledge, coextensive with many other parts, yet irreducible in its insistence on its own finite existence. It is the purpose of literature, however, to constantly remind us that we belong to a complex world of meanings and values where choice and responsibility are the burdens of our humanity. No system, no totalized structure, however grand, can relieve us of our humanity. If Lévi-Strauss teaches us that man dwells in a world that was not intentionally made for man's benefit, we are admonished even more strongly that man must assume his commitment to himself and that world, and Lévi-Strauss has provided not a refutation of Sartre nor a denial of the privilege of literary humanism, but a plea that man and the literary endeavors he so persistently projects must accept the role assigned to them. In such a world no action is trivial.

Specifically in part 2, and frequently elsewhere in this essay, I have associated literature with the realm of language itself, as occupying a middle position between Cassirer's two extremes of conscious activity: the lower level of ineffable, indeterminate experience and the upper level of ineffable, determinate, and transcendental knowledge. Literature embraces the conflict between these realms within the freeplay of metaphor and metonymy, risking the irrational obsession with particulars on the one hand and the rational obsession with universals on the other hand. It sways between the radicalism of anarchy and the radicalism of conservatism, but it is never wholly one or the other. It is wrong, I believe, to confuse literature with pure perception, philosophy, myth, or history, but it is blindly narrow to forget that literature, as a quintessential testing of language's capacity for meaning, touches all of these realms of experientiality and discourse. Literature is not, therefore, mere language; it is not a particular kind of game played by an eccentric manipulator of language's codes. Literature has a privileged role among all discourses precisely because it embraces, at all times, the extreme possibilities of self-consciousness and anonymity.

This is why neither a pure romanticism nor a pure classicism, neither an existentialism nor a structuralism, is adequate to a fully developed literary hermeneutics. It is more instructive to look at the impurities of such theories, for here one senses the deeply humanistic urges in both Sartre and Lévi-Strauss reaching toward one another. Even if literary discourse is not "mirrored" experience, nor history, nor myth, it may be said to be a profound imitation of all three. The literary artist is far more self-conscious than the philosopher or historian, far more so, for example, than the exaggerated picture of the objective, scientific anthropologist painted by some misguided followers of Lévi-Strauss. (It is this critical self-consciousness, the lure of metaphor, that infuses *Tristes tropiques* with its powerful literary qualities.) A fear of "literariness" has led Barthes and Foucault to posit ideal worlds and to blindly live in them; it has distorted the creative talents of John Barth into the writing of novels about novels. These men have failed to learn one crucial lesson taught by the structuralist ideology that they, in their different ways, espouse—a lesson forcefully emphasized by Derrida. We are all victims of language's enslaving tendencies; we are trapped by the "prison-house" of language,[50] bound off from reality and truth by what Sartre calls our fetishizing of the "word." All language, I believe, reaches toward authentic experience at one extreme and toward totalizing systematicity at the other, but it is confessedly inadequate to both. Literature, by its very nature, resists fetishizing by calling attention to itself as both a possibility for articulation to experience and as a fragmentary, degenerate medium that resists such articulation.

In his recent study of what he calls "structural autobiography" Jeffrey Mehlman argues rather convincingly that Sartre's philosophy represents a kind of egoistic martyrdom. In *The Words* Sartre's obsessive concern with his "lack of a father," his lack of a "supergo" as he calls it,[51] disguises a mode of philosophical self-justification. It is a form of psychic "resistance" to the Symbolic Order (the Oedipal father-function), which intensifies and explains the egoism of Sartre's perspective as *pour soi*. The missing father, the missing cultural order that the father symbolizes, results in what Sartre calls the overpowering of *de trop*, the "contingency" of experience that Sartre's alter ego, Roquentin, reacts to with "nausea."[52] Mehlman has clearly identified certain philosophical and psychological excesses in Sartre's thought, but those excesses are, in fact, countered in the later developments of Sartre's philosophy. The old existentialist idea of man's alienation, the necessity of commitment to the subjectivity of the "other" was essentially a static dialogistics, although one impregnated with experiential meaningfulness. Sartre has now evolved a more complex sense of this dialogue by transforming the old binary confrontation into a trinary structure of communication. The self-other conflict takes place only in the context of identifiable sociohistorical structures. Fredric Jameson, speaking of the *Critique de la raison dialectique*, describes the importance of this advance. "By showing that interpersonal experience can never precede group experience, it immediately forces the argument of the *Critique* to transcend the individualistic level at which the analyses of *Being and Nothingness* had been undertaken, and moves at once to the ways in which the solitary individual tries to overcome his ontological and socioeconomic weakness by the invention of collective acts and collective units."[53] Of most importance here is the overthrow of the rigid "existence-precedes-essence" formula of the early philosophy. Essences creep into this new schema in the form of cultural-historical structures, and if Levi-Strauss is correct, such experiential-historical systems are always in an organic relationship with the universalizing mythic structures that are pervasive in human society.

The tensions besetting the individual subject, therefore, are both personal (I-thou dialogues) and collective, and at present I see no way (and no need) to resolve them or collapse them into a unity. This is the basis of man's finitude (a rather orthodox definition of man that both Sartre and Lévi-Strauss profess), and it is this finitude that the finite literary text reproduces. Every literary artist (the term is unavoidably honorific) is necessarily committed and revolutionary, but commitment and revolution mean neither existential aloneness nor militant iconoclasm. If man is trapped in the prison-house of language, enslaved by his cultural institutions, it is the freeplay of signifiers within the structure that enables the anonymous to give way to the emergence of being—even to the thrust toward identity (whatever the mixed blessing such a confirmation bestows). One cannot simply renounce one's position in culture, and one must not live blindly and anonymously in culture's givens. The former is a willful denial of finitude, a dehumanizing surrender of the particularity assigned to man by a world he did not create but of which he is a *distinct part*. Such a denial is an expression of the sinful pride of romantic egoism wherein man loses both his sense of belonging and his power to alter the terrifying state of his existential alienation. This is the fate of Faulkner's Ike McCaslin; his blindness to the consequences of his withdrawal from life traps him more forcefully than ever in the perpetuation of the very evils he sought to end. No matter how admirable his goals as they are presented in the abstract, they are impotent at best—and destructive at worst—when they achieve no being through action. On the other side one cannot "decide for" ego loss, for anonymity; any such decision is an assertion of the ego, however faintly so. We should again recall Borges's dilemma in "The Library of Babel"; his convincing demonstration that man cannot articulate his own nonexistence without breaking the silence of that nonexistence. Once more I will call on Heidegger to describe the situation. "Saying [in the sense I have used the term *langage*, as system or design] is in need of being voiced in the word. But man is capable of speaking only insofar as he, belonging to saying, listens to Saying, so that in resaying it he may be able to say a word. That needed usage and this resaying lie in that absence of something in common which is neither a mere defect nor indeed anything negative at all." From the point of view of the "subject," we cannot "know" the nature of *langage* (Saying); that is a transcendental view like Wittgenstein's idea of *logische Raum*. That is, also, "not a defect . . . but rather an advantage by which we are favored with a special realm, that realm where we, who are needed and used to speak language, dwell as *mortals*."[54]

Our discussion here returns us one more time to Faulkner's

story "Pantaloon in Black" whose pivotal function in the text of the novel illustrates the very principle I am trying to define. As the reader juxtaposes the worlds of Rider and the sheriff, he experiences the tension between the individualized hero (whose identity cannot be reduced to generalized history) and the sheriff's stereotyping of that hero into an anonymous cultural pattern. Through the agonizing struggle of Faulkner's metaphorical/metonymical style, an agony that reproduces the profound feelings of his hero, the moments of expansive meaningfulness held precariously against the inevitable flow of time, we see Rider emerge as a particular, individual being out of the buzz and flux of the world in which he dwells. The sheriff's reductions of this hard-won identity are irritating, and morally reprehensible, but they are the means through which we experience Faulkner's purposeful "accidentalism," the insertion of a particularized, individual element into a systematic world that can neither absorb nor reject it. This is the "gift" of *langage*, that its place of dwelling is for all men, that belonging is truly egalitarian. The sheriff's troubled questioning is evidence of this intrusion and serves to intensify our awareness of Rider's heroic "presence."

Moreover, sweeping across the full range of language's capabilities, from defamiliarized, metaphoric individuality to demythologized, metonymic anonymity, "Pantaloon in Black" is a paradigm of the "finite text." Literature's privileged finitude will allow us neither the illusion that the work is a discrete, organic object with symbolic pretensions nor a game of transforming existing codes into pale shadows of themselves. Literary discourse is a radical version of what Ricoeur calls a "language-event"; it is temporally specific (finite), proclaims a subjective voice, reveals the world of endless systematicities as its background, and addresses itself dynamically, hermeneutically, to a reader.[55]

The finite text is not, of course, simply ephemeral. It is not an object in any literal sense. Its finitude, its Heideggerian coming into being, derives from its holding in tension two infinities of different orders. Literature resists the infinite particularities of discrete metaphors by embedding them in the infinitely expansive orderliness of metonymy. Such a text is the result of a delicate balance, of the creative labors of the writer manifest in his style. At this point, therefore, we must abandon the narrow conception of hermeneutics (with its comforting scientific methodology) advocated by Ricoeur, Betti, and Hirsch. The text, itself inadequate to experience, to the orderly discourses of history and to myth, nevertheless offers itself as a focus for them all, and as a consequence, interpretation defies precise methodology. Literature's privileged functioning invites rather than closes off the vast worlds of moral and political action, scientific and philosophical thought. It tests the potential meaningfulness of all systems by speaking them to particular experience, and threatens its readers with an awareness of "immensities" of radically different kinds. If the text has no ontic status, it is surely ontological; if it embodies no single system of knowledge, it is nonetheless epistemological in its design.

Among the immensities of man's world, literature can achieve the enduring qualities of its finite being only through its weakness. Not in its dependence on ink and paper, but in spite of its dependence on these materials, does the dynamic force of the work rise to the status of text; in the act of articulation literature's privileged status is earned. No longer can we think of literature as an ideal ordering of life's chaotic plenitude; it is frequently that, but it is also and always a challenge to its own ordering powers. In this it presents us not life, but an experience that belongs to life; its privileged status comes not from its power to sum up and round off experience, but from the fact of its difference. Literature belongs to culture but it is not merely a reflection of it; it belongs to language but it is not merely language. It is the rightful place of human action, the place of the articulation of the freedom to be and to belong, and of the concern that all men owe to this ideal of freedom. This power of weakness Shakespeare, perhaps the most enduring writer of the western world, knew well.

> Since brass, nor stone, nor earth, nor boundless sea,
> But sad mortality o'ersways their power,
> How with this rage shall beauty hold a plea,
> Whose action is no stronger than a flower?
> O! how shall summer's honey breath hold out
> Against the wrackful siege of battering days,
> When rocks impregnable are not so stout,

> Nor gates of steel so strong, but Time decays?
> O fearful meditation! where, alack,
> Shall Time's best jewel from Time's chest lie hid?
> Or what strong hand can hold his swift foot back?
> Or who his spoil of beauty can forbid?
> O! none, unless this miracle have might,
> That in black ink my love may still shine bright.
>
> Sonnet 65

Here the personal experience holds its own in the dynamic qualities of the poet's art, in the fragility of the poem as substance, for that ink and paper are no more than a rough but essential manifestation of the true poem, the power of feeling and thought, personal experience and abstract idea, the "trace" of one who was (and "is") there, the mark of Friday's footprint.

Notes

Part 1

1. Northrop Frye, *Anatomy of Criticism* (Princeton, 1957), see particularly pp. 33-52. See also Angus Fletcher, "Utopian History and the *Anatomy of Criticism*," in *Northrop Frye in Modern Criticism*, ed. Murray Krieger (New York, 1966).

2. See Northrop Frye, "Myth, Fiction, and Displacement," *Fables of Identity* (New York, 1963).

3. Fearing the confusion of literature and myth, John J. White, in *Mythology in the Modern Novel* (Princeton, 1971), manages no more than a revised allusionism; see particularly chap. 1.

4. Claude Lévi-Strauss, *The Raw and the Cooked*, trans. John and Doreen Weightman (New York, 1969), p. 6.

5. Ernst Cassirer, *An Essay on Man*, (New Haven, 1944), p. 87; see also G. S. Kirk's discussion of Cassirer in *Myth: Its Meaning and Function in Ancient and Other Cultures* (Cambridge and Berkeley, 1973), pp. 11-13, 31.

6. Claude Lévi-Strauss, *Tristes tropiques*, trans. John Russell (New York, 1972), pp. 326-28, 390-92.

7. See Fredric Jameson, "Metacommentary," *PMLA* 86 (January 1971): 9-18.

8. Ludwig Wittgenstein, *Tractatus Logico-Philosophicus* (London, 1922).

9. Lévi-Strauss, *The Raw and the Cooked*, p. 12.

10. The term *function* has been frequently contrasted with the term *form*; the former, therefore, implies movement, dynamics, and the latter implies stasis, shape, a closed system. In fact, I am not sure that the two can be so easily separated, for "form" carries with it the idea of "informing" or the activity of creating form; its function is to come into being and hold its being or shape against the ever present threat of formlessness.

11. See Jeffrey Mehlman, "The Floating Signifier: From Lévi-Strauss to Lacan," *Yale French Studies* 48 (1972):10-37.

12. Noam Chomsky, "Form and Meaning in Natural Languages," *Language and Mind* (New York, 1972).

13. Jacques Derrida, "Structure, Sign, and Play in the Discourse of the Human Sciences," in *The Languages of Criticism and the Sciences of Man*, eds. R. Macksey and E. Donato (Baltimore, 1970).

14. I use the term *accommodation* here as one of a pair (including *assimilation*) defined by Jean Piaget; see his *Structuralism*, trans. C. Maschler (New York, 1968), p. 63. This idea of surplus of experientiality seems to be what the recent structuralist movement most ardently wants to deny. There is, therefore, an antirealism and antiexistentialism in structuralists as widely different from one another as Derrida, Foucault, and Barthes. I am willing to accept the idea, taken from Lévi-Strauss, that "the [external, experiential] universe is never charged with sufficient meanings and [that] the mind always has more [potential] meanings available than there are objects to which to relate them." See Lévi-Strauss, *Structural Anthropology*, trans. C. Jacobson and B. G. Schoepf (Garden City, 1967), p. 178. Yet the idea of a surplus of signifier (potential meaningfulness) implies, to use an old metaphor, a voracious vacuum that strives to be filled. I would, then, get the "experientially real" back into the system through a naive view of "meaning" (to be discussed at length below). The performative act of articulation is an assertion of "being-there," an assertion of one's "self" into an existential dimension. Meaning arises only in this activity (even if it does not speak aloud or write it down), and we find that we never fully exhaust either the infinite potential of the system nor the (at least seemingly) infinite supply of particularized, "experience" (in the Kantian sense), the supply of "events" to which the system can be applied.

15. G. Charbonnier, *Conversations with Claude Lévi-Strauss* (London, 1969), p. 55.

16. I reflect here Jean Piaget's definition of what he calls "constructivism," *Structuralism*, p. 13.

17. In *The Scope of Anthropology* Lévi-Strauss seems to express regret for the traditional split in hermeneutic theory between the positivistic, descriptivistic, logical methodology and an intuitionist, mystical, even irrationalist approach. Interpretation in its fullest sense involves both descriptive "analysis" and intuitive "understanding." For the anthropologist, he says, "logical certainty is not enough," and he argues for the role of "empathy," the "trying" of "intimate experiences of another upon oneself," which is "less a proof, perhaps, than a guarantee." (Lévi-Strauss, *The Scope of Anthropology*, trans. S. O. and R. A. Paul [London, 1967], p. 16; see also Richard E. Palmer, *Hermeneutics* [Evanston, 1969] on the various hermeneutical methodologies.)

18. Lévi-Strauss, *The Raw and the Cooked*, p. 2.

19. See Mary Louise Pratt, *Toward a Speech Act Theory of Literary Discourse* (Bloomington, 1977), pp. 103–4, and Pierre Macherey, *Pour une théorie de la production littéraire* (Paris, 1971) in his discussion of a literary "contract."

20. Lévi-Strauss, *The Raw and the Cooked*, pp. 10–18.

21. Ibid., p. 28.

22. Martin Heidegger, "The Origin of the Work of Art," in *Poetry, Language, Thought*, trans. A. Hofstadter (New York, 1971), pp. 44–45.

23. Lévi-Strauss, *The Raw and the Cooked*, p. 28.

24. Ernst Cassirer, *The Philosophy of Symbolic Forms* II, trans. R. Manheim (New Haven, 1955), p. 13.

25. The best expression of this paradox, I believe, is in the remarkable insistence of contemporary structuralists (Lévi-Strauss, Foucault, Chomsky) that "system" or "structure" does not imply sameness or conformity. Following the philosophy of Gilles Deleuze, structure is seen to arise through "difference"—on the basis of making systematic distinctions. It is an idea of enormous importance to social and political ideology, for it tends to counter the argument that immersion into the collective whole necessitates a surrender of personal identity (as in some forms of totalitarian Marxism). The issue of "individual" versus "system" is a very complicated one. In a fascinating article, "Of Structuralism and Literature," in *Velocities of Change*, ed. R. Macksey (Baltimore, 1974), Eugenio Donato discusses the theories of Lévi-Strauss and Jacques Lacan, defining how each presents a different view of the individual's assertion of identity. For Lévi-Strauss (particularly in his *Elementary Structures of Kinship*) Donato says the "*ego* is spoken by system but *ego* does not speak the system" (p. 162). In the societies studied by Lévi-Strauss there is a peculiar division between the individual and his function (identity conferring) in the social system (kinship), and Lévi-Strauss is most interested in describing the latter, even to the point that identity seems determined by the individual's function in a closed system of genealogical relationships. My interest in the myth singer as individual is quite different and somewhat more simplistic. His function is "special" and identity conferring. He is, in one sense, a protector of the system; he preserves the elaborate differential character of its systematicity by meeting the eventualities of the experiential world with the infinite terms of the myth's explanatory power, by localizing the system. In this, and in all cases of individual functioning in the system, it is perhaps justifiable to claim that the ego preserves some of its own individuality by virtue of its function. Systematicity does not absorb the individual but projects an identity for him. The essence of such a system is not homogeneity, but difference. This idea leads Lévi-Strauss to speculate that "men can coexist on condition that they recognize each other as being all equally, though differentially, human" (*Tristes tropiques*, p. 149). A society unable to do so will, I think, either subordinate the individual to sameness or reduce the vast majority of individuals to absolute subservience to the ruling few.

26. See Elli Köngäs Maranda, "Five Interpretations of a Melanesian Myth," *Journal of American Folklore* 86: 3–13; see also the classic text by Albert B. Lord, *The Singer of Tales* (New York, 1973), particularly p. 4. That there is a significant element of what we traditionally call "creative" genius in such performances seems undeniable, but we had best be careful about such honorific titles when applied to myth singers, tellers of epic poems, or even writers of literary texts. I am, I believe, moving toward the position of Roland Barthes when he argues that "there exists, of course, an art of the storyteller: it is the ability to generate narratives (messages) based on the structure (the code); this art corresponds to the notion of *performance* as defined by Chomsky, and it is far remote from the notion of authorial 'genius' Romantically conceived as a

personal, hardly explicable, secret" ("An Introduction to the Structural Analysis of Narrative," *New Literary History* 6 (1975): 238, fn. 2). The degree of remoteness or nearness of my theory to romantic "genius" is a trivial question, but my sense of the performative act of storytelling carries with it the idea of asserting oneself existentially into the world, into being there. It is not mere "repetition" but repetition-toward, repetition that informs through the nonreversible act of individual *parole*.

27. By "occasion" I mean not simply the appointed ritual event but the broad historical and geographical milieu of the performance. In terms of language it is similar to what R. Jakobson calls "context" ("Closing Statement: Linguistics and Poetics," in *Style in Language*, ed. T. Sebeok [Cambridge, Mass., 1960], pp. 350–77), the referential dimension of language that brings into the structure of the speech act the full range of the speaker's empirical being. The occasion encompasses the threat of surplus experience, the "too much" reality, that seems to defy the totalizing drive of structure.

In effect I am rejecting the antiexistentialism of Jacques Derrida ("Structure, Sign, and Play") or perhaps reintroducing the experiential into the systematicities that Derrida borrows from Lévi-Strauss.

28. Lévi-Strauss, *The Scope of Anthropology*, p. 19.

29. I do not wish to minimize the distinction between oral and written modes of articulation; I will take up this issue in more detail in part 2.

30. This makes the writer an imitation of what Lévi-Strauss calls a *bricoleur*, the craftsman-artist who composes his work out of the bits and pieces of materials that are found "at hand" (Claude Lévi-Strauss, *The Savage Mind* [Chicago, 1968], pp. 16–22).

31. See Cleanth Brooks, *William Faulkner: The Yoknapatawpha Country* (New Haven, 1963).

32. The chronology of Faulkner's career, therefore, results in an expansive sense of the province of Yoknapatawpha County. Because Faulkner must create the occasion for each performance-work, he both repeats and adds to the details of the background. In the process he also creates a sense of change, diachrony, or history; it is not, however, a simple linear, homogeneous history, but cumulative, multicentered, and experiential. See my "History, Presence, and the Limits of Genre Criticism," MMLA *Bulletin* (Fall 1973), pp. 38–54.

33. This theme is taken up in detail in David L. Minter, *The Interpreted Design as a Structural Principle in American Prose* (New Haven, 1969); see particularly chap. 9.

34. See Susanne K. Langer, *Feeling and Form* (New York, 1953).

35. Frye, *Anatomy of Criticism*; see particularly the second essay, "Ethical Criticism: Theory of Symbols," pp. 71–130.

36. José Ortega y Gasset, *History as a System and Other Essays Toward a Philosophy of History* (New York, 1961), p. 216.

37. William Faulkner, *Faulkner in the University*, ed. F. L. Gwynn and J. L. Blotner (New York, 1959), pp. 3–4, 273.

38. Roberto DaMatta, "Myth and Anti-myth among the Timbira," in *Structural Analysis of Oral Tradition*, ed. P. and E. K. Maranda (Philadelphia, 1971), pp. 271–91.

39. See Walter Brylowski, *Faulkner's Olympian Laugh* (Detroit, 1968), for an excellent treatment of the traditional mythical approaches in Faulkner criticism.

40. An earlier story, "A Justice," details how Sam got his name and, not incidentally, gives us fuller information on Sam's mixed racial heritage. Sam was originally called "Had-two-fathers," an interesting bit of "doubling" that Ike seems unaware of in *Go Down, Moses*. In the earlier story it is not Ike who listens to Sam's tales but Quentin Compson; by changing the characters and shortening Sam's name Faulkner rather cleverly conceals information that would surely strike Ike as significantly parallel to the racial confusion in his own family. But the contrast between the two family histories is very significant for the reader in separating the worlds in which the two characters dwell. Sam's doubled patronym is a form of "dispersion," a kind of denial of the importance of direct male-line descent. The world of Sam's ancestors was remarkably free in the use of proper names; the central figure of "A Justice," Ikkemotubbe, adopts and casts off names at will. Ikkemotubbe "solves" a dispute over Sam's parentage by calling him "Had-two-fathers." On the other hand, Ike's discovery of a genealogical doubling through incest in the McCaslin family intensifies and emphasizes the importance of direct male-line descent.

41. William Faulkner, *Go Down, Moses*, Modern Library Edition (New York, 1942). Page references to this edition are given in the text.

42. We might claim here a literary implementation of the now famous Sapir-Whorf hypothesis: that Sam's language represents a different reality from that of Ike. "The worlds in which different societies live are distinct worlds, not merely the same world with different labels attached" (Edward Sapir, *Language* [New York, 1921], p. 209). This hypothesis has been called into some doubt by Jane and William Bright, "Semantic Structures in Northwestern California and the Sapir-Whorf Hypothesis," *American Anthropologist* 67 (October 1965): 249–58, but as yet it provides insight into the cultural dimension of language usage. It is a point I will refer to in future discussions of the power of language to constitute the world in which we dwell.

43. In "A Justice" Sam's father is not Ikkemotubbe, and Sam has no hereditary claim to being chief. But the burden of this early story is in itself a denial of such hereditary rights. Ikkemotubbe usurps the position of chief through "magic" and intimidation.

44. Sam is a Chickasaw, a tribe that had a "deer" clan. See Alexander C. Kern, "Myth and Symbol in the Criticism of Faulkner's 'The Bear,'" in *Myth and Symbol: Critical Approaches and Evaluations*, ed. B. Slote (Lincoln, 1963), pp. 152–61.

45. See Claude Lévi-Strauss, "The Structural Study of Myth," in *Structural Anthropology*, pp. 202–28. Here Lévi-Strauss demonstrates how such a theme enters into the structure of myth and literature.

46. Cassirer, *The Philosophy of Symbolic Forms* II, p. 175.

47. Ibid., p. 177.

48. Ibid., p. 51.

49. Ibid., p. 35.

50. Harold Toliver, *Animate Illusions: Explorations of Narrative Structure* (Lincoln, 1974), particularly pp. 37–49.

51. Émile Benveniste, *Problèmes de linguistique générale* (Paris, 1966), p. 25 (my translation).

52. Again we should note here that in "A Justice" the role of Ike is filled by another of Faulkner's storyteller/story-listener characters, Quentin Compson. The change is interesting as a reflection of Faulkner's own stance toward his own stories. He is the teller and reteller whose versions are not always the same. But through the fact of these variations we discover the essential patterns of cultural or mythical understanding that describe the issues, the limits of Faulkner's world. The relationship between Ike and Quentin has been developed at some length by Faulkner scholars (Estella Schoenberg, *Old Tales and Talking: Quentin Compson in William Faulkner's "Absalom, Absalom!" and Related Works* [Jackson, 1977], pp. 17–20), and such a discussion is beyond the scope of this essay. Nevertheless, several general points should be noted here. The reading of Faulkner's novels in the "mode" of folktales (not *as* folktales) leads to a violation of the belief that each novel stands as an independent unit. The most problematic issue in Faulkner studies concerns the "blending" of *Absalom, Absalom!* and *The Sound and the Fury*, but the appearance of other blends (like that of Quentin and Ike) is equally important in revealing the deep patterns that weave the Faulknerian world. Just as folklore, therefore, can be said to exist "only potentially" (Pratt, pp. 9–10), so too the Faulknerian world must be seen as the horizon for every particular articulation. If Sam's stories reveal his world, the order and patterns of his way of being in the world, so too are Faulkner's stories the opening to his way of being. Crucially, the world or horizon emerges only through the actual telling without which the world remains habitual, unconscious, and mute. Storytelling is intimately involved in belonging to one's world.

53. Edmund Leach, *Genesis as Myth and Other Essays* (London, 1971), p. 27.

54. Ibid., p. 11.

55. See Carl Rowan, *South of Freedom* (New York, 1952) on the "white goddess complex," and Lillian Smith, *Killers of the Dream* (Garden City, 1963) on the confusion of women and slaves in the South's caste system. Also Elizabeth M. Kerr, *Yoknapatawpha: Faulkner's 'Little Postage Stamp of Native Soil'"* (New York, 1969), discusses at length the very social and kinship codes that I am at pains to develop here; see particularly p. 110, where she claims that the rape of a Negro woman was "regarded as a physical impossibility."

56. For an elaborate development of Jacques Lacan's rewriting of Freud's Oedipus complex, wherein the son symbolically replaces the father by taking his name, see Jeffrey Mehlman, *A Structural Study of Autobiography* (Ithaca, 1974).

57. R. D. Laing, *The Politics of the Family and Other Essays* (New York, 1972), see particularly pp. 117–24.

58. I do not wish to engage here in the ongoing debate about how widespread was the sexual abuse of female slaves in the antebellum South. Statistical factuality is not at issue. I wish only to describe a myth that was at least unconsciously functional and was a basis for a code of behavior even if most white slave owners had the decency *not* to exercise what they would, perhaps, never have questioned as a cultural privilege.

59. Charles Sanders Peirce, *Collected Papers*, vol. 2 (Cambridge, 1931–58).

60. Herbert Marcuse, *One-Dimensional Man* (Boston, 1964).

61. See Paul Davidson, "A Keynesian View of Friedman's Theoretical Framework for Monetary Analysis," in *Milton Friedman's Monetary Framework*, ed. R. J. Gordon (Chicago, 1974), pp. 90–110 for an outline of a monetary model of exchange that shows remarkable similarities with the patterns I have been developing.

62. Julia Kristeva, "La Semiologie: Science critique et/ou critique de la science," *Theorie d'ensemble* (Paris, 1968).

63. For example, this means that no black woman could substitute for a white woman in the marriage convention, a substitution that Zack Edmonds risks with Lucas's wife Mollie. Lucas, therefore, has this negative law on his side in his confrontation with Zack.

64. Gilles Deleuze and Félix Guattari, *Anti-Oedipus: Capitalism and Schizophrenia*, trans. R. Hurley, M. Seem, and H. R. Lane (New York, 1977), pp. 104, 114–15.

65. Claude Lévi-Strauss, *The Elementary Structures of Kinship*, trans. J. H. Bell and J. R. von Sturmer (Boston, 1969), see particularly chap. 1.

66. Compare Jacques Derrida on Rousseau, *Of Grammatology*, trans. G. C. Spivak (Baltimore, 1976), pp. 220–24, 260–67.

67. Lévi-Strauss, *Tristes tropiques*, particularly his discussion of the Caduveo culture, pp. 151–97.

68. Derrida, *Of Grammatology*.

69. C. G. Jung, *Four Archetypes*, trans. R. F. C. Hull (Princeton, 1959), p. p. 151.

70. I offer here a somewhat different view of "failure" as a theme in Faulkner's novels than that developed by Walter J. Slatoff, *Quest for Failure: A Study of William Faulkner* (Ithaca, 1960).

71. Cassirer, *The Philosophy of Symbolic Forms* II, p. 200, an idea he borrows from Herman K. Usener.

72. See Zeno Vendler, *Res Cogitans: An Essay in Rational Psychology* (Ithaca, 1972), p. 199.

73. The idea is taken from V. Sklovskij; see Ewa Thompson, *Russian Formalism and Anglo-American New Criticism* (The Hague, 1971), pp. 67 ff., for an excellent discussion of this point. The terms "deconstruction," "demystification," and "defamiliarization" are much in vogue of late, a fact that causes much confusion. My use of them is partly derivative and partly my own invention; the possible confusion I hope will be clarified by my text. See also R. H. Stacy, *Defamiliarization in Language and Literature* (Syracuse, 1977).

74. See Geoffrey Hartman, *Beyond Formalism* (New Haven, 1970), particularly part 1.

75. Piaget's term, see fn. 14 above.

76. See Thompson on this point, fn. 73 above.

77. See fn. 14 above.

78. Roland Barthes, *Critical Essays*, trans. R. Howard (Evanston, 1972), pp. 215, 216.

79. Paul Ricoeur, *The Symbolism of Evil*, trans. E. Buchanan (Boston, 1967), p. 18.

80. Barthes, *Critical Essays*, p. 217.

81. Leach, *Genesis as Myth*, p. 26.

82. Lévi-Strauss, *The Scope of Anthropology*.

83. Barthes, *Critical Essays*, p. 217.

84. J. L. Austin, *How to Do Things with Words* (New York, 1962). See also Jacques Derrida, "Signature Event Context," and John R. Searle, "Reiterating the Differences: A Reply to Derrida," *Glyph: Johns Hopkins Textual Studies*, 1 (Baltimore, 1977): 172–97, 198–208. See also Stanley Fish, "How to Do Things with Austin and Searle: Speech Act Theory and Literary Criticism," *MLN* 91 (1976): 983–1025, and "What Is Stylistics and Why Are They Saying Such Terrible Things about It?," *Approaches to Poetics*, ed. S. Chatman (New York, 1973), pp. 109–52.

85. Of the endless arguments against closed textuality that have come to the fore in recent years I am still most persuaded by the sociological approach of Lucien Goldmann in *The Hidden God*, trans. P. Thody (New York, 1964), particularly pp. 7–21. See also Roland Barthes's wonderful *S/Z*, trans. R. Miller (New York, 1974).

86. Barthes, *S/Z*, and Jacques Derrida, *La dissémination* (Paris, 1972) and *Of Grammatology*.

87. Lévi-Strauss, *Structural Anthropology*, p. 176.

88. E. D. Hirsch, Jr., *Validity in Interpretation* (New Haven, 1967).

89. Benveniste, *Problèmes*, p. 25: "It is in effect in and through *langue* that individual and society are mutually determined" (my translation).

90. Umberto Eco, *A Theory of Semiotics* (Bloomington, 1976), p. 172.

91. Ibid., p. 188 (italics original).

92. Ibid., p. 270.

93. Louis Althusser, *For Marx*, trans. B. Brewster (New York, 1969), pp. 62–63.

94. See Louis Althusser and Étienne Balibar, *Reading Capital*, trans. B. Brewster (New York, 1970), particularly for Althusser's development of the ideas of the "epistemological break" and "critical reading."

95. Claudio Guillén, *Literature as System* (Princeton, 1971), pp. 139–40. See also Harry Berger, Jr., "Naive Consciousness and Cultural Change: An Essay in Historical Structuralism" *Bulletin of the Midwest Modern Language Association* 6 (1973): 1–44.

96. Michel Foucault, *The Order of Things*, trans. A. M. Sheridan-Smith (New York, 1970).

97. Guillén, p. 48.

98. Cassirer, *The Philosophy of Symbolic Forms* II, p. 23.

99. For an excellent discussion of literary periods see Guillén, fn. 95 above.

100. Benveniste, p. 25.

101. I express here my substantial disagreement with the "neo-Aristotelian" school (see *Critics and Criticism* [Chicago, 1952]) and with similar views put forth by Frank Kermode in *The Sense of an Ending* (New York, 1967), see particularly pp. 133–39.

102. For an excellent discussion of history as explanation see William Dray, *Laws and Explanation in History* (London, 1957).

103. See Lévi-Strauss, *The Savage Mind*, particularly chap. 9, "History and Dialectic."

104. Barthes, "An Introduction to the Structural Analysis of Narrative," p. 261.

105. Robert Scholes, *Structuralism in Literature* (New Haven, 1974), pp. 166–67.

106. Barthes, "An Introduction to the Structural Analysis of Narrative," p. 266.

107. See Georg Lukács, *The Theory of the Novel*, trans. A. Bostock (Cambridge, 1971); Julia Kristeva, *Le texte du roman* (The Hague, 1970); Margaret Schlauch, *The Gift of Language* (New York, 1942); Arnold Kettle, *An Introduction to the English Novel* (New York, 1951).

108. Robert Weimann, *Structure and Society in Literary History* (Charlottesville, 1976), p. 259.

109. Jonathan Culler, *Structuralist Poetics: Structuralism, Linguistics, and the Study of Literature* (Ithaca, 1975), p. 203.

110. Barthes, *S/Z*, pp. 20–33.

111. Tzvetan Todorov, "Les catégories du récit littéraire," *Communications* 8 (1966): 125–51; Toliver, *Animate Illusions*.

112. Vladimir Propp, *Morphology of the Folktale*, trans. L. Scott (Austin, 1968).

113. See A. J. Greimas, *Semantique structurale* (Paris, 1966); and discussion by Scholes, *Structuralism in Literature* and Fredric Jameson, *The Prison-House of Language* (Princeton, 1972), particularly p. 126.

114. See Fredric Jameson, "Magical Narrative: Romance as Genre," *New Literary History* 7 (Autumn 1975): 135–64, and Louis A. Wagner's preface to Propp's *Morphology of the Folktale.*

115. Faulkner, *Faulkner in the University*, p. 273.

116. See Malcolm Cowley, *The Faulkner-Cowley File* (New York, 1966), p. 113. Faulkner said that "Rider was one of the McCaslin Negroes," but that fact is missing from the text itself and is relatively insignificant even if we know it while reading the story.

117. Ferdinand de Saussure, *Course in General Linguistics*, trans. W. Baskin (New York, 1966), pp. 131–34.

118. Benveniste, pp. 49–55.

119. Ibid., p. 55.

120. My emphasis on the violent disruption of metaphor as a twofold movement of presencing and absencing has parallels in the theory of Gerard Genette, particularly in what he defines as the rhetorical functioning of the "figure." See *Figures* (Paris, 1966) and the discussion of Genette in Scholes, pp. 157–67.

121. Eugenio Donato, "Of Structuralism and Literature," pp. 153–78.

122. André Bleikasten, *The Most Splendid Failure: Faulkner's "The Sound and the Fury"* (Bloomington, 1976), sees Caddy as "a figure of absence," as "an empty signifier," p. 56.

123. See Tony Tanner, *The Reign of Wonder: Naivety and Reality in American Literature* (London, 1965).

124. See Geoffrey Hartman, *Wordsworth's Poetry* (New Haven, 1964).

125. Immanuel Kant, from "The Critique of Judgment" in *Critical Theory Since Plato*, ed. Hazard Adams (New York, 1971), pp. 377–99, particularly the selections on "the sublime;" Ernst Cassirer, *Language and Myth*, trans. Susanne K. Langer (New York, 1946); James Joyce, *Dubliners* (New York, 1971); Eliseo Vivas, *The Artistic Transaction* (Columbus, 1963).

126. Roland Barthes, *The Pleasure of the Text*, trans. R. Miller (New York, 1975).

127. Sigmund Freud, "The 'Uncanny,'" *New Literary History* 7 (Spring 1976): 619–45. See also a remarkably similar definition of the uncanny in Martin Heidegger, *An Introduction to Metaphysics*, trans. R. Manheim (New York, 1961), pp. 125 ff.

128. Richard P. Adams, *Faulkner: Myth and Motion* (Princeton, 1968), p. 145. Adams appears to be speaking of the sheriff's racism.

129. Chomsky, *Language and Mind*, see fn. 12 above.

130. See T. S. Eliot, "Tradition and the Individual Talent," reprinted in *Critiques and Essays in Criticism*, ed. R. W. Stallman (New York, 1949), and Frye, *Anatomy of Criticism*.

131. John Barth, "The Literature of Exhaustion," *The Atlantic* 220 (1967): 29–35; Robert Scholes, "The Illiberal Imagination," *New Literary History* 4 (1973): 521–40.

132. See Lévi-Strauss, *The Savage Mind*, chap. 9, "History and Dialectic," and Lionel Abel, "Sartre vs. Lévi-Strauss," in *Claude Levi-Strauss: The Anthropologist as Hero*, ed. E. N. and T. Hayes (Cambridge, 1970).

133. Barth, "The Literature of Exhaustion."

134. Ricoeur, *The Symbolism of Evil*, pp. 143–48.

135. See Deleuze and Guattari, *Anti-Oedipus*.

136. Edward W. Said, *Beginnings: Intention and Method* (New York, 1975).

137. Edward W. Said, "Quest for Origins and Discovery of the Mausoleum," *Salmagundi* 12 (Spring 1970): 68-69.

138. Adams, *Faulkner: Myth and Motion*, p. 153.

139. Ricoeur, *The Symbolism of Evil*, p. 82.

140. Ibid., pp. 161-62.

141. Mircea Eliade, *Myth and Reality*, trans. W. Trask (New York, 1963).

142. See Fredric Jameson, *Marxism and Form: Twentieth-Century Dialectical Theories of Literature* (Princeton, 1971), particularly chap. 4 on Sartre.

143. The term *vision* is a difficult one. I use it here close to the sense defined by Murray Krieger, "Mediation, Language and Vision in the Reading of Literature," in *Interpretation: Theory and Practice*, ed. C. S. Singleton (Baltimore, 1969). Krieger says that he seeks to describe "the vision that comes to be created in the work *as* the work." But I am not sure that I can accept the strictures of a full-blown contextualism that limits us to the structure of the work *as* work. Vision involves, as I see it, an element of self-projection, self-creation, a coming to stand in the world. The text becomes, then, a complex embodiment of the "I" of the author as it emerges into being at a particular place and time, swirling out of the rich experiential plenitude of the author's reality and the complex myths and/or cognitive systems that in-form the culture to which he belongs.

PART 2

1. See Murray Krieger, *The New Apologists for Poetry* (Bloomington, 1963).

2. Ewa Thompson, *Russian Formalism and Anglo-American New Criticism* (The Hague, 1971), and Fredric Jameson, *The Prison-House of Language* (Princeton, 1972).

3. René Wellek, "The Literary Theory and Aesthetics of the Prague School," *Discriminations* (New Haven, 1970).

4. Leo Spitzer, *Essays on English and American Literature* (Princeton, 1962), particularly pp. 193-95.

5. Krieger, *The New Apologists.*

6. Samuel Taylor Coleridge, *Biographia Literaria*, ed. J. Metcalf (New York, 1926), p. 236.

7. Ibid., p. 194.

8. Ibid., p. 197.

9. Ibid.

10. Karl D. Uitti, *Linguistics and Literary Theory* (Englewood Cliffs, 1969), pp. 95, 104.

11. Henri Bergson, *Creative Evolution*, trans. A. Mitchell (New York, 1944).

12. Benedetto Croce, *Aesthetics*, trans. D. Ainslie (New York, 1909), and R. G. Collingwood, *The Principles of Art* (London, 1938).

13. John Crowe Ransom, "Poetry: A Note on Ontology," in *Critiques and Essays in Criticism*, ed. R. W. Stallman (New York, 1949).

14. Gilbert Ryle, "Systematically Misleading Expressions," *Proceedings of the Aristotelian Society*, 1931–32.

15. F. W. Bateson, "The Responsible Critic: Reply," in *A Selection from Scrutiny* II, ed. F. R. Leavis (Cambridge, 1968), particularly pp. 305–6.

16. Benedetto Croce, *What Is Living and What Is Dead in the Philosophy of Hegel*, trans. D. Ainslie (London, 1915), p. 89.

17. I. A. Richards, *Principles of Literary Criticism* (New York, 1925).

18. Jacques Derrida, *Of Grammatology*, trans. G. C. Spivak (Baltimore, 1976).

19. Jacques Derrida, "Structure, Sign, and Play in the Discourse of the Human Sciences," in *The Languages of Criticism and the Sciences of Man*, ed. R. Macksey and E. Donato (Baltimore, 1970).

20. Georges Poulet, "Phenomenology of Reading," *New Literary History* 1 (October 1969): 55.

21. Max Black, *A Companion to Wittgenstein's Tractatus* (Ithaca, 1964), p. 6.

22. Francis M. Cornford, *Plato's Theory of Knowledge* (New York, 1957).

23. Ibid., p. 197.

24. Ibid., pp. 310–15.

25. Gottlob Frege, "Über Sinn und Bedeutung," *Zeitschrift fur Philosophie und philosophische Kritik* (1892).

26. Aristotle, *Poetics*, in *Critical Theory since Plato*, ed. H. Adams (New York, 1971); see particularly chap. 24.

27. Ludwig Wittgenstein, *Tractatus Logico-Philosophicus* (London). Propositions are cited by number in the text.

28. Ernst Cassirer, *The Philosophy of Symbolic Forms* I, trans. R. Manheim (New Haven, 1955), p. 158.

29. Martin Heidegger, *An Introduction to Metaphysics*, trans. R. Manheim (New York, 1961), also defines the term "logos" to mean a "gathering" or "arranging."

30. Black, p. 11.

31. See Uitti, pp. 77–87, for a discussion of the Cartesian rationalist Condillac who seems to find parallels in Wittgenstein's later theory.

32. Richard Kuhns, *Structures of Experience* (New York, 1970), p. 35.

33. Jean Piaget, *Structuralism*, trans. C. Maschler (New York, 1968), p. 83.

34. Kuhns, p. 227.

35. Ibid., p. 225.

36. Ibid., p. 219.

37. Anthony Kenny, *Wittgenstein* (Cambridge, 1973), p. 93.

38. Kuhns, p. 229.

39. Ibid., p. 259.

40. Wilhelm von Humboldt, *Linguistic Variability and Intellectual Development*, trans. G. C. Buck and F. A. Raven (Coral Gables, 1971), p. 27.

See also Gerald L. Bruns, *Modern Poetry and the Idea of Language* (New Haven, 1974), particularly pp. 44–45; and Martin Heidegger, comments on Humboldt, *On the Way to Language*, trans. Peter Hertz (New York, 1971), particularly the essay "The Way to Language."

41. Kenny, p. 80.

42. Ernst Cassirer, *An Essay on Man* (New Haven, 1944), p. 145.

43. Ibid., p. 169.

44. Kenny, p. 78.

45. Ernst Cassirer, *Language and Myth*, trans. Susanne K. Langer (New York, 1946), p. 37.

46. Ibid., p. 41.

47. Bronislaw Malinowski, "The Problem of Meaning in Primitive Languages," in *The Meaning of Meaning*, by C. K. Ogden and I. A. Richards (New York, 1946).

48. Kenny, p. 85; see also Bruns, p. 26.

49. Jean Piaget, *Genetic Epistemology*, trans. E. Duckworth (New York, 1970), pp. 16–17.

50. Sigmund Freud, *Beyond the Pleasure Principle*, Norton Edition, trans. J. Strachey (New York, 1961).

51. Roland Barthes, *Elements of Semiology*, trans. A. Laver and C. Smith (New York, 1967), pp. 22–23.

52. Cassirer, *Language and Myth*, p. 57.

53. Cassirer, *Essay on Man*, p. 126.

54. Cassirer, *Language and Myth*, p. 88; see also *Essay on Man*, p. 109.

55. Kenny, p. 75: "The *Tractatus* has very little to say about change."

56. Derrida, "Structure, Sign, and Play."

57. Derrida, *Of Grammatology*, p. 238.

58. Ibid., p. 167.

59. Cassirer, *Language and Myth*, p. 58.

60. Ibid., p. 81.

61. Murray Krieger, *The Play and Place of Criticism* (Baltimore, 1967).

62. Cleanth Brooks, *The Well Wrought Urn* (New York, 1947).

63. Jonathan Culler, among others, has argued that the methods of linguistics do not "provide a method for the interpretation of literary works" (*Structuralist Poetics: Structuralism, Linguistics, and the Study of Literature* [Ithaca, 1975], p. 109). This is, of course, true, but my interest here is in the ideology that the methodology reveals, and thus in his stance toward language Chomsky tells us much about language's many functions, even poetic ones.

64. Noam Chomsky, *Cartesian Linguistics* (New York, 1966), pp. 32–33.

65. John Lyons, *Noam Chomsky* (New York, 1970), p. 120.

66. Noam Chomsky, "Current Issues in Linguistic Theory," *Janua Linguarum* 38 (London, 1964): 21.

67. Chomsky, *Cartesian Linguistics*, pp. 69–71.

68. Ibid., p. 54.

69. Ibid., p. 60.

70. Chomsky, *Language and Mind* (New York, 1972), p. 91. A similar argument from an avowedly "structuralist" point of view has more recently been made by Thomas Kuhn, *The Structure of Scientific Revolutions* (Chicago, 1970).

71. Chomsky, *Cartesian Linguistics*, p. 71.

72. Ibid., p. 35.

73. Kenny, see fn. 55 above.

74. Derrida, "Structure, Sign, and Play."

75. See Jeremy J. Shapiro, "One-Dimensionality: The Universal Semiotic of Technological Experience," in *Critical Interruptions: New Left Perspectives on Herbert Marcuse*, ed. P. Breines (New York, 1972).

76. There is no single movement here; I will simply cite works referred to elsewhere in this text by Jacques Lacan, Gilles Deleuze and Félix Guattari, Jeffrey Mehlman, R. D. Laing, and even the works of Michel Foucault, Jacques Derrida, and Claude Lévi-Strauss should be included.

77. Derrida, *Of Grammatology*, pp. 141–64.

78. Jacques Derrida, *Speech and Phenomena: Other Essays on Husserl's Theory of Signs*, trans. D. B. Allison (Evanston, 1973), pp. 94–95.

79. Ibid., p. 86.

80. Heidegger, *Introduction to Metaphysics*, pp. 53–58.

81. Evan Watkins, *The Critical Act: Criticism and Community* (New Haven, 1978), p. 86, and Derrida, *Of Grammatology*, p. 71.

82. Jacques Lacan, *Écrits: A Selection*, trans. A. Sheridan (New York, 1977), pp. 159–71. See also Anthony Wilden's discussion of Lacan's concepts of the "mirror stage" and the "Symbolic Order" in *The Language of the Self* (Baltimore, 1968).

83. Bruns, p. 242.

84. Ibid., p. 261.

85. Émile Benveniste, *Problèmes de linguistique générale* (Paris, 1966), p. 261.

86. Ibid., p. 263.

87. John R. Searle, "Reiterating the Differences: A Reply to Derrida," *Glyph: Johns Hopkins Textual Studies* 1 (Baltimore, 1977): 208.

88. Jacques Derrida, "Signature Event Context," *Glyph: Johns Hopkins Textual Studies* 1 (Baltimore, 1977).

89. Edward W. Said, *Beginnings: Intention and Method* (New York, 1975), particularly chap. 6 on Vico.

90. Piaget, *Genetic Epistemology*, pp. 8–9.

91. Piaget, *Structuralism*, p. 93.

92. Piaget, *Genetic Epistemology*, pp. 9, 47.

93. Ibid., pp. 10, 11.

94. Ibid., p. 15.

95. Ibid., p. 77.

96. Lucien Goldmann, *Pour une sociologie du roman* (Paris, 1964), p. 213; see also Robert Weimann, *Structure and Society in Literary History* (Charlottesville, 1976), p. 159.

97. Derrida, *Of Grammatology*, see fn. 77 above.

98. Ihab Hassan, *The Literature of Silence* (New York, 1967), p. 27.

99. Ferdinand de Saussure, *Course in General Linguistics*, trans. W. Baskin (New York, 1966), pp. 67 ff.

100. Claude Lévi-Strauss, *Tristes tropiques*, trans. John Russell (New York, 1972), p. 58; see also Jameson, *The Prison-House of Language*, pp. 142–43.

101. Derrida, "Structure, Sign, and Play," p. 263.

102. Wilden, pp. 240–43.

103. Ibid., p. 200.

104. Ibid., p. 264.

105. Ibid., p. 243.

106. John T. Irwin, *Doubling and Incest/Repetition and Revenge* (Baltimore, 1975).

107. Derrida, *Of Grammatology*, p. 266.

108. Benveniste, p. 131.

109. Kenneth Burke, "Literature as Equipment for Living," *Critical Theory Since Plato*, pp. 944–45.

110. Michel Foucault, *The Archaeology of Knowledge*, trans. A. M. Sheridan-Smith (New York, 1971).

111. Derrida, "Structure, Sign, and Play."

112. Lionel Trilling, *The Opposing Self* (New York, 1955).

113. Umberto Eco, *A Theory of Semiotics* (Bloomington, 1976), p. 43.

114. Ibid., p. 44.

115. Ibid.

116. Ibid., p. 58.

117. Ibid., pp. 254–56.

PART 3

1. For the debate on the meaning of the term *style* see: Nils Enkvist, "On Defining Style," in *Linguistics and Style*, ed. J. Spencer and M. Gregory (London, 1964); R. A. Sayce, "The Definition of the Term 'Style,'" *Proceedings of the Third International Comparative Literature Association* (The Hague, 1962); Seymor Chatman, "Semantics of Style," *Social Sciences Information* 6 (1967): 77–99; Roland Barthes, *Writing Degree Zero*, trans. A. Lavers and C. Smith (Boston, 1967); Donald Bryant, ed., *Rhetoric and Poetic* (Iowa City, 1965). For a debate on the relationship of linguistics and literary criticism one might start

with the following: Karl D. Uitti, *Linguistics and Literary Theory* (Englewood Cliffs, 1969); Thomas Sebeok, ed., *Style in Language* (Boston, 1960); Rene Wellek, *Discriminations* (New Haven, 1970), pp. 327-43; Nils Enkvist, "On the Place of Style in Some Linguistic Theories," in *Literary Style*, ed. S. Chatman (London, 1971); Leo Spitzer, *Linguistics and Literary History* (Princeton, 1948), pp. 1-29.

2. Spitzer, *Linguistics and Literary History*, pp. 1-29.

3. Michael Riffaterre, "Criteria for Style Analysis," *Word* 15 (1959): 155.

4. Richard Ohmann, "Generative Grammar and the Concept of Literary Style," *Word* 20 (1964): 427.

5. Louis T. Milic, "Introductory Essay," *Stylists on Style* (New York, 1969), pp. 1-24.

6. Louis T. Milic, "Information Theory and the Style of *Tristram Shandy*," in *The Winged Skull: Papers from the Lawrence Sterne Bicentenary Conference*, ed. A. H. Cash and J. M. Stedmond (Kent State University Press, 1971), pp. 237-46.

7. Gerald L. Bruns, *Modern Poetry and the Idea of Language* (New Haven, 1974), see particularly chap. 1.

8. John Crowe Ransom, *The New Criticism* (Norfolk, 1941), pp. 294-336.

9. Uitti, particularly pp. 129-30.

10. Barthes, *Writing Degree Zero*, p. 12.

11. Ibid., pp. 13, 52.

12. Jonathan Culler, *Structuralist Poetics: Structuralism, Linguistics, and the Study of Literature* (Ithaca, 1975), p. 140.

13. Ibid., p. 259.

14. Ibid., p. 133.

15. Ibid., see particularly the opening pages of chap. 3.

16. Ibid., pp. 219-25.

17. Ibid., p. 118.

18. Ibid., p. 116.

19. Ibid., see chap. 8.

20. S. R. Levin, "Deviation—Statistical and Determinate—in Poetic Language," *Lingua* 12 (1963): 218. See also Bernard Bloch, "Linguistic Structure and Linguistic Analysis," *Report of the Fourth Annual Round Table Meeting on Linguistics and Language Teaching*, 1953, particularly p. 42.

21. Ibid., p. 285.

22. S. R. Levin, "Internal and External Deviation in Poetry," *Word* 21 (1965): 233.

23. Roman Jakobson, "Two Aspects of Language and Two Types of Aphasic Disturbances," *Selected Writings*, II (The Hague, 1971), p. 259.

24. Roland Barthes, "Style and Its Image," in *Literary Style*, ed. S. Chatman (London, 1971), p. 4.

25. Harry Berger, Jr., "Naive Consciousness and Cultural Change: An Essay in Historical Structuralism," *Bulletin of the Midwest Modern Language Association* 6 (1973): 1-44.

26. Richard Ohmann, "Literature as Act," in *Approaches to Poetics*, ed. S. Chatman (New York, 1973), p. 94.

27. Uitti, p. 150.

28. Edward Sapir, *Language* (New York, 1921), pp. 246-47.

29. Sapir clearly defines a tradition that is fully developed in cultural historians like V. L. Parrington, V. W. Brooks, Edmund Wilson, and R. H. Pearce. For a discussion of this tradition see Wesley Morris, *Toward a New Historicism* (Princeton, 1972).

30. Quoted in Uitti, pp. 143-44.

31. R. H. Stacy, *Defamiliarization in Language and Literature* (Syracuse, 1977), presents a great variety of examples.

32. Martin Heidegger, *An Introduction to Metaphysics*, trans. R. Manheim (New York, 1961), p. 144.

33. Ibid.

34. Ibid.

35. See Harry Levin, *The Gates of Horn* (New York, 1963), p. 21.

36. Roy Harvey Pearce, *The Continuity of American Poetry* (Princeton, 1961), particularly pp. 12-13.

37. Roman Jakobson, "Concluding Statement: Linguistics and Poetics," in *Style in Language*, ed. T. Sebeok (Boston, 1960), p. 358.

38. S. R. Levin, "Linguistic Structures in Poetry," *Janua Linguarum* 28 (1962).

39. Ohmann, "Generative Grammar," pp. 428-30.

40. Levin, "Linguistic Structures in Poetry," p. 51.

41. William Strunk and E. B. White, *The Elements of Style* (New York, 1972), p. 43.

42. Murray Krieger, "The Ekphrastic Principle and the Still Movement of Poetry: Laokoön Revisited," *The Play and Place of Criticism* (Baltimore, 1967); see also Joseph Frank, "Spatial Form in Modern Literature," *The Widening Gyre* (New Brunswick, 1963).

43. See W. K. Wimsatt and Monroe C. Beardsley, *The Verbal Icon* (Lexington, 1954).

44. Riffaterre, "Criteria for Style Analysis," p. 139.

45. Ibid., pp. 157-58; see also W. Ullman, *Style in the French Novel* (Cambridge, 1957), pp. 2 ff.

46. Ibid., p. 167.

47. Michael Riffaterre, "Stylistic Context," *Word* 16 (1960): 207-9.

48. Spitzer, pp. 1-29.

49. I. A. Richards, *Principles of Literary Criticism* (New York, 1925), pp. 223-27.

50. Jakobson, "Two Aspects of Language," p. 259. The discussion of the metaphor/metonym interplay that I develop herein has much support in recent literary theory. For excellent practical examples see Herbert N. Schneidau, "Style and Sacrament in Modernist Writing," *The Georgia Review* (Summer 1977): 427-53, and David Lodge, *The Modes of Modern Writing: Metaphor, Metonymy, and the Typology of Modern Literature* (London, 1977).

51. Jakobson, "Concluding Statement," *Selected Writings* II (The Hague, 1971), p. 356.

52. Ibid.

53. Georg Henrik von Wright, *Explanation and Understanding* (Ithaca, 1971), p. 29.

54. Jakobson, "Concluding Statement," p. 358.

55. Jakobson, "Two Aspects of Language," p. 258.

56. Jakobson, "Concluding Statement," p. 370. It is clear that my reading of Jakobson differs somewhat from that of Murray Krieger, *Theory of Criticism* (Baltimore, 1976), particularly p. 198, fn. 23. I am arguing that metonymy is never wholly transformed into metaphor, nor should we see this as an "as if" transformation for the sake of marking the limits of the "literary." I am afraid that too often we come to believe in our "as if's" and forget that necessary "impurity" that is the basis for a rich meaningfulness.

58. Umberto Eco, *A Theory of Semiotics* (Bloomington, 1976), p. 258.

59. Mary Louise Pratt, *Toward a Speech Act Theory of Literary Discourse* (Bloomington, 1977), pp. 103-4.

60. Bruns, p. 96; see also Barthes, part 1, fn. 97.

61. Eco, p. 314; see also p. 317, fn. 1, for a list of those who have developed the concept through debate.

62. See Gilles Deleuze and Félix Guattari, *Anti-Oedipus: Capitalism and Schizophrenia*, trans. R. Hurley, M. Seem, and H. R. Lane (New York, 1972).

63. Jorge Luis Borges, "The Library of Babel," *Labyrinths* (New York, 1962), p. 58.

64. Martin Heidegger, "The Way to Language," *On the Way to Language*, trans. Peter Hertz (New York, 1971).

65. Krieger, "The Ekphrastic Principle."

66. Roland Barthes, *Sur Racine* (Paris, 1963).

67. von Wright, pp. 4-5. Of this general approach, which goes under the title of "covering law theory," von Wright says "it consists . . . in the subsumption of individual cases under hypothetically assumed general laws of nature, including human nature"; it is "in a broad sense causal" and opposed to idealistic theory, which "wants to grasp the individual and unique features of their objects." See also Dray, *Laws and Explanations in History* (London, 1957).

68. See T. S. Eliot, "Four Quartets," *Collected Poems: 1909-1962* (London, 1963).

PART 4

1. Quoted in Richard Palmer, *Hermeneutics* (Evanston, 1969), p. 43.

2. Ibid., p. 47.

3. Ibid., p. 107 ff.

4. Wilhelm Dilthey, *Meaning in History*, ed. H. P. Rickman (London, 1961), pp. 67–68.

5. Palmer, p. 114, fn. 31.

6. E. D. Hirsch, Jr., *Validity in Interpretation* (New Haven, 1967), p. 218.

7. Ibid., p. 110; see also Noam Chomsky, *Language and Mind* (New York, 1972), p. 78.

8. Leo Spitzer, *Linguistics and Literary History* (Princeton, 1948), pp. 33–35, fn. 10.

9. Ibid.

10. Hirsch, p. 78.

11. In Palmer, p. 42.

12. See Murray Krieger, *Theory of Criticism* (Baltimore, 1976), pp. 198–206, for a discussion of the "miraculism" of poetic metaphor and the critic's "as if" commitment to this "fiction."

13. Martin Heidegger, "The Origin of the Work of Art," in *Poetry, Language, Thought*, trans. A. Hofstadter (New York, 1971), p. 23.

14. Ibid.

15. Jonathan Culler, *Structuralist Poetics: Structuralism, Linguistics, and the Study of Literature* (Ithaca, 1975), p. 19.

16. A distinction must be made here between what I have called translation and Roland Barthes's concept of textual criticism as "transcription." Barthes's interpretive rewriting of the text is restricted to a process of deconstructing and reassembling the linguistic codes of the work. He deliberately brackets the crucial questions of historical meaningfulness that concern me most directly; the text for Barthes is opaque, revealing little about the author or his world. Yet the basic operations on the text of Barthes's transcription seem to me to be valid and profitable.

17. In Palmer, p. 131.

18. Martin Heidegger, *An Introduction to Metaphysics*, trans. R. Manheim (New York, 1961), p. 121.

19. Heidegger, "Origin of the Work of Art."

20. Heidgger, *Introduction to Metaphysics*, p. 144.

21. In Palmer, p. 201.

22. Martin Heidegger, *On the Way to Language*, trans. Peter Hertz (New York, 1971), p. 90.

23. Ibid., pp. 86, 88, 89.

24. I find myself both in agreement with Krieger on the substantiality of metaphor and also concerned that this status not be allowed to rigidify to that of objectivity.

25. Heidegger, *On the Way to Language*, p. 94.

26. In Palmer, p. 189.

27. See Michel Foucault, *The Order of Things*, trans. A. M. Sheridan-Smith (New York, 1970).

28. Thomas Carlyle, *Sartor Resartus*, from *A Carlyle Reader*, ed. G. B. Tennyson (New York, 1969). Page references are cited in the text.

29. Georges Poulet, *Les metamorphoses du cercle* (Paris, 1961).

30. Maurice Merleau-Ponty, *Phenomenology of Perception*, trans. C. Smith (New York, 1962).

31. Michel Foucault, *The Archaeology of Knowledge*, trans. A. M. Sheridan-Smith (New York, 1971), p. 76.

32. Jacques Derrida, "Structure, Sign, and Play in the Discourse of the Human Sciences," in *The Languages of Criticism and the Sciences of Man*, ed. R. Macksey and E. Donato (Baltimore, 1970).

33. Thomas Carlyle, "Letter to Mr. Fraser," *A Carlyle Reader*, p. 21.

34. Ibid.

35. Kreiger, *Theory of Criticism*, p. 184.

36. Gilles Deleuze and Félix Guattari, *Anti-Oedipus: Capitalism and Schizophrenia*, trans. R. Hurley, M. Seem, and H. R. Lane (New York, 1972).

37. Joseph Conrad, *Heart of Darkness*, ed. R. Kimbrough (New York, 1963), p. 150.

38. Robert Scholes, *Structuralism in Literature* (New Haven, 1974), particularly pp. 194–97. Scholes's account of this debate is clear and concise, but he tends to accept the idea that Sartre and Lévi-Strauss defend either/or positions. The consequence of this kind of polemics is to denature the extremes. In fact, Lévi-Strauss seems more open to allowing history an important place in his philosophy than Sartre is to giving anthropology some degree of legitimacy (that anthropology defined by the structuralists, anyway). But it is clear that each man responds to the challenge of the other and this makes possible a third position that acknowledges both. See also Mark Poster, *Existential Marxism in Postwar France: From Sartre to Althusser* (Princeton, 1975), particularly pp. 306–39.

39. Foucault, *The Order of Things*, particularly p. 330.

40. Derrida, "Structure, Sign, and Play."

41. Hugh M. Davidson, "Sign, Sense, and Barthes," in *Approaches to Poetics*, ed. S. Chatman (New York, 1973), p. 45.

42. For a somewhat contrary view see Monroe K. Spears, *Dionysus and the City* (New York, 1970).

43. See Jean-Paul Sartre, *Existentialism and Humanism*, trans. P. Mairet (London, 1946).

44. Ernst Cassirer, *Language and Myth*, trans. Susanne K. Langer (New York, 1946), p. 63.

45. Ibid., p. 71.

46. See Scholes, *Structuralism in Literature*, particularly the final chapter.

47. Jean-Paul Sartre, *Search for a Method*, trans. H. E. Barnes (New York, 1967), p. 174.

48. Ibid.

49. Claude Lévi-Strauss, *The Scope of Anthropology*, trans. S. O. and R. A. Paul (London, 1967), p. 26.

50. Fredric Jameson, *The Prison-House of Language* (Princeton, 1972).

51. Jean-Paul Sartre, *The Words*, trans. B. Frechtman (New York, 1954).

51. Jeffrey Mehlman, *A Structural Study of Autobiography* (Ithaca, 1971), particularly pp. 151–86.

53. Fredric Jameson, *Marxism and Form: Twentieth-Century Dialectical Theories of Literature* (Princeton, 1971), p. 244.

54. Heidegger, *On the Way to Language*, p. 134.

55. Paul Ricoeur, "The Model of the Text: Meaningful Action Considered as a Text," *New Literary History* 5 (Autumn 1973): 92.

Index